Passing the Torch

The Vietnam Experience

Passing the Torch

by Edward Doyle, Samuel Lipsman, Stephen Weiss, and
the editors of Boston Publishing Company

Boston Publishing Company/Boston, MA

Boston Publishing Company

President and Publisher: Robert J. George
Vice President: Richard S. Perkins, Jr.
Editor-in-Chief: Robert Manning
Managing Editor: Paul Dreyfus

Staff Writers:
 Edward Doyle, Samuel Lipsman, Terrence
 Maitland, Stephen Weiss
Research Assistants:
 Kerstin Gorham, Scott Kafker, Matthew H.
 Lynch, Frederick C. Ruby

Senior Picture Editor: Julene Fischer
Picture Editors:
 Ann Leyhe, Maren Stange
Picture Researchers:
 Shirley L. Green (Washington, D.C.),
 Wendy K. Johnson, Kate Lewin (Paris)

Historical Consultants:
 David P. Chandler, Thomas J. Corcoran,
 Vincent H. Demma, Lee Ewing
Picture Consultant: Ngo Vinh Long

Assistant Editors:
 Karen E. English, Jeffrey L. Seglin

Production Coordinator: Douglas B.
 Rhodes
Production Editor: Patricia Leal Welch
Editorial Production:
 Elizabeth S. Brownell, Pamela George,
 Elizabeth Hamilton, Amy P. Wilson

Design: Designworks, Sally Bindari

Marketing Director: Linda M. Scenna
Circulation Manager: Jane Colpoys
Business Staff:
 Darlene Keefe-Bonney, James D. Burrows,
 Christine E. Geering, Jeanne C. Gibson,
 Elizabeth Schultz

About the editors and authors

Editor-in-Chief *Robert Manning*, a long-time journalist, has previously been editor-in-chief of the *Atlantic Monthly* magazine and its press. He served as assistant secretary of state for public affairs under Presidents John F. Kennedy and Lyndon B. Johnson. He has also been a fellow at the Institute for Politics at the John F. Kennedy School of Government at Harvard University.

Staff Writers: *Edward Doyle*, an historian, received his masters degree at the University of Notre Dame and his Ph.D. at Harvard University. *Samuel Lipsman*, a former Fulbright Scholar, received his M.A. and M.Phil. in history at Yale. *Terrence Maitland* has written for several publications, including *Newsweek* magazine and the *Boston Globe*. He is a graduate of Holy Cross College and has an M.S. from Boston University. *Stephen Weiss* has been a fellow at the Newberry Library in Chicago. An American historian, he received his M.A. and M.Phil. at Yale.

Historical Consultants: *David P. Chandler*, a former U.S. foreign service officer, is research director of the Centre of Southeast Asian Studies at Monash University in Melbourne, Australia. His major publications include *In Search of Southeast Asia: A Modern History* (coauthor) and *The Land and People of Cambodia*. *Thomas J. Corcoran*, a career foreign service officer, now retired, served in various posts in Indochina between 1951 and 1977 as well as in the U.S. State Department and Pacific military command (CINCPAC) headquarters in Honolulu. *Vincent H. Demma*, an historian with the U.S. Army Center of Military History, is currently working on the center's history of the Vietnam conflict. *Lee Ewing*, editor of *Army Times*, served two years in Vietnam as a combat intelligence officer with the U.S. Military Assistance Command, Vietnam (MACV) and the 101st Airborne Division.

Picture Consultant *Ngo Vinh Long* is a social historian specializing in China and Vietnam. Born in Vietnam, he returned there most recently in 1980. His books include *Before the Revolution: The Vietnamese Peasants Under the French* and *Report From a Vietnamese Village*.

Cover photographs:
(Upper left) Two French soldiers run for cover during a Vietminh artillery barrage at the battle of Dien Bien Phu, March 1954.

(Upper right) A pro-French Vietnamese soldier arrests a North Vietnamese peasant suspected of aiding the Communists.

(Lower left) A Moroccan member of the French Foreign Legion stands in the rain after a battle in the Red River Delta.

(Lower right) Captain Gerald Kilburn, a United States Army adviser, leads Vietnamese troops on a hunt for Communist hideouts in the Mekong Delta.

Library of Congress Catalog Card Number: 81-68920

ISBN: 0-939526-01-8

10 9 8 7 6
5 4

Contents

Asia in Ferment

With the end of World War II in 1945 came hope for an era of peace and tranquility and high expectations for the future. Nowhere were those expectations higher than in Asia. After being dominated by westerners for four hundred years, the people of Asia demanded nothing short of independence.

Asian nationalists looked to the United States to insure that Europeans did not continue to dominate their countries. America set an example by granting full independence to the Philippine Islands. On July 4, 1946, while Americans were celebrating the 170th birthday of their country, Filipinos celebrated the birth of their own independent nation.

After some hesitation, the British soon followed. Realizing that Great Britain no longer possessed the strength to rule a large empire, British leaders granted independence to India and Burma in 1948. The Dutch proved more stubborn in their vast colony of Indonesia. Only when the United States used all of its powers in support of the Asian nationalist movement was Indonesia able to gain its independence in late 1949.

Like the French in Indochina, the Dutch had been displaced as rulers of Indonesia by the Japanese at the outbreak of World War II. After the war the Dutch, like the French in Indochina, attempted to

---

A Fourth of July for the Philippines (above): Filipinos celebrated their independence in 1946 with an old-fashioned American fireworks display.

General Douglas MacArthur's dramatic return to the Philippine Islands in October 1944 signaled to the Americans the beginning of the end of World War II. To Filipinos it marked the return to the path of self-government promised by the Americans in 1916 and decreed by Congress in 1932.

reclaim their colonial empire. The British occupation army, which accepted the Japanese surrender in Indonesia, permitted the reentry of Dutch troops. Indonesian nationalists led by Achmed Sukarno resorted to guerrilla warfare.

When negotiations between Indonesian nationalists and the Dutch government proved unsuccessful, Indonesia seemed headed for the same fate that was to befall Vietnam: a bitter, protracted guerrilla war. But in late 1948 the American government made good its pledge to support independence in Asia, presenting the Dutch with an ultimatum: If they did not grant Indonesia full independence immediately, all Marshall Plan aid would be terminated. Within a year all of the treaties and agreements were signed, and Indonesia took its place among Asia's newly independent nations.

In all, nearly one-half billion people had won independence. Their future, however, was far from settled. With the withdrawal of European rulers, religious, ethnic, and political rivalries erupted into violence. War and famine claimed millions of lives. But for the Asians there was a crucial difference: The solutions would be of their own choosing. The era in which Europeans determined the fortunes of Asia was over, almost.

But while almost one-half billion Asians rejoiced, there was little joy in French Indochina. There, Laotians, Cambodians, and Vietnamese remained under French rule. America called this an "internal French matter" and refused to intervene as it had done in Indonesia. Washington preferred instead the comfort of a policy of neutral noninvolvement. For the Indochinese it was a betrayal of America's commitment to anticolonialism. For Americans this policy of neutrality was to be short-lived.

The Philippines

The independence won by the Philippine Islands on July 4, 1946, ended over four hundred years of colonial rule, first by Spain and then by the United States.

As most Filipinos rejoice at their newly won independence, sentries watch over the Spanish walls of old Manila, a reminder of the Philippines' former Spanish rulers. Guerrilla violence followed closely on the heels of independence.

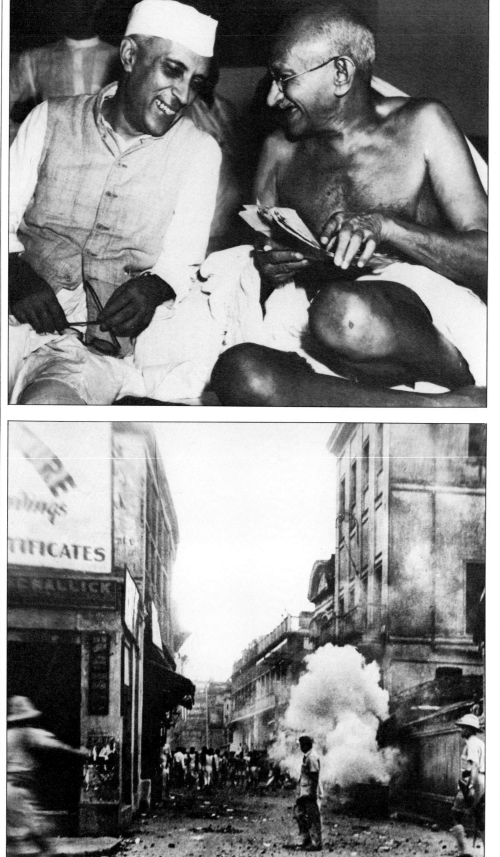

India

The independence attained by India in August 1947 came only after a long campaign of nonviolent opposition to British rule by Indian nationalists. For nearly a century, Indian demands for independence had been met only with British promises of independence in the future—a future that never seemed to arrive. The election of the first Labor government in Great Britain provided the final impetus: The new government promised a British withdrawal if Moslems and Hindus could settle their differences. The result was partition, the creation of two countries—India and Pakistan—on the subcontinent.

Burma

A century of British colonial rule ended for Burma in January 1948. The British originally conquered Burma and incorporated it into its Indian territories, largely to protect its Indian borders against Burmese claims and later to prevent encroachments by France from Laos to the east. Like the French in Laos, the British also hoped that Burma would provide an overland trade route to China.

India's two great nationalist leaders, Jawaharlal Nehru (left) and Mohandas Gandhi (right), enjoy a light moment at the opening of the Indian National Congress meeting in 1946 (above). The congress formally agreed to partition.

Calcutta police lob tear gas bombs at Moslem nationalists after their attempt to burn a Hindu temple during five days of rioting in 1947. Moslems and Hindus clashed even before the British had completed their withdrawal from India; the toll was five hundred lives.

An astrologer leads Burma's independence celebration on January 4, 1948 (right). Burmese nationalists left it to astrologers to determine the best time to begin national independence. Their choice of 4:20 A.M. forced all of Burma to rise in the middle of the night to proclaim, "We are free."

Indonesia

The former Dutch East Indies, Indonesia, won freedom with a bloody guerrilla struggle, ended only after the newly formed United Nations pressed the Netherlands government to withdraw. American insistence on independence forced the issue in the U.N.

Speaking near a burned-out railway station, Indonesia's charismatic nationalist leader and the country's first president, Achmed Sukarno, exhorts his countrymen (above). When Sukarno moved closer to Communist China in the mid–1960s, he was ousted by a pro–American military coup.

Out with the old (left). Indonesians remove a reminder of their former Dutch colonial masters after Independence Day in 1949. Portraits of all former Dutch governors general were taken from the palace in Djakarta to dramatize independence.

Vietnam

Vietnam was in step with its Asian neighbors in declaring its independence immediately following the capitulation of the Japanese ending World War II. As in the Philippine Islands, India, Burma, and Indonesia, a native independence movement had spent the war years preparing for liberation. But Vietnam's struggle was to be the longest and costliest in all of Asia. Suddenly finding itself caught up in the emerging Cold War, Vietnam found the "independence" that Ho Chi Minh declared on September 2, 1945, to be a hollow pronouncement until the Geneva Peace Conference nearly ten years later.

A jubilant Hanoi crowd listens to Ho Chi Minh quote the American Declaration of Independence in proclaiming Vietnam's independence. Lacking the kind of support other Asian countries received from the United States, Ho and his followers were forced to fight an eight-year war with the French to make good his proclamation and another eleven years to achieve his goal of a unified nation.

The French Return

It began in Saigon and it ended in Saigon. Between the first battle of Saigon and the last, three decades passed. A generation of Vietnamese was born and reared and reached adulthood without knowing true peace. Uncounted lives were lost: French, German, Laotian, Cambodian, American, Korean, Australian, British, Indian, Moroccan, Senegalese, and hundreds of thousands of Vietnamese. The debris of war, billions of dollars worth, littered the Vietnamese landscape. It began in Saigon, the Paris of the Orient, and it ended in Saigon, Ho Chi Minh City.

Early on the morning of Sunday, September 23, 1945, a small group of French soldiers led personally by the French commissioner designate for Cochin China, Colonel Jean Cédile, stormed the city hall, arrested the members of the Vietminh committee that had run the city since the Japanese surrender, and once again hoisted the French Tricolor above the streets of Saigon. Other French troops simultaneously occupied the

British General Douglas Gracey released many Japanese prisoners to aid him in resisting the demands of the Vietminh. Here a Japanese soldier posts Gracey's Proclamation No. 1, a declaration of martial law in southern Vietnam on September 21, 1945.

post office and secured police headquarters. In the month of August, when the Vietminh governed the country almost without opposition or interference, only one Frenchman had been killed. But on the day of the French return, scores of Vietnamese were killed, attacked, or taken prisoner, with what one British eyewitness described as "maximum ineptitude and considerable cruelty."

It was a day of revenge for the French—revenge for the Japanese coup on March 9, 1945, which had robbed them of their power, revenge for the frustration they felt as Ho Chi Minh had declared Vietnam's independence and moved to consolidate his power, revenge for the "ingratitude" that the Vietnamese displayed after nearly one hundred years of France's

Preceding page. The French return: Occupation troops bound for Vietnam leave Marseilles in November 1945, soon after French forces had retaken Cochin China.

"civilizing" rule. In this atmosphere of revenge the French invented a new crime: to be Vietnamese. Old men, women, and children had their ears boxed by French matrons trying to reestablish the "natural" order in Saigon.

But the Vietnamese were unwilling to revert to the colonial role of good-natured children, beloved by their French masters. They had tasted independence. One Saigonese, a middle-aged man who had traveled the world in the French navy, told an American reporter of his fondness for the French when he visited France. "But Frenchmen here?" he asked himself, "I hate them. We all hate them with a hatred that must be inconceivable to you, for you have not known what it is to live as a slave under a foreign master."

The French coup was not only cruel but, as the British observer reported, also inept. The Vietminh committee apparently had some inkling of the impending strike by the French forces, and its leaders were able to escape to the safety of the countryside. There they joined with their political enemies, the Cao Dai and Hoa Hao religious sects and the Binh Xuyen bandits, to begin their guerrilla resistance. After the coup all of the southerners were united against the French.

The British occupation of Vietnam

The man responsible for the outbreak of violence in Saigon was neither French nor Vietnamese. He was General Douglas D. Gracey, a British war hero, the right-hand man of Lord Louis Mountbatten, supreme commander of all British forces in Asia. Mountbatten would later gain world respect for his probity in guiding British policy during India's transition to independence. But his choice of General Gracey to fulfill England's responsibility to accept the Japanese surrender in Vietnam south of the sixteenth parallel was a poor one. Gracey's fame rested on his effective command of Indian troops, to many Asians the most visible sign of European domination of their continent. Gracey lacked the finesse required in the tense situation of Vietnam in September 1945. Gracey identified with the French soldiers wanting to reclaim their empire. He was incapable of acting as an objective mediator between the French and the Vietminh.

Gracey later recalled with evident pride his first meeting with Vietminh representatives after his arrival in Saigon on September 13, 1945. To welcome him, the Vietminh had hung English-language ban-

The arrival of British troops in Saigon after World War II brought a captor-prisoner turn around. French colonialists, many of whom were held prisoner by the Japanese occupation troops during World War II, confront British-held Japanese prisoners.

ners proclaiming, "Welcome to the Allies, to the British and the Americans, but we have no room for the French." But then the Vietminh, in Gracey's words, "came to see me and said 'welcome' and all that sort of thing. It was an unpleasant situation and I promptly kicked them out."

Mountbatten's orders to Gracey were clear and sharply limiting. It was his job to disarm the Japanese, to repatriate the prisoners of war, and to maintain order. But he was specifically forbidden to exercise "any measure of administrative authority outside key areas," and he was not "to reestablish French sovereignty." Between the French and the Vietminh he was to remain neutral. No matter how explicit Mountbatten's orders were, Gracey was well aware that British policy in Asia was to do nothing that might jeopardize British claims to its own empire, especially in India. Gracey acted accordingly.

Gracey expressed pride in refusing to meet with

the Vietminh committee, but he quickly came under intense pressure from the other side. Colonel Cédile made repeated entreaties to Gracey, arguing that the French citizens of Saigon would be helpless against a Vietminh attack and pleading that the detained French prisoners of war be immediately armed. He also argued that a majority of the Vietnamese supported the French regime and lived in fear of the Vietminh. To counter this last argument, the Vietminh staged a general strike in Saigon on September 17. In response Gracey ordered the Vietnamese press closed and all Vietnamese disarmed. The Vietminh protested the "gross interference with their political liberties and aspirations." But Gracey was not listening to the Vietminh.

Gracey declares martial law

For the next thirty years Saigon was often to experience the harshness of martial law. But that it should first be proclaimed by the British soldier whom the Vietnamese hoped would aid their fight for inde-

Colonel Jean Cédile, acting French commissioner for Cochin China, capitulated to the demands of the French population in Saigon for strong action against the Vietnamese. With British General Gracey's aid, he launched the takeover of the Vietminh Committee of the South in September 1945.

pendence was particularly disheartening to them. Until he declared martial law on September 21, General Gracey had performed, with some stretching of the limits, within the boundaries of his orders. But by issuing Proclamation No. 1, a declaration of martial law, not only in Saigon but throughout southern Vietnam, Gracey clearly exceeded his orders to maintain order only in "key areas." Gracey later argued that the proclamation was issued in response to the general strike of September 17. But the date of its printing suggests that it was considered and drafted prior to the strike. Martial law was more the result of Cédile's pleas than of the Vietminh's peaceful strike.

Having declared martial law, Gracey was now responsible for maintaining order south of the sixteenth parallel. With a force of only some twenty thousand Indian soldiers at his disposal, many of whom had not yet arrived, Gracey looked elsewhere for support. He finally gave in to Cédile and, on Saturday, September 22, armed the French troops, prisoners of the Japanese since the March coup.

The next morning Cédile and his newly armed troops staged their brutal coup. Gracey's proclamation of martial law, designed to insure order, had achieved the opposite effect. Gracey tried to reverse the situation by disarming the French population and confining French troops to their barracks. But on Tuesday, September 25, French and Eurasian citizens in a Saigon suburb were brutally massacred by Vietnamese. An estimated one hundred and fifty people died. The French and Gracey were quick to blame the Vietminh. Perhaps they found it impossible to differentiate between the various political factions operating in Saigon. But a later investigation by the British government concluded with impressive evidence that the Cochin China "mafia," the Binh Xuyen bandits, was responsible for the massacre, perhaps as an effort to discredit the Vietminh or perhaps to show the Vietnamese that they were more "radical" than Ho Chi Minh's forces.

The British response was to rearm the Japanese soldiers and to undertake the pacification of Cochin China, the southern part of Vietnam. The Vietminh blockaded the roads leading out of Saigon and attempted to starve the city. They urged the entire Vietnamese population to evacuate the city, much as their ancestors had done in 1859 when the French first claimed it. The Indian troops of the British army and the Japanese then began a slow, village-by-village pacification effort. They made some progress but, as the next thirty years would show, progress is elusive in guerrilla warfare. Gracey's orders to his troops described the problems of pacification, problems that no antiguerrilla army was ever able to solve:

There is no front in these operations. We may find it difficult to distinguish friend from foe ... beware of 'nibbling' at opposition. Always use maximum force available to insure wiping out any hostilities we may meet. If one uses too much, no harm is done. If one uses too small a force, and it has to be extricated, we will suffer casualties and encourage the enemy.

For the British the war in Vietnam was mercifully short. By the end of December, when their obligations to supervise the Japanese surrender ended, they began to withdraw their troops. By April 1946 the final British soldiers left, replaced by French troops clothed, armed, and supported with supplies provided by the British. The British, with their home economy devastated by six years of war, could provide the French only with lend-lease materials given them by America. To the Vietnamese watching the reentry of the French troops, the clean new uniforms, the shiny jeeps, and the modern firearms all bore the unmistakable imprint of their supplier: "Lend–Lease—Provided by the Government of the United States of America."

Few Americans were aware of these events taking place in a remote corner of Asia. News coverage was sparse. Events in China, India, even in Indonesia were more important. But at least one American was indignant. Following the fighting from his command in Tokyo, General of the Army Douglas MacArthur remarked:

If there is anything that makes my blood boil, it is to see our allies in Indochina ... deploying Japanese troops to reconquer the ... people we promised to liberate. It is the most ignoble kind of betrayal.

The Chinese are coming

To the events in Saigon, over seven hundred and fifty miles from Vietminh headquarters in Hanoi, Ho Chi Minh could only make an ineffective protest to British Prime Minister Clement Attlee. Unrecognized as a head of state, Ho found his protests unanswered, and he was virtually without resources to control the

Vietnamese nationalists are taken to prison under French guard after violence erupted in Saigon in September 1945.

events in the South. He had no influence over the extreme antiwestern elements operating in the South. And he even found it difficult to restrain his own Vietminh followers, who were under heavy pressure to prove that they were as anti-French as the religious sects. But Ho knew as well that his strength lay in the densely populated Tonkin Delta. It was Tonkin that was uppermost in Ho's mind, because once again the Chinese were coming.

The Allies had assigned Chiang Kai-shek the responsibility of accepting the Japanese surrender north of the sixteenth parallel. But Chiang could ill afford to give the job to one of his crack northern units, now needed to confront Mao Tse-tung's guerrillas. Instead he dispatched a ragtag force from south China under the command of General Lu Han. While the British had arrived in the South with a force of 20,000 troops, Lu Han commanded almost 200,000 Chinese soldiers. But more important to Ho than the 200,000 soldiers were the few hundred Vietnamese

Ho's provisional government sought financial support in 1945 through voluntary contributions, especially during the "Gold Week" campaign. This campaign poster asks citizens to "Make a sacrifice—Donate gold to the nation."

who traveled with them—the remnants of Vietnam's old Nationalist party and the official protégés of Chiang Kai-shek.

As the Chinese forces moved through northern Tonkin, they evicted the Vietminh committees from power in the villages and replaced them with members of the Nationalist party. Fighting broke out between Vietminh partisans and the Chinese, but Ho quickly ordered that the Chinese occupation be accepted peacefully. He had his own strategy for dealing with Lu Han and was anxious to avoid violence in the North. By the end of September, the Vietminh remained in power only in Hanoi. The Nationalists, backed by Chinese troops, controlled the rest of the countryside, but the Vietminh waited quietly for opportunities to act.

Ho deals with the Chinese

Ho's long experience in dealing with Chinese Nationalists, especially during World War II, had taught him what was necessary to protect his government. A tidy sum of money would be more attractive to Lu Han than a few Vietnamese allies. But the whole operation would have to be done delicately, so the Chinese could "save face." Ho declared the week of September 16 through 22 "Gold Week." Voluntary contributions were requested to enable the nearly bankrupt Vietminh government to purchase weapons on the open market. The fund-raising drive was enormously successful. Over eight hundred pounds of gold and 20 million piasters were raised. Ho's only disappointment was that few wealthy Vietnamese contributed. Most of the money came from poor peasants least able to afford it.

Some purchases of weapons were made, perhaps as a cover. But most of the money was used to make General Lu Han and his senior officers wealthy men. In exchange, Lu Han adopted a policy of noninterference in Vietnam's political affairs (while further enriching himself by manipulating Vietnam's foreign exchange market) and permitted the Vietminh committee in Hanoi to continue to govern the city.

To avoid appearances that the Chinese had sold out their Vietnamese Nationalist allies, Ho reached a series of agreements with the Nationalists. A Nationalist was named vice president of the provisional government, and in early November 1945, Ho dissolved the Indochina Communist party with the explanation that "my party is my country."

The first National Assembly of the Democratic Republic of Vietnam meets in January 1946 to establish a government headed by Ho Chi Minh.

Ho then introduced a series of reforms designed to win broader support for the Vietminh by ending the most hated of French colonial policies. The use of opium was banned and the alcohol monopoly ended. The salt tax and head tax were abolished. Ho won the support of the major Catholic bishops in the North and soon the Nationalist party itself split, one-half of it merging with the Vietminh.

In the meantime Ho had been making preparations for the election of a National Assembly, which would draft a constitution and end the provisional nature of the independent Vietnamese government. Ho originally called for elections to take place on December 23, 1945. But the Nationalists wanted more time to prepare, and Ho agreed to postpone the elections for two weeks. As the time for the elections grew near, the Nationalists realized that their cause was hopeless. The popularity of the Vietminh was too great. Since Lu Han's troops still controlled Tonkin, Ho reached another agreement with the Nationalists. No matter how poorly they did, they would be awarded seventy seats in the new parliament, would retain the office of vice president, and be awarded two ministers' portfolios. The national elections—the first in Vietnamese history—took place on January 6, 1946, without incident and amid great festivity. An estimated 90 percent of the eligible voters exercised their new right.

The results were a great victory for the Vietminh. Had they not been guaranteed their 70 seats, the Na-tionalists would have won only 48. All 254 of the other representatives elected belonged to the Vietminh front. But the new parliament was hardly stacked with Communists. Only 10 Marxists were elected. The other Vietminh seats were won by those described as Socialists, democrats, and independents. When the assembly convened, its Catholic president asked Ho to form a new government. Of the twelve cabinet members only three had been comrades of Ho in the old Indochina Communist party. Ho, who became president, was the only other Communist. The other eight positions went to the Nationalists, leaders of the Catholics, and independents. It was still the "Government of Union."

Ho's deft political moves had broadened his base within Vietnam and neutralized the Nationalists, who in a showdown could still have counted on the force of the Chinese occupational troops. It was clear now that the Chinese troops had broader intentions than merely accepting the Japanese surrender. Ho could only recall with horror that the first time the Chinese came they had stayed for one thousand years. But he knew that the future of the Chinese occupation no longer depended upon him but upon the French officials conducting negotiations with Chiang's representatives in Shanghai.

By early fall it was apparent to Ho that Chiang's real goal in occupying Tonkin was to wring concessions from the French in China. Between February 28 and March 14, 1946, the French signed a series of agreements with the Chinese, relinquishing their pre–World War II rights in China. In exchange, China was willing to hand Vietnam back over to its colonial rulers. With these agreements the Chinese began withdrawing their troops, a process that lasted until the end of October, paving the way for the return of French forces.

A decision for peace

Now the focus shifted back from Shanghai to Hanoi. The question: How would the French return? By force, against the wishes of the Vietnamese? Or peacefully, following agreement with the Vietminh?

At this critical juncture France was fortunate. The top representatives Charles de Gaulle sent to Hanoi—both military and civilian—were men possessed with a decidedly non-Gaullist pragmatism and common sense. Their deep Gaullist patriotism and firm hope that France would return to glory did not blind them to the realities of the Vietnamese political situation.

Jean de Hautecloque was a name virtually unknown to his fellow Frenchmen, except perhaps as that of the scion of an aristocratic family. Yet the man's fame as a general was exceeded only by that of de Gaulle himself. De Hautecloque had escaped from France at the beginning of the Nazi occupation and had raised the first Free French Army in the French colony of Chad. His soldiers fought in Libya and then joined the Allies in the North African campaign. His black African troops spearheaded the French effort in the liberation of Paris. But fearful lest his leadership in the Free French Army provoke Nazi reprisals against his family in France, de Hautecloque had changed his name. Thus it was that General Jacques Philippe Leclerc, hero of the Free French, came to command French forces in Vietnam.

Leclerc's experiences in the guerrilla fighting around Saigon convinced him that a return to the prewar colonial relationship was impossible. On February 5, 1946, Leclerc announced at a press conference that the French pacification of southern Vietnam was complete. But he warned, "France is no longer in a position to control by arms an entity of 24 million people."

Leclerc's conclusion was shared by Jean Sainteny, the commissioner designate of Tonkin in the North. Sainteny had been the first Frenchman flown into Hanoi after the Japanese capitulation, arriving with the American Office of Strategic Services (OSS) advance team. His presence so upset the Vietnamese population of Hanoi that the Japanese, responsible for maintaining order until relieved by the Chinese, suggested that he separate himself from the Americans and move into the governor general's palace. Leaping at the chance to reclaim the symbol of French power, Sainteny agreed. The Japanese then argued that his mere appearance on Hanoi's streets could provoke a disturbance and forced him to remain within his "golden cage."

On February 18, Leclerc, temporarily serving as high commissioner in Indochina, assigned to Sainteny the task of conducting negotiations with Ho Chi Minh for the return of French troops to Tonkin. Ho was attacked by his closest advisers for his willingness to participate in these negotiations. Pham Van Dong and Vo Nguyen Giap considered force, not negotiations, to be the only means of liberating Vietnam from the French. The Vietminh newspaper printed an article entitled "Calm but Ready" which said, "We are preparing to negotiate, but at the same time we are preparing to resist, and the negotiations will succeed only if we get independence and freedom."

The negotiations did succeed. On March 6, 1946, Ho and Sainteny signed a preliminary agreement—a promising start toward decolonization without bloodshed. Under the terms of the agreement, France recognized Ho's government as a "free State, having its own Government and Parliament, and forming part of the Indochinese Federation within the French Union." France also agreed to a national referendum in Vietnam to determine whether the colony of Cochin China would be joined with Tonkin and Annam to form a reunited Vietnam. In return, the Vietnamese granted the French army the right to replace the Chinese troops north of the sixteenth parallel and to remain there for five years.

The March Agreement was followed by a series of good will gestures on both sides. Leclerc ordered that French army vehicles fly both French and Vietminh flags. Giap, the intractable, spontaneously shook hands with Leclerc before France's Tomb of the Unknown Soldier in Hanoi. The temporary Socialist prime minister of France, Léon Blum, was in complete accord with his representatives in Hanoi: "We have achieved much for the peoples of distant In-

Some Hanoi residents climbed the trees lining the boulevard to catch a glimpse of French Commissioner of Tonkin Jean Sainteny (left), Vo Nguyen Giap, then Ho's minister of the interior (center), and the commander of French forces in the Far East, General Jacques Philippe Leclerc (right), as they lead off a caravan to the Tomb of the Unknown Soldier in March 1946.

dochina. . . . We have but one end there: to insure a sufficient degree of order and civilization that all citizens, in accordance with the principles of the United Nations Charter, can make a free choice about the political future of their country."

A turn for the worse

In March 1946 it appeared that France, the country that had made *liberté* the political dream of Europe in 1789, would precede both England and Holland in emancipating its colonies. Indochina might become independent before India or Indonesia.

The moderates—Ho and Sainteny—quickly came under attack from extreme elements in both their camps. Ho was sharply criticized by the pro-Nationalist Chinese elements within the Vietminh who wanted the government to encourage the Chi-

nese troops to remain in Tonkin to prevent the reentry of the French. Ho countered this argument with Vietnamese history:

You fools! Don't you realize what it means if the Chinese stay? Don't you remember your history? The last time the Chinese came, they stayed one thousand years! As for me, I prefer to smell French shit for five years, rather than Chinese shit for the rest of my life.

Ho's continued popularity, both within the Vietminh and in the country as a whole, insured that he would prevail over his opponents. But the position of Leclerc and Sainteny was not so secure.

Sainteny had been appointed commissioner for Tonkin, but over the regional commissioner presided the Gaullist high commissioner for all Indochina, a post equivalent to the prewar governor general. He was a man with a very different mind, Admiral

Georges Thierry d'Argenlieu. D'Argenlieu had served in both World War I and World War II as a high-ranking French naval officer. Between the wars he had retreated to a Carmelite monastery. One of his staff members sardonically described him as the "most brilliant mind of the twelfth century." Even before Leclerc had begun paving the way for negotiations, d'Argenlieu had complained to de Gaulle about Leclerc's "defeatist attitude." As soon as the March Agreement was signed, d'Argenlieu began to undermine it.

The tactics employed by d'Argenlieu were those long employed by French colonial administrators: to make a unilateral policy decision, to try to persuade officials in Paris to accept the policy, and failing that, to carry out the policy all the same and present Paris with a fait accompli. The government would then be left with the face-losing choice of either publicly disagreeing with its officials in front of the "natives" or accepting the policy. D'Argenlieu dispatched a four-man team to Paris to argue that Cochin China should be exempted from the March Agreement because the people in the South had no desire to be reunited with the North.

D'Argenlieu had one powerful weapon: the French constitution. Tonkin and Annam were only protectorates whose relationship to France was governed by treaties, that is, by acts of the parliament. But Cochin China was a colony whose legal status was embedded in the French constitution. Any change in its status would require an amendment to the constitution. For the time being Paris ignored d'Argenlieu's argument and instructed him to continue the negotiations begun by Sainteny.

The failures of Da Lat and Fontainebleau

On April 18, 1946, French and Vietminh officials met in Da Lat, a French resort in Vietnam's highlands, to begin defining precisely what was meant by the part of the March Agreement that said that Vietnam was to be a "free State . . . forming part of the Indochinese Federation within the French Union." Giap led the Vietminh delegation while Max André, a member of the Christian-Democratic party and a former banking official in Saigon, headed the French. Giap was one of the most inflexible opponents of the French while André, a former colonist, was sure to insist on considerable French influence in the new Vietnam.

The Da Lat conference made no progress. The French definition of membership within the French Union provided little real power for the new "free State" of Vietnam. Foreign affairs were to be controlled solely by Paris, while Vietnam (as well as Cambodia and Laos) was to control its own internal affairs. The French made some important exceptions. The Departments of Justice, Social Security, Economic Planning, Transport, Customs, Communications, Immigration, and even Hygiene were all to remain under French control. Apparently, the Vietnamese were not even to be given power over collection of their own garbage.

André described this proposal as "major" and "final." Had Ho accepted that as France's last word, he would have cut off the negotiations. Instead, the Vietminh issued a statement at the conclusion of the Da Lat conference hoping for more progress at a conference to be convened at Fontainebleau near Paris—away from French and Vietnamese extremists in Vietnam.

Ho and his negotiating team, led by Pham Van Dong, departed by boat for Paris on May 31, 1946. Ho wisely left Giap behind. Moderation was essential if these new negotiations were to be productive. When the Vietnamese delegation arrived in Paris, however, they were greeted by a new bombshell from Saigon.

On June 1, the day after Ho's departure, d'Argenlieu proclaimed the "autonomous" Republic of Cochin China. D'Argenlieu appointed Dr. Nguyen Van Thinh prime minister. The Consultative Council—a reorganized Colonial Council, elected on a very restricted suffrage—only had the power to confirm the choice of prime minister and approve the budget. The French high commissioner remained the real power in Saigon. The Vietminh considered d'Argenlieu's action a stab in the back. Unification had been a goal second in importance only to independence. Showing an enormous reservoir of self-restraint, Ho dismissed d'Argenlieu's actions as a "misunderstanding" which the negotiations would clear up.

To the French negotiators in Paris little clarification was necessary. Max André again led the French delegation. He refused to use the March Agreement that implied Vietnamese independence as a basis for discussions and instead placed on the bargaining table his unacceptable proposal made at Da Lat. Both sides blundered during the negotiations. Ho received a delegation of Algerians demanding their independence, a sign of solidarity that greatly angered the French government. D'Argenlieu held a second Da

A Vietminh "death volunteer" stands ready with an anti-tank bomb in Hanoi in late 1946. The "death volunteers" attached bombs to their bodies and flung themselves at French tanks, exploding the bombs on impact.

Lat conference, inviting delegates from Cochin China, Cambodia, and Laos, but ignoring Ho's government in Hanoi. A final communiqué was issued on September 12, announcing some French economic and financial concessions to the Vietnamese. But Max André refused to agree to a further discussion of the issues—essentially telling the Vietnamese to "take it or leave it." He refused to make any commitment to a referendum in Cochin China in which the southerners themselves could decide whether they wanted reunification with the North. On September 13, the Vietnamese delegation left Paris for Haiphong.

A chance for peace

But Ho, who had "come to make peace," refused to leave Paris without "France's company." Sainteny urged Ho to return to Hanoi, where he was afraid that extremists would get the upper hand in Ho's absence. But Ho replied, "What could I do if I return empty-handed?" On September 14, Ho met with Sainteny, Prime Minister Georges Bidault, and Minister of Overseas Territories Marius Moutet. Ho was now begging the French: "Do not leave [me] this way. Arm me with something against those who seek to outdo me. You will not regret it." But Ho continued, "If we must fight, we will fight. You will kill ten of our men, and we will kill one of yours. Yet, in the end, it is you who will tire."

At midnight on September 14, Ho signed a modus vivendi with the French. Ho conceded to the French practically all of their demands. In return he gained only two promises: a referendum in Cochin China and resumption of negotiations no later than January 1947. Neither would come to pass.

Before leaving for Vietnam Ho met for the last time with David Schoenbrun, an American journalist whom he had befriended in Paris. His optimism had disappeared. He spoke of his opponents in Vietnam and called the agreement which he had just signed his "death warrant." He predicted that unless the French proved more flexible in the future, war was inevitable. About the nature of that war, Ho had no illusions:

It will be a war between an elephant and a tiger. If the tiger ever stands still, the elephant will crush him with his mighty tusks. But the tiger will not stand still. ... He will leap upon the back of the elephant, tearing huge chunks from his side, and then he will leap back into the dark jungle. And slowly the elephant will bleed to death. That will be the war of Indochina.

The American journalist was just one of many Americans in those years who became enchanted with Ho Chi Minh. One week after Ho's arrival in Hanoi on August 15, 1945, an advance team of American officials from the OSS, led by Major Archimedes Patti, flew into the capital to insure the welfare of American prisoners of war in Japanese camps and to make preliminary arrangements on behalf of Chiang

Kai-shek for the Japanese surrender. A similar team, led by Major A. Peter Dewey, landed in Saigon. The OSS officials outraged the French who accused them of siding with the Vietminh. In truth, the OSS officials gave the impression of supporting Ho's forces. They met with Vietminh officials and transmitted messages from Ho to the American government.

But the OSS officials did not exceed their authority. Part of their responsibility was to insure that the Japanese continue to maintain civil order in the occupied lands, as commanded by U.S. Army General MacArthur. Since the Japanese chose to rely upon the Vietminh committees, the Americans worked with these forces. On an informal basis, the early American arrivals made friendly overtures to the Vietnamese. One of the early participants was General Philip Gallagher, who assisted Lu Han's Chinese occupation army. Gallagher agreed with the Vietminh that a student exchange between the U.S. and Vietnam would be a "good idea."

America and Vietnam— a budding friendship?

Although Ho occasionally glossed over his Communist associations, he generally made no secret of them. He told the Americans that independence for Vietnam came first. At one point Ho told Major Patti that he had learned a great deal about political organization and tactics from Moscow, but considered his twenty years of work for the Comintern as sufficient repayment. He now considered himself a free agent. Later he argued that Vietnam would not be ready for communism for "fifty years" and slyly remarked that by then even the United States might be Communist. Perhaps then the Americans wouldn't mind so much if Vietnam was as well.

Between August and December 1945 Ho made at least seven appeals directly to the American government. Adhering to diplomatic protocol, which refused to acknowledge correspondence from unrecognized governments, the U.S. answered none of the communications. At one point the Vietminh asked "to be placed on the same status as the Philippines for an undetermined period," that is, to be made an American colony. Ho tried to entice the American government with promises of economic advantages and stated that they "would like to see the economy of Vietnam geared to America's if possible."

The Vietnamese were disappointed in the American response. Their pleas ignored, they slowly began to stop believing that America would aid them in their struggle for independence. When French troops began to arrive in Vietnam, supplied with American-made equipment, the Vietnamese felt betrayed. They now argued that the Americans were supporting the French.

The Americans were not, not exactly. But American policy had changed somewhat since President Roosevelt's death in April 1945. Roosevelt had insisted on an end to French rule in Vietnam, either directly through independence or by making Vietnam a trust territory of the United Nations. In May 1945, however, U.S. Secretary of State Edward R. Stettinius informed the French government that the U.S. was not "questioning, even by implication, French sovereignty over Indochina." Further clarification from the State Department revealed that America was expecting considerable reform by the French colonial administration "with eventual self-government as the goal."

The guiding statement of American policy came in October 1945 as the French prepared to return south of the sixteenth parallel. The State Department repeated that it was not opposed to a return to French control, but added:

it is not the policy of this government to assist the French to reestablish their control of Indochina by force, and the willingness of the U.S. to see French control reestablished assumes that [the] French claim to have the support of the population of Indochina is borne out by future events.

In other words, if the French claim that the vast majority of the Vietnamese were happy living under French rule were true, there would be no need for force, and the U.S. would accept French reoccupation. In the meantime, the U.S. would give no military support to the French effort. The American government refused to transport French troops or weapons to Indochina and insisted that no military aid given to the French government be sent to the South China Sea. But it was not difficult for the French to secure American equipment. The English continued to provide their lend-lease American equipment, and the military aid given to Paris by the United States simply freed funds to purchase American equipment on the open market.

Still, the American position can accurately be called neutrality, a position that did not change until 1950. But there were two problems with such neutrality. When the "French claim to have the support of the population" was *not* "borne out by future events" the U.S. did not change its "willingness ... to see French control reestablished." More important, as the *Pentagon Papers* confirm, a policy of neutrality was "tilted" toward the French, as the recognized sovereign power. As long as the U.S. did nothing the French were free to do as they pleased. Only direct aid by the American government to Vietnamese nationalists would have tilted the policy in the opposite direction.

And what about the Soviet Union? Vietnamese Communists were at best cynical about Russian aid. They knew that the Soviet economy itself was too weak to provide much aid for Vietnam. Moreover, as one Vietminh told an American reporter, "The Russians are nationalists for Russia first and above all. They would be interested in us only if we served some purpose of theirs."

It was apparently when Ho Chi Minh understood the full implication of the American policy that he began negotiating with the French. No help was expected from the Soviet Union, the United States had refused to intervene, and the Chinese were only to be feared. In late 1945 Ho dejectedly told an American reporter, "We apparently stand quite alone. We shall have to depend on ourselves."

To a Vietnam standing alone the French were most unwilling to make important concessions. The result was the breakdown in negotiations after the promising beginning in March 1946. To the Americans the promise of the March Agreement had seemed to put France on the road toward fulfilling a major American goal—the eventual independence of Indochina. That further progress was not made at Da Lat and Fontainebleau was disappointing, but then the negotiations by the English with India and by the Dutch with Indonesia could also have been characterized as "two-steps-forward-one-step-back."

The short road to war

When Ho returned to Vietnam from Paris on October 20, 1946, with only the poor modus vivendi to show for his efforts, he was greeted by the Hanoi population "with rapture," according to reports of that day. But he knew that many in the government were sharply critical of his postconference agreement. Accordingly, at the meeting of the Vietnamese National Assembly on November 9, 1946, Ho dramatically tendered his resignation. In effect, he asked the assembly to accept both him and the agreement or to reject them both. The assembly chose Ho and he reaccepted the position of president. In the meantime, the assembly made arrangements for the worst. They gave wide powers to a standing committee, empowering it to act in the assembly's name should the assembly be unable to meet, that is, in the event of a war of resistance. The government was reorganized to insure a broad national front. Of its fifteen members, six were Communists.

Colonial attitudes died hard in Saigon. Despite the uncompromising attitude shown by the French government toward the negotiations, d'Argenlieu and his extremist followers in Saigon were still unhappy over the restraint shown by Paris. D'Argenlieu criticized the fact that the French were even negotiating with Ho. As the Fontainebleau Conference opened, d'Argenlieu voiced his dismay. "I can assure you," he boasted to the press, "that if General de Gaulle were still prime minister of France, Ho Chi Minh would not get away with such impertinence. He would be obliged to keep his place." Neither d'Argenlieu nor anyone in the French government made much of Ho's Communist affiliations. To the old colonists this was beside the point. More important to them, Ho was a dangerous rabble-rouser, a Vietnamese who didn't know his place.

The fragile peace was shattered in mid-November 1946. On November 20 French and Vietnamese customs officials clashed in Haiphong over who had the legal right to collect import duties. During the next few days isolated gunfire was exchanged between Vietminh militia and French soldiers. Fearful that a slow war of attrition was beginning, the French decided to give the Vietnamese a hard lesson. The Vietminh were given two hours to evacuate the Chinese quarter of Haiphong. Two hours was not even sufficient time to forward the message to Hanoi for consideration by the government. When the time ran out the French shelled the city, killing at least six thousand Vietnamese civilians.

The incident appeared to be an overreaction—later described by Moutet as a "foolish and criminal mistake"—to a series of isolated outbreaks of violence. But other French officials later admitted that the attack had been planned far in advance to be used when the opportunity arose. At a meeting of the French Committee of National Defense in early November, an attempt was made to convince Prime Minister Georges Bidault that war was not inevitable. But Bidault replied, *"Il faut tirer le canon."* ("It is necessary to fire the cannon.")

At the outbreak of hostilities in December 1945 the Vietminh government fled to mountains northwest of Hanoi. Here Ho Chi Minh leads a session of the government steering committee in a mountain cave.

The "Haiphong incident" won the day for Ho's more extreme followers. Giap began making preparations for a war of resistance. On November 28 the French demanded full control of the Hanoi-Haiphong road, until then shared with the Vietminh. Giap countered by erecting barricades in Hanoi and by ordering the population to pierce holes in the walls of their homes to permit direct communication without the use of streets.

In Paris, Sainteny was quickly dispatched to Hanoi, arriving there on December 2, in the hopes that his good relations with Ho Chi Minh might yet save the situation. After one brief meeting with Sainteny, Ho refused to meet with his old friend again. Moreover, Giap began slowly to withdraw his regular troops from Hanoi, leaving police chores to the popular militia.

The war begins

As so many future Vietminh attacks would, it began at nightfall. At eight o'clock in the evening of December 19, 1946, Vietminh guerrillas—for they were now guerrillas again—destroyed the electric power plant in Hanoi, plunging the city into darkness. Homes of French civilians were attacked and mines exploded in Hanoi's streets. Sainteny himself was injured when a mine blew up his car.

That night French installations throughout Vietnam were attacked. But the attacks were more a good-bye than a concerted effort to destroy the French in one blow. Ho Chi Minh and his government fled to a preplanned mountain retreat even before the attack was staged, much as the Emperor Ham Nghi had done sixty-two years earlier when the Vietnamese had waged their first war of resistance against the French. French officials predicted the war would be over in three months. Not quite soon enough to get the boys home by Christmas.

"The First American Casualty"

Death seldom seemed so tragic, so much a matter of bitter misfortune, as in the Vietnam War, a war that knew no front lines and entailed few pitched battles. A missed step, the wrong place in formation, was often the only explanation for a combat fatality. That this would be the Vietnam War Americans came to know was tragically foreshadowed in its earliest days—in 1945, during the first battle of Saigon.

Major A. Peter Dewey was not unlike many of the American officers who would arrive in Vietnam twenty years later. He was young and intelligent, the nephew of New York Governor (and GOP presidential candidate) Thomas Dewey, and the son of a Chicago millionaire. He had graduated from Yale University where he studied French history and culture. An officer in the OSS, he was assigned to Saigon at the end of World War II largely because of his knowledge of French. In Saigon he headed the U.S. mission that cared for Americans interned by the Japanese during the war.

On September 26, 1945, Major Dewey was headed for reassignment to India. At 9:10 A.M. he arrived at Tan Son Nhut Airport, only to be told that his plane was delayed. Returning to the airport shortly after noon, he was told that there would be a further delay. Major Dewey decided that there was enough time to lunch at OSS headquarters not far from the airport. For the first time that day Major Dewey took the wheel, chatting with his companion, Captain Herbert Bluechel, as they traveled the narrow roads of Saigon's suburbs.

For nearly a week Saigon's back roads had been blocked by Vietminh guerrillas attempting to stop the movement of French and English troops. But as an American, Major Dewey had never experienced any difficulties passing the roadblocks. Americans were still admired in Vietnam, and Major Dewey had grown to have a fondness for the Vietnamese and a deep respect for the Vietminh.

At approximately 12:30 P.M. Dewey and Bluechel approached the last road-block at a turn in the road 500 yards from OSS headquarters. Dewey slowed to a speed of only eight miles per hour. Suddenly a burst of machine–gunfire struck the vehicle. A bullet entered the left side of Dewey's head, near the ear. Major Dewey died instantly, the first American to be killed by Vietnamese guerrillas.

Bluechel was unharmed. He ran behind a row of hedges to OSS headquarters where a few American soldiers and a couple of war reporters held off the attacking Vietminh. No other Americans were injured, but at least eight Vietnamese were killed before the guerrillas retreated. By 5:00 P.M. OSS headquarters had been evacuated for the security of the Continental Hotel in downtown Saigon. When he heard about the incident, Ho Chi Minh immediately sent an emissary to OSS headquarters in Hanoi to apologize. But the deed had been done.

Why had the guerrillas attacked an American vehicle when so many had previously passed the same roadblock unharmed? Captain Bluechel was convinced that the blame lay with British General Douglas Gracey, commanding general of the Allied Control Commission, which accepted the Japanese surrender. Gracey had ordered that no military vehicle display an identifying national flag. Bluechel testified that Dewey was "killed through being mistaken of being a nationality other than American. If the jeep in which he was riding at the time of the incident had been displaying an American flag, I feel positive that the shots would not have been fired." The official War Department investigation of Dewey's death concluded that when Gracey prohibited the use of national flags "he was thinking too much in terms of his own personal prestige rather than in terms of the safety of his own and American soldiers."

Fourteen years later, when the Pentagon reported the first official American combat death in Vietnam, it was not a matter of mistake. The American flag had become the target.

A World War I mountain gun borne into battle on mule's back near Mon Kay on the Chinese border.

Teenaged Vietnamese volunteers answering the French recruitment call arm themselves with grenades.

A caravan carries dead from a battle in the Red River Delta as one of the survivors, a Moroccan legionnaire, watches in the rain.

Vietnamese women in Nam Dinh, south of Hanoi, mourn the dead in a military cemetery for French and Vietnamese soldiers.

The Tiger and the Elephant

The French boys did not make it home for that Christmas. Nor for the next. They fought in Vietnam for eight Christmases after the incidents in Haiphong and the Vietminh attack on Hanoi in December 1946. These eight years of fighting have been called the French Indochina War. Initially the sole French goal in the war was to retain its control and influence in Indochina, to fight for its empire. But the colonial war evolved into a second war: France fighting to contain Communist aggression. In private, French policy makers never gave up hope of winning the first war, the colonial war, but in public they increasingly defended this war by invoking the need to fight the second, to stop Communist expansion. It is difficult to assign a specific date to this change. The two wars merged. But that a second war would begin was decided on December 15, 1949

Mao's victory

The small French outpost in the Vietnamese village of Chi Ma looked across the border to the Chinese village of Ai Diem. For days the French troops had been waiting, peering nervously across the frontier. On the morning of December 15, 1949, all remained quiet in Ai Diem. But at three o'clock in the afternoon, the French soldiers in Chi Ma suddenly heard a din from the Chinese side of the border. About thirty Chinese soldiers started to run toward the French position. Machine gun batteries were pointed from each side, and the thirty men rushed back to Ai Diem. Colonel Charton, commander of the Chi Ma post, decided to approach the Chinese. Fifty yards from the frontier he met with a group from the other side waving their pistols in the air. Charton's interpreter tried to determine who these men were. Suddenly a gleam of recognition appeared in his eye. He tore himself loose from the meeting at the border and ran back to the French post at Chi Ma shouting, "The Communists! The Communists!"

The Communists had arrived on the Indochina border. It came as no surprise. For months the French had known that Chiang Kai-shek would be defeated. That prospect, strangely enough, was not altogether displeasing to the French command. General Marcel Alessandri, French commander in Tonkin, said to a reporter, "I am glad the Chinese Communists are settling in next to us. That will bring a little order into things." Frenchmen such as Alessandri, experienced in the Far East and secure in their "understanding of the Oriental mind," never believed that Mao Tse-tung would be able to convert the Chinese to communism. But he might be able to establish order along the frontier where the Nationalist troops had so often threatened chaos.

The major concern of the French officers at the frontier was what would happen when the Nationalist troops, fleeing the soldiers of Mao's Chinese People's Army, reached the French border. Would they pour across the frontier? Would they surrender to the French? Would Mao's troops follow in pursuit of the Nationalists, and even try to liberate Indochina from the French? The one thing the French knew was that they would be powerless to determine the events.

On December 8, General Marcel Carpentier, commander of all French forces in Indochina, had as-sembled his senior officers stationed on the China border. He described to them what might happen: "It may be an avalanche. Perhaps there will be a million Chinese. Two million Chinese. We don't know. If that happens, we shall need reinforcements." Then, almost as an afterthought, he added, "Perhaps I will be able to send you a company."

In fact, the French did not even need an additional company. A French missionary, acting as an envoy from the Nationalist army, offered the entire Nationalist army to the French. Together the two armies would fight the Communists—Vietnamese and Chinese alike. The French politely refused the offer. The Nationalists then threatened to storm the border. Heated negotiations took place, but the French refused to budge an inch. The Nationalists would be protected by the French, but they must surrender their weapons on crossing into Vietnam. The French would give Mao no excuse for crossing the frontier.

On the evening of December 11, the Chinese gave in. On December 12 and 13, thousands of Chinese Nationalist troops, the remnants of Chiang Kai-shek's once-proud armies, surrendered to the French. They were wrapped in rags, suffering from hideous wounds, and undernourished. Eventually, the French would transport them to Taiwan where they could nurture Chiang's dream of returning and reconquering the mainland. On December 15, the Communist troops arrived on Vietnam's border.

Within two months the entire Chinese frontier was occupied by the Chinese Communists, from Laos to the Gulf of Tonkin. They did not cross the border, but their presence changed the war. First, the Vietminh could now train in friendly Chinese Communist territory. More important, until the Communists arrived on the Chinese border, the two great superpowers, the United States and the Soviet Union, had simply watched from the sidelines, cheering their respective allies on, often with reluctance. But the presence of Mao's troops changed that. The war in Indochina was now a part of the Cold War. The war that the French were fighting to save their empire—the "dirty little war" as the French Communists called it—suddenly became part of the great crusade to save the free world.

The French were not unhappy to see this change take place. In the first war, the colonial war, the French and Vietminh were irrevocably stalemated. The greatest of the French generals, Jean de Lattre de Tassigny, admitted as much. France was no longer fighting for victory, but for negotiations. The

second war saved France from the stalemate of the first. But later France would learn that this reprieve from the stalemate only saved them for the ordeal at Dien Bien Phu.

The guerrilla war

The word "guerrilla" came into the English language early in the nineteenth century. Roughly, it is Spanish for "little war" and was first applied to the Spanish partisans who helped Wellington's army harass Napoleon's occupying troops in the Iberian Peninsula. From 1946 to 1950, the French Indochina War was a pure guerrilla struggle. As one French army technician recalled: "It was an abnormal war. . . . Things were only good when we were in bed." A French sergeant who commanded the Dak To post in the mountains of central Vietnam was more descriptive:

It is only little by little that you come to understand how terrible it is. You can starve to death there, with flowers all around you. You can die of thirst in spite of the enormous monsoon rains, because the water just goes straight down the cracks in the limestone. Everything rots, and your flesh rots first of all. You get fevers, and horrible great boils,

A column of soldiers from Chiang Kai-shek's defeated Chinese Nationalist Army streams across the border into northern Vietnam after Mao's victory.

and the least scratch sets up an inflammation that can't be cured. . . . You can't stop because the enemy is following you and you are following him. . . .

In the end the Vietminh relied on their great advantages of being able to make allies of the population and their knowledge of local geography. They were fighting in terrain they knew, under conditions that were a part of their daily life. A French noncommissioned officer resigned himself to his fate:

Monsieur, we are finished here, we French. We can't live in the jungles like the Annamites. We get cholera and malaria, and die. Or they sneak into our camps and cut our throats. There are ten thousand Annamites for every hundred Frenchmen. Out of every hundred soldiers only five go home alive.

From the outset of the war the French made every effort to engage Giap's troops in a "set piece" battle, a decisive confrontation they were sure they could win. But Giap's strategy, to which he adhered with only one major exception—a terrible blunder in the spring of 1951—was to refuse such an engagement until he was sure he could win with superior force.

In the early years of the war the French believed that the capture of Ho, as the capture of Emperor Ham Nghi in 1888 had ended an earlier insurrection, would quickly end the rebellion. In the fall of 1947, they launched Operation Lea. They threw fifteen thousand men and reserves in three columns against Ho's mountain outpost, which consisted of forty thousand men defending a triangle of nearly inaccessible Tonkin jungle and mountains one hundred miles wide and one hundred miles long northwest of Hanoi. With its Spitfires, ancient German-built "Junkers-52" trimotor aircraft, American-built C-47 transports, and French Morane reconnaissance aircraft, the entire Fourth Fighter Group gave air support to the ground forces, made up of three battalions each of armor, infantry, and artillery. The third column, 1,137 paratroopers, landed directly over Ho's headquarters at dawn on October 7. It was nearly a total surprise. The paras, as the French called their para-

troopers, found Ho's mail on his work table awaiting his signature. They captured a ranking Vietminh minister. But Ho and Giap had escaped.

Operation Lea continued, as the armored and infantry columns pushed slowly forward encircling the Vietminh troops. But whole Vietminh regiments could still walk undetected through French lines, along secret jungle paths where nighttime visibility barely stretched the length of a soldier's arm. One month after it began, Lea ended inconclusively. The French had gained an enormous expanse of territory. But they lacked the manpower and equipment to secure it. In December, the French pulled back to the lowlands. Giap's army had survived again, and in a guerrilla war, survival is a form of victory.

As the belief in a quick victory faded, the French Union force settled in for a long war of pacification. The French Expeditionary Corps was the classic example of a colonial army. Its forty thousand man strength was a "united nations" unto itself. Senegalese, Moroccans, Cambodians, Laotians, and Vietnamese—all soldiers from French colonies—were commanded by an all-volunteer force from France. The French were already weary of the war. Mindful of that, the French parliament had banned the use of conscripts in Indochina.

In addition, the French depended on their famed Foreign Legion, whose ranks were swelled after

---

An abandoned boot shows the effectiveness of primitive weapons employed by the Vietminh. "Punji-traps," designed to maim and disable, were made of barbed iron or wood spikes dipped in poison and set in camouflaged pits.

World War II by many who had need of disguising their actions when the Nazis ran Europe. Germans formed the largest contingent within the Foreign Legion, amounting to about one-third of the total legion forces. So ubiquitous was the Foreign Legion that German sometimes seemed to be the second language of the war. First designated as the French Union forces, the army would later be reorganized into the Expeditionary Corps, eventually numbering one hundred and fifty thousand men, not counting Indochinese natives.

The French chose as their basic tactic the plan that had worked sixty-five years earlier when they had first "pacified" Vietnam. The French high command concentrated troops in isolated outposts—known as hedgehogs—in hostile territory. From there, the troops would spread military control of the area like an oil slick. But the guerrillas were far better organized and led than they had been sixty-five years earlier, and they refused to engage in direct combat. Pacification proved elusive, as the Vietminh troops slipped away from French patrols only to return when the French had left.

One, two, many guerrilla wars

This guerrilla war was really a series of smaller wars. Each had its own characteristics, but all were dominated by the increasing frustration of the French in failing to catch an enemy they knew they could crush—if only it would stand still.

In the jungle the French fought against foes who effectively exploited the natural dangers as well as ancient means of warfare. Mats of palm leaves hid "punji-traps," shallow pits lined with four-inch spikes. Other traps were fashioned with bayonets designed to penetrate a man's calf and body in the fall. Punji sticks and bayonets alike were poisoned with toxic plants or rotting meat, which along with the jungle climate would quickly transform a minor wound into a raging infection. In the brush overhead were huge creepers balanced to fall at the slightest jostle. Bushes bent in two at the side of the trail would often trigger an arrow down the path at chest level. The Vietnamese also made effective use of crossbows and poisoned darts.

The Vietminh seldom used the roads running through the jungles. They cut their own secret paths, wide enough for but one man. The jungle growth recovered the path so quickly that French soldiers found it difficult to trace the guerrillas' course. But the Vietminh could always find it.

French and Vietnamese forces seeking out the hidden population of a captured village uncover women and children in a haystack.

This same kind of war took place in the jungle-covered mountains, but mountain warfare had its own peculiarities. In the highlands both the French and the Vietminh fought for the loyalty of the native tribes. In the case of the Meo Tribe in Laos, for instance, it came down to competition over the purchase of that year's opium poppy crop. One French noncommissioned officer had welded young men of the Sedang tribe into a fighting unit, but he had to be careful to respect their customs and taboos. If the Sedang column heard a stag cry on the right, the sergeant reported, he had to order a retreat or his soldiers would desert him. The belling stag was a Sedang omen of exceedingly bad luck.

The French did their best to adapt to the peculiarities of this warfare. One soldier, recalling "when the war was amusing" in 1948, told of a commando unit made up entirely of Frenchmen. "They were lions!" he said. "Nothing they couldn't do. Their specialty was to attack naked, but well greased all over, with their ammo slung round their bellies." One night, he continued, the commanding officer "was reviewing a detail in combat order; he was in the raw, everybody was. He saw the chaplain in line, and was *shocked*. 'Father, not you!' he said. 'At least put your shirt on!' "

The delta war

Fighting was fiercest in the highlands, but the prizes of the war were the Red and Mekong river deltas. As in the jungle, two governments, one French and one Vietnamese, sought control of the people. But in the water-covered paddy lands, there was another prize, the rice crop. By controlling the deltas the French thought they could deprive the Vietminh of their major food source. Whenever the battle turned against them, the Vietminh would maintain a low profile in the deltas. But when the initiative again passed to the guerrillas they would resurface, collecting their taxes and propagandizing among the people. More than anywhere else, the people of the deltas were the water sustaining Giap's guerrilla "fishes."

A French colonel recalled an operation that General René Cogny, then a division commander in Tonkin, led against a "little bamboo village" where Vietminh troops were known to be. Two mobile battalions surprised and evacuated the village. Then they went over it with "a fine-toothed comb and found no one," according to the colonel. Three days later a few guerrillas crawled out from beneath the bulldozed village esplanade.

The Vietminh militia fled in the face of superior force and the same colonel said, "We always had the feeling we were plunging a knife into water." Some guerrillas actually "hid under water and breathed through bamboo," he added.

The large cities, Hanoi, Saigon, and Haiphong, were, with brief exceptions, firmly in the control of the French throughout the war. They gave the appearance of cities secure from the Vietminh guerrillas. But the French couldn't keep the Vietminh out of the urban centers. "The Vietminh has secret cells in Hanoi and in every city we hold," said a French officer. "There must be at least three thousand Viets here in Hanoi." He threw up his hands. "Nobody knows who the Vietminh chief is. He may be the little clerk there, so intent on his papers, or he may be the servant at home now with my wife and children." He shrugged. "Who knows? This rebellion is like a plant that you cut and cut and it still comes back. You can't kill it. The only way would be to bring in half a million troops and go from village to village, sweeping the whole thing clean." Twenty years later Americans found that even a half million troops were not enough.

More than anywhere the war was fought in the mountains of Tonkin along the Chinese frontier and near the Laotian border, in Vietnam's most isolated regions. Ho Chi Minh and the Vietminh government found their refuge there. Before 1950 Giap's best troops received their training in the secrecy afforded by the limestone cliffs of Tonkin's mountains. It was in these mountains that all of the frustration, futility, and failure of the French strategy ultimately merged into catastrophe.

The battle of Dong Khe

France's war to retain its colonial grip would climax at a small mountain outpost in Tonkin. Chiseled into the high limestone cliffs between Lang Son and Cao Bang was a pathway barely the width of two GMC trucks; this was the RC 4, Route Coloniale 4. The key to the war in the mountains, thought the French military strategists, was control of this highway. RC 4 provided locations for the construction of hedgehogs. The French believed that control of this, the only road

French sentries at Dong Khe fortress Observation Post No. 2 peer at the surrounding hills in 1950. From these hills seemingly invisible Vietminh troops launched their first major offensive of the war, reducing Dong Khe to a pile of rubble within days.

traversing the mountains along the Chinese frontier, would permit them to cut Vietminh supply routes and stop troop movements. Within a year after the beginning of the war, however, the Vietminh cut two footpaths running parallel to RC 4 through the mountainous jungle.

Although the hedgehogs of RC 4 controlled little more than the land within their boundaries, they became symbols of French control deep in guerrilla-held territory. Defense and supply of the outposts became their own ends, a measure of French ability. Every day convoys of French trucks passed along RC 4, resupplying the hedgehogs, and daily the Vietminh watched them pass. They were always there, but they could never be seen. Were there only ten of them? One hundred? Surely Giap could never mass a thousand troops there in secrecy. Would today's convoy pass without incident? Or would the Vietminh attack, ambush the convoy, and capture for themselves the supplies intended for the French? The French never knew. As one foreign legionnaire said, "The Route Coloniale No. 4 is a road a man travels only once alive."

The civilian dress worn by many Vietminh supporters made the French suspicious of all Vietnamese, inspiring propaganda such as this 1947 caricature of the "smiling Vietnamese," who hides a gun behind the "skirt" of traditional mandarin robes. The exaggerated "slanted eyes" and wispy Ho Chi Minh beard complete the stereotyped image of shiftiness and connivance.

In early 1950, soon after the Chinese Communists had gained control of their side of the frontier, the guerrilla fighting along RC 4 became full-scale war. Where before the Vietminh had ambushed convoys on RC 4, now they blocked the road with full regiments dug into the hillsides. French infantrymen scoured the hills in advance of each convoy to seek out the Vietminh. But the guerrillas were as invisible in the mountains as they were in the deltas. As Giap's ambushes ground down the defenders of the key French posts of Cao Bang, Dong Khe, and Lang Son, his army pulled into place during the dry season of 1950. The French command did little.

Thick cumulus clouds hung over the peaks around Dong Khe, and heavy rains fell into the dense green forest that surrounded the distant French stronghold at the end of May 1950. The monsoon rains had struck, and with them came the Vietminh. One heavy and four light battalions, the first to be trained in China, appeared noiselessly on the limestone crags.

With precision and ease, their mortars and howitzers pounded the French post. Desperate radio calls for air support went out. But nothing could fly in the monsoon storms. In Hanoi, French pilots played cards or drank in bars, eyeing the sky nervously.

Exactly forty-eight hours after the shelling had begun, Vietminh infantry poured over the battered concrete walls of the French citadel. At 3:00 A.M. on May 28, 1950, all resistance ended.

After the battle of Dong Khe the fighting would continue for another four years. To France it was still a war to maintain its influence in Indochina; it was no longer private, but an international war whose repercussions were already being felt on the battlefield. The Vietminh forces at Dong Khe, trained in China, were modeled after Mao's Chinese People's Army.

The end of "neutrality"

Within days after Dong Khe fell, in June 1950, several American transport planes, DC-3 Dakotas, arrived at Tan Son Nhut airfield. The Dakotas represented the first tangible evidence of what had been a gradual shift in American policy. The previous neutrality, which in truth gave the French a free hand, evolved into an alliance with France in a common struggle against Chinese, and hence Soviet, expansion.

The shift from neutrality to open support of the French was gradual, reflecting a tug of war between the two American policies of anticolonialism and anticommunism. When war erupted between the French and Vietminh in December 1946, the U.S. State Department informed the French government that its general willingness to sell arms would be denied "in cases which appear to relate to Indochina." One month later the U.S. ambassador in Paris informed the French premier that "colonial empires . . . are rapidly becoming [a] thing of [the] past." But the ambassador also explained that the U.S. was aware that "Ho Chi Minh has direct Communist connections." In the end, the ambassador admitted, "Frankly we have no solution of [the] problem to suggest." The United States would let France handle the war its own way.

There was one troubling aspect to the American analysis: The State Department had no evidence of Ho's "direct Communist connections." In July 1948 the department concluded that it "has no evidence of direct link between Ho and Moscow but assumes it exists." In the fall of 1948, in a wide-ranging review of Communist activities in Southeast Asia, the State Department Office of Intelligence Research stated, "To date the Vietnam press and radio have not adopted an anti-American position. It is rather the French colonial press that has been strongly anti-American . . . to the point of approximating the official Moscow position." The report concluded, "If there is a Moscow-directed conspiracy in Southeast Asia, Indochina is an anomaly so far."

Even so, the State Department was well aware that, under the name of Nguyen Ai Quoc, Ho Chi Minh had labored for the Communist International, the Comintern, during the 1920s and 1930s. Finding no direct evidence that Ho was still operating under Moscow's orders or supervision in Vietnam after World War II, the department simply asserted that

---

Bogging Down: Road-bound French troops wrestle a truck up the muddy slope of Route Coloniale 4 on the Chinese border. Vietminh troops choked off the outposts along RC 4 by ambushing the truck caravans used by the French to supply their isolated "hedgehogs."

such a link must exist. In the immediate postwar years, before Tito had established a Yugoslavia independent of the Soviet Union and long before Mao broke with Moscow, it seemed inconceivable that a Communist could be a dedicated nationalist. In other words, American policy makers assumed that Ho would always place the interests of the international Communist movement above the interests of Vietnam.

With the great advantage of hindsight, later policy makers and students of the Vietnam conflict have wondered if there were no direct links between Ho and Moscow whether it would have been possible for an independent Vietnam under Ho's leadership to have developed into an "Asian Yugoslavia." Might Ho have established a neutral state opposed to Chinese and Russian domination?

If answers to these questions existed they were buried with Ho in 1969. But for American policy makers to have even considered this possibility in the 1940s would have required a vision of the role of emerging nations—the Third World—which seemed to elude Americans at least until the 1960s. To the dominant figures in the State Department, Southeast Asia was considered to be little more than an appendage of Europe. U.S. policy toward Southeast Asia was

thus to be determined by the colonial powers. France was of much graver concern to the United States in the late 1940s than was Vietnam, so American policy in Indochina was subordinated to American policy toward France.

France's postwar problems

No country in post–World War II Europe seemed as important to the United States as France, and no country seemed to be beset with so many problems. Not only had France's economic life been completely disrupted, even destroyed, by the Nazi occupation; France was also suffering from deeply troublesome political instability. The Communist party had emerged from the war as France's strongest party, gaining over 25 percent of the popular vote. With the party's popular support it was impossible to form a French government without Communist participation.

At the other end of the political spectrum stood the august figure of Charles de Gaulle. De Gaulle and his supporters, contemptuous of the strong parliamentary government, called for a strong presidential system. Not achieving that, he retired from politics, but his supporters formed a large party on the

A fast paint job is applied to a U.S.–supplied Fairchild C–119 transport plane at Haiphong air base, transforming the white star of the U.S. Air Force into the French Tricolor.

Ho sits in his mountain headquarters in 1951. Fearing capture by the French, he spent the war years in hiding, where he shunned contact with western journalists and deepened his mystique as a revolutionary.

right. The Gaullists were always animated by an anti-American impulse; they considered America's influence in Europe a threat to French power. The Communists, of course, became increasingly anti-American as the Cold War took shape. Thus, as the United States formed its postwar policy toward France, it had to tread carefully to avoid nourishing these anti-American sentiments. Any attempt by the United States to influence French policy toward Vietnam would immediately be attacked by both the Gaullists and Communists—with some justification—as interference in French politics.

This policy dilemma became more critical as the Cold War heightened in 1948 and 1949. The fall of Czechoslovakia to Soviet domination, the Berlin blockade, and the Soviet Union's ending of the United States' atomic monopoly all made the situation in Europe even more critical. The Marshall Plan and the North Atlantic Treaty Organization (NATO) were the economic and military responses of the United States intended to create a strong alliance between America and Europe. Germany still lay divided, devastated, and disarmed—by agreement of all four occupying powers. More than ever the U.S. looked to France as the defensive bulwark of Europe. This demanded a continuation of America's Indochina policy of neutrality, neutrality "tilted" toward France.

All vestiges of the anticolonial policy of the United States were, however, not lost. The American government continued to press the French to institute reforms in Vietnam and to prepare the way for a national movement leading to eventual independence. In January 1949 the American ambassador told the French government that the State Department "is desirous of the French coming to terms with . . . any truly nationalist group which has a reasonable chance of winning over the preponderance of the Vietnamese" from the Vietminh.

Vice President Richard Nixon meets a Vietnamese nationalist soldier near Dong Giao during his trip to Asia in late 1953. Nixon told the Vietnamese that while the U.S. supported their wish for self-rule, they must continue to cooperate with the French.

The "Bao Dai solution"

American pressure on the French government did not go unheeded. On March 8, 1949, Emperor Bao Dai signed an agreement with the president of the French Republic recognizing Vietnam's independence "within the French Union," giving birth to the new State of Vietnam. The Elysée Agreement, as this pact was known, was later confirmed in the Franco-Vietnamese treaty of December 30, 1949, granting Vietnam the status of an independent nation.

The French signed preliminary agreements with Bao Dai in December 1947 and mid-1948 in which France finally recognized Vietnam's "right to unity and independence," the first time the word independence had been used. But there were no references to an independent Vietnamese army or foreign policy, as Ho had consistently demanded.

The Elysée Agreement consummated these negotiations. Bao Dai received the right to raise an independent army but could enjoy full diplomatic relations only with Nationalist China, Thailand, and the Vatican. The French retained special privileges for their citizens and army in Vietnam. Bao Dai thought he had done well, but would the Vietnamese accept this new independence and support him?

The answer was forthcoming at elections held in Cochin China in April 1949 to decide whether the southern colony would join with Annam and Tonkin to form a unified Vietnam. Calling the Bao Dai government a sham, the Vietminh called for a boycott of the election. The people of Cochin China followed the Vietminh. Of the 3 million qualified voters in Cochin China, only 1,700 voted.

These 1,700 Cochin Chinese voted overwhelmingly to join in the new State of Vietnam. When Bao Dai returned to Vietnam in June, however, the mood, according to French journalist Lucien Bodard, was far from festive:

There were many flags fluttering colorfully in the breeze; there were policemen and there were bowing civil servants. From the people, there came not a living soul.

The stillbirth of the State of Vietnam was nowhere more evident than in the documents signed by French and Vietnamese officials. Whereas the document granting Burma independence from England in 1948 had run four legal-sized pages in length, the Franco-Vietnamese agreement was a 258-page volume filled with restrictions and responsibilities limiting Vietnam's independence.

America becomes involved

Still, this independence was good enough for the U.S. State Department. By late 1949, with the Chinese Communists poised on the frontier, American policy makers were looking for any justification to shift from a neutral pro-French position to one of active aid.

On February 7, 1950, the United States government recognized the State of Vietnam, a recognition that Ho Chi Minh had begged for nearly five years earlier. Now there were two Vietnams: Bao Dai's State of Vietnam and Ho Chi Minh's Democratic Republic of Vietnam (DRV). Few expected both entities to survive the Indochina War.

On February 27, 1950, the National Security Council (NSC) met in Washington for its first session exclusively devoted to Indochina. The report adopted by the council and President Harry S Truman established as official a new analysis of the situation in Vietnam and formulated the basis of a new policy: "It is recognized that the threat of Communist aggression against Indochina is only one phase of anticipated Communist plans to seize all of Southeast Asia." The report instructed the Departments of State and Defense to "prepare as a matter of priority a program of all practicable measures designed to protect United States security interests in Indochina."

The recognition of Bao Dai's government gave the United States a conduit through which it could funnel military and economic assistance without accusations that it was aiding European colonialism. The first result was the arrival of the DC-3 Dakotas in June 1950. But these aircraft, the symbol of a heightened U.S. commitment to the French cause, quickly became a cause of Franco-American jealousies. As soon as the Dakotas landed, French maintenance men appeared on the runway with small pots of paint. The white star of the U.S. Air Force was quickly replaced with the red, white, and blue rings of the French Tricolor.

In March 1950 General Marcel Carpentier, then commander in chief of French forces, came to the United States to work out an agreement for military assistance. Before leaving America, he told the *New York Times* that he would "never agree to equipment being given directly to the Vietnamese." He threatened to "resign within twenty-four hours" if the

Commander in Chief Vo Nguyen Giap reviews troops of the Vietnam People's Army. Giap skillfully adapted Mao Tse-tung's Chinese model for a revolutionary army to the situation in Vietnam.

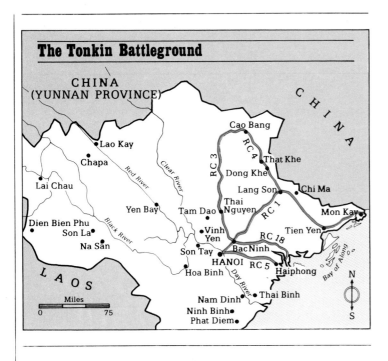

The Tonkin Battleground

CHINA (YUNNAN PROVINCE)

CHINA

LAOS

Lao Kay
Chapa
Lai Chau
Yen Bay
Dien Bien Phu
Son La
Na San
Cao Bang
That Khe
Dong Khe
Lang Son
Chi Ma
Tam Dao
Thai Nguyen
Mon Kay
Vinh Yen
Tien Yen
Son Tay
Bac Ninh
HANOI
Hoa Binh
Haiphong
Nam Dinh
Thai Binh
Ninh Binh
Phat Diem

Red River
Clear River
Black River
Day River
Bay of Along

RC 3
RC 4
RC 1
RC 18
RC 5

Miles
0   75

N
E   W
S

United States insisted. The French were to continue to run the show. The United States relented, and on May 1, 1950, President Truman signed a bill authorizing $10 million in military assistance, all to be controlled by the French.

The Americans—especially those in Vietnam—bristled under the restrictions. An economic assistance program was also developed, one which in theory, at least, permitted direct contact between Americans and the Vietnamese. But the French continued to be suspicious. To them America's anti-colonial rhetoric and insistence that Vietnam's independence be respected seemed to be little more than a screen behind which the Americans were trying to replace French influence in Vietnam with their own.

Ultimately, the French position prevailed because they had to do the fighting. As the war dragged on, the French government came under increasing pressure from opposition parties and the public to negotiate a settlement. After the outbreak of war in Korea, however, American policy makers saw the war in Indochina as the second front in the battle to contain Communist China, a view which they pressed on the French government. Ultimately, the war in Indochina became more important to the United States than to France, and so it was fought on France's terms, with increasing amounts of U.S. aid.

Having come to the conclusion that winning the Indochina War was crucial to containing China, American policy makers worked to deter a Chinese invasion of Vietnam, that is, to avert a repetition of Korea. Contingency planning to aid the French with

the direct intervention of American troops was limited to countering such a Chinese invasion. This policy blinded American officials to the colonial character of the Indochina War even though it had been internationalized by the Chinese and American involvements. The United States consistently underestimated the strength and will of the Vietminh. American officials were certain that American aid would bring victory to France and the free world.

Giap, however, reasoned otherwise. The victory of communism in China had provided France with America's aid in its quest for victory, but Giap had already insured that the resources of China and the Soviet Union were at the disposal of the Vietminh. The result was another stalemate.

U.S.S.R. cool toward Ho

Until the victory of Mao Tse-tung in China, the attitude of the Soviet Union toward Ho Chi Minh was even cooler than that of the United States toward France. Stalin's advice to Ho, like his advice to Mao, was to hold back; the time was not yet ripe for communism in Asia. According to orthodox Marxist thought, liberation for colonized people (and semi-colonized people like the Chinese) would come only after the Western capitalist states had fallen to communism. Neither Mao nor Ho would listen. Stalin gave Ho no military support and refrained from recognizing Ho's government. All that changed in December 1949.

Mao's victory certainly spurred the French to come to an agreement with Bao Dai and establish an independent Vietnamese government to compete with Ho's. China would probably have recognized Ho's government in any case. But the agreement with Bao Dai and the American recognition of his government either forced China and the Soviet Union or enabled them more easily to take sides. In January 1950 the DRV gained its first international recognition from the People's Republic of China. The Soviet Union, fearing that China was trying to gain the upper hand in the Third World followed suit two weeks later. Within days, the DRV was recognized by the entire Soviet bloc.

A few months after the Chinese recognition of the DRV, Vietnamese peasants built four roads from Chinese supply depots to the Vietnamese border. Over these roads modern equipment from the Soviet Union, Czechoslovakia, and China would be transported to the border, and from there Vietnamese peasants would carry it to Giap's army. Much of the Vietminh's equipment, however, was American made, captured from the French or bought on the open market. To standardize parts, the Chinese supplied Giap heavily with American equipment captured in Korea.

Chinese aid to the Vietminh, however, never reached the level of U.S. assistance to the French. In 1951 when the assistance became measurable, the United States was shipping a monthly average of 7,200 tons of military equipment to the French, the Chinese only 10 to 20 tons per month to the Vietminh. By the end of 1953 the Chinese had increased their assistance to 500 to 600 tons per month, but U.S. aid to France had increased to 10,000 tons per month. Of course, Vietminh military hardware tended to be lighter and less sophisticated than France's. The Vietminh, for example, had no air force. And Giap continued to depend upon captured French weapons.

Building a people's army

More important to the Vietminh than the Chinese military help was Chinese ideological assistance. Already at the Battle of Dong Khe in May 1950 the Vietminh had displayed the new strength gained by organizing their forces across the border in China. But Chinese Communists did more than train Vietnamese peasants in the art of warfare; they also trained them in the art of political revolution. After 1950 the Vietminh front became more aggressively Communist. "Unreliable elements" were purged. Within a year Giap's regulars and irregulars became a "people's army" after Mao's model. By the end of 1950 a Vietminh infantry battalion had as much firepower—submachine and heavy machine guns, mortars, bazookas, and American-made recoilless guns—as a French Expeditionary Force battalion. And the weapons were equally modern. But as General L. M. Chassin noted of the Chinese training that turned illiterate peasants into fighting machines:

In the day's work of the Red soldier, the Marxist political lesson plays as important a part as the arms manual. Taken in hand by intelligent leaders, the armed peasant rapidly becomes a fanatic, an apostle of the new religion.

Both peasant-soldiers and peasant civilians, serving largely as porters, were indoctrinated with militant anticolonialism. Such men were capable of enormous discipline and of making enormous sacrifices. The Vietminh "death volunteer" units whose

Organization of the civilian population was as important to the Vietminh as raising the army. This Vietnamese woman proudly displays the "hero of the resistance" medal she received in 1953 for model service in the war effort.

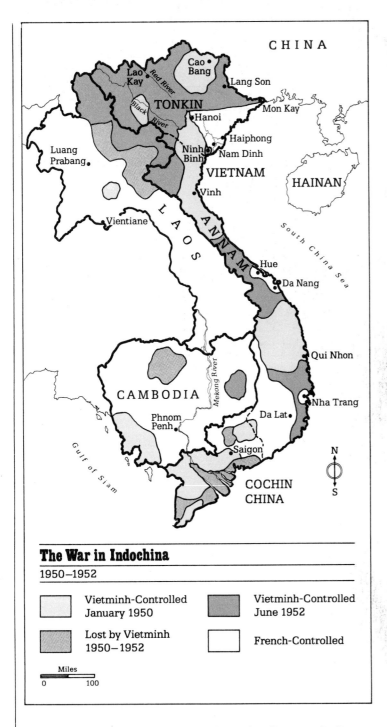

The War in Indochina

1950–1952

- Vietminh-Controlled January 1950
- Vietminh-Controlled June 1952
- Lost by Vietminh 1950–1952
- French-Controlled

Miles
0   100

Responsibility for maintaining discipline came from the political cadres attached to each unit. They, not the military commanders, made the final decisions. This power was given to the political cadres to insure that the Vietminh army would never be anything but the military wing of the Vietminh front and eventually the Communist party. The political leaders insured that the single most important goal of the party was never forgotten: Support of the civilian population was the key ingredient to victory.

This discipline was enforced whenever Vietminh troops came in contact with the civilian population. Any soldier accused of rape was handed over to the village authorities for punishment. Even the use of terror fell under the rules of political discipline. The Vietminh, as well as the French, were nonetheless guilty of terrorist actions against the civilian population. But French terror was often the result of undisciplined anger or frustrations and to the Vietnamese wholly unpredictable.

Giap's terror followed careful rules. It was employed only against those who violated the principles of the revolution. It was as vicious, if not more so, as that employed by the French. The peasants may have hated it, but they understood it and its lesson: If one follows the right path, one is immune from Vietminh terror. The French were as likely to harm their allies as their enemies.

From guerrilla war to people's war

The Chinese Communist victory had shown Giap that Mao Tse-tung's theory of revolutionary warfare could work. As the Vietminh's leading military strategist, Giap was surely aware of Mao's analysis of guerrilla warfare long before 1950. But after 1950 it became the guiding strategy of the Vietnam People's Army (VPA). Mao's theory, adapted by Giap to Vietnamese conditions, called for victory in three stages. In the first stage, the revolutionaries would be on the defensive. Their only objective was to survive, to avoid a confrontation. Their tactics: hit, run, hide, but mostly hide.

These tactics would eventually frustrate the enemy, who would then concentrate on consolidating the gains already made. This would lead directly to the second phase. As the enemy adopts a more defensive posture, the tide turns. The guerrillas become more daring and attack the enemy as they attempt to defend their position. But the attacks are more a harass-

men strapped dynamite to their bodies and threw themselves against tanks or bunkers were a weapon that the French could never counter.

Giap actually trained his men to do only a few things, but through numbing repetition they learned to do those few things well. A French prisoner once witnessed the Vietminh preparations for battle. The peasants built scale models of the French fortifications out of sand, and the soldiers then practiced the attack repeatedly. "Each soldier rehearsed his job fifty times, maybe one hundred times," the French prisoner of war said. "*C'est formidable.* When they attack, they move like machines."

ing technique. The tactics are still hit-and-run. Pitched battle is avoided.

The second phase is designed to further the demoralization of the enemy and to increase the ranks of the guerrillas. When the revolutionaries finally gain numerical and military superiority they pass to the third stage—the general counteroffensive (GCO). With a frontal assault on the now demoralized enemy troops, the revolutionaries achieve final victory.

After his victory at Dong Khe in early 1950, Giap thought that the Vietminh was ready to pass from the second phase to the GCO. A few preliminaries were still necessary, but fortified by Chinese training and weapons, the Vietminh were predicting that Ho would celebrate Tet in Hanoi. It was Giap's only great mistake of the war.

The battle for Route Coloniale 4

The Vietminh victory at Dong Khe in May 1950 was merely a rehearsal for the most important battle of the war until Dien Bien Phu. A few days after the fall of Dong Khe, when the skies had cleared, French paras flew into the village and within hours recaptured it for France. During the height of the rainy sea-son, from July to September, the war in the mountains of Tonkin remained quiet. Quiet except for the Vietminh loud-speakers blaring into the French camps: "You are prisoners already! In a few weeks you will be in our power." The French command did little.

On September 18, 1950, as the last of the torrential rains beat the soft earth of Tonkin, the Vietminh again overran Dong Khe. The French garrison was swallowed up by the attack. No one escaped. No paras from Hanoi leaped to the rescue, no reinforcements fought up jungle paths. Still, French generals argued among themselves and did not believe in the guerrillas' strength.

One by one the French evacuated the hedgehogs, their forts along RC 4. By October 10, the whole northeast frontier lay open to the Vietminh south to Lang Son, a provincial capital of one hundred thousand and a symbol of French power. If the Vietminh captured this fortified town, they would be in striking distance of Hanoi. Lang Son was abandoned in panic before the Vietminh had even drawn near, and the thirteen hundred tons of ammunition, food, equipment, and artillery left there were not blown up.

The *Paris-Presse* wrote late in October that "Everybody, from our cabinet minister down to the

French soldiers mount an attack during the battle of Na San, a major French victory. Moving toward Laos in late 1952, General Giap badly underestimated the French outpost's strength and lost half his 308th Division trying to take it. After the stunning defeat, Giap ordered his troops to bypass the fort on their way to Laos.

man in the street, realizes now that the massacre ... is the outcome of five years of neglect, hesitation, intrigues, and balmy optimism." Never had a French army been so demoralized. The tough North African troops deserted in panic. There was fear that Mao might throw Chinese troops into the battle—as he had done in Korea—and plans were made to evacuate women and children from Hanoi. French military planners feared that the Expeditionary Force would not be able to retreat to Haiphong and escape by the sea. It might be another Dunkirk, but without the final escape. Giap brought his regular troops to the perimeter of the Tonkin Delta. He was ready to pass over to the general counteroffensive, and Hanoi was his target.

The French government refused to give in. Instead on December 17, 1950, it underlined its commitment to the Expeditionary Force with the appointment of General Jean de Lattre de Tassigny as both high commissioner and commander in chief of French forces. De Lattre was a hero of World War II, a tough disciplinarian, France's MacArthur. He knew how desperate the situation in Indochina was and might have been excused if he had refused the assignment, choosing to live out his career in greater comfort. But he accepted, because "it is my duty."

De Lattre's first task was to restore morale to the Expeditionary Force. He canceled the evacuation of women and children from Hanoi. "As long as the women and children are here," he said, "the men won't dare to let go." He brought his wife to Hanoi to live, where he spent most of his time, unlike many of his predecessors who preferred the more amiable environment of Saigon.

The battle of Vinh Yen

De Lattre had little time to work his miracle. On January 13, 1951, Giap began the GCO. His force outnumbering the French three to one, Giap attempted to take the French fortified city of Vinh Yen, the last major French stronghold northwest of Hanoi. If Giap were successful, Hanoi might well be in Vietminh hands by the Tet festival.

In the first day of fighting the Vietminh completely surrounded Vinh Yen, cutting it off from all French forces. The next day de Lattre flew into the besieged outpost in his private two-seater plane. When his chief of staff pleaded that Vinh Yen was about to be overrun, de Lattre ordered, "Well, break through and get me out."

The French counterattacked. On one flank a detachment of Muong soldiers—hill people from what they called the "Country of the Killing Water"—moved forward against Vietminh machine-gunfire. On the other flank turbaned Moroccans attacked, chanting, "There is no God but Allah." By three o'clock in the afternoon the French had recaptured two hills overlooking Vinh Yen. The Vietminh attempted two more assaults, throwing human waves of infantrymen at the French for the first time. But de Lattre threw all available resources into battle, and Vinh Yen became the scene of the largest aerial bombardment of the war. By January 17 the guerrillas were through. The Vietminh retreated. Vinh Yen claimed six thousand Vietminh dead and five hundred prisoners, while French casualties were reported as less than a tenth of the enemy's. The French had prevailed because of superior firepower, control of air, and—thanks to de Lattre—superb discipline.

De Lattre had succeeded. Hanoi was safe, at least for the time being. But the victory came at a tremendous personal cost. His only son, Bernard, fell in May in the aftermath of the GCO. De Lattre himself was soon forced to return to France, complaining of ill health. One year later, in January 1952, "King John," General Jean de Lattre de Tassigny, died of cancer in a Paris nursing home.

Stalemate again

De Lattre's death was a double blow to France. Alone among France's leaders de Lattre had possessed the prestige enabling him to negotiate a settlement with the Vietminh short of complete victory. On the battlefield, French forces were again commanded by a series of lackluster generals.

Giap's forces again slipped away, wounded but surviving. Giap began a new offensive in the highlands near the Laotian border. He openly confessed his error in prematurely beginning the GCO. In the future he would be much more cautious. He moved back to the second stage of resistance, harassing the French at every opportunity. During 1952 and 1953 he captured a huge expanse of territory across the border in Laos after fierce combat against French Union forces. With this improved tactical position he swept eastward, securing the position of the Vietminh in Vietnam's "central spine." Then he headed back to the highlands. And somewhere, near the Laotian border, not far from an unknown outpost named Dien Bien Phu, he waited patiently.

Algeria-
The
Dirty War
Continued

Less than seven months after the fall of Dien Bien Phu a revolt began in the French colony of Algeria. This bloody and violent struggle would result in terrorism and torture, the death of thousands of Frenchmen and Algerians, the fall of France's Fourth Republic, and eventually the independence of Algeria. It, too, was a part of France's Vietnam experience.

"You came to fight us," a Vietminh political officer said, "and you are returning to your country bearing our mark and deep down the mark of our revolution." This statement could have been directed at any of the Vietminh's antagonists, but it is particularly relevant to the North Africans who fought side by side with the French against the Vietminh and later turned against them in their own struggle for independence in Algeria. This dramatic turnabout was influenced and even inspired by the lessons the Algerians and their fellow North Africans—Tunisians and Moroccans—learned in Indochina.

"Dien Bien Phu," Ferhat Abbas, the leader of the Algerian independence movement, said after the battle, "was not only a military victory. It was the affirmation of the Asiatic and African man against the European man." The notion of the invincibility of the colonial power had been dispelled at last. The North Africans had seen with their own eyes the defeat of the French forces by a guerrilla army.

North African perceptions had begun to change even before Dien Bien Phu. A French officer commanding a Moroccan division noticed a difference in attitudes as early as 1949: "They were already thinking about independence," he said, "and then we sent them to fight in a country which was already in the midst of the same problem." The fact that the North Africans were fighting for France, the country from which "they themselves were trying to get away," only intensified France's dilemma.

The Vietminh cadres developed a separate propaganda campaign to nourish the North African's budding nationalism. The man they chose to lead this effort, known only by his revolutionary alias, Maarouf, had ideal credentials for the task. Maarouf was not only a tribal leader from Morocco's Atlas Mountains and a leader in the Moroccan Communist party, but also a decorated veteran of France's World War II North African army. His goal in Indochina was twofold: to spread antiwar feeling in the North African ranks and prepare these men to liberate their own countries. The propaganda leaflets he distributed to Algerian, Moroccan, and Tunisian units called for North Africans to end their war against the Vietminh and join in the struggle against colonialism.

The indoctrination of prisoners of war provided him with his greatest opportunity. He separated Algerians and other North Africans from French POWs and treated them in a special manner. They were counted not as prisoners but as potential freedom fighters. After complimenting them on their heroic struggle in Vietnam, Maarouf or Vietminh interrogators asked them, "And since you are such good soldiers why do you fight for the colonialists? Why don't you fight for yourselves and get yourself a country of your own?" To promote this idea Maarouf organized political and cultural consciousness-raising sessions and made sure his prisoners were well treated and released promptly. In response to anyone who questioned his methods, Maarouf replied, "They will form the cadres of our wars. . . . You will see. . . ."

Maarouf was right. After eight years of war in Indochina, France endured eight more in North Africa. The first war left its mark on France: The country was divided on the question of continued warfare against colonial independence movements. In turn the French army was demoralized by its defeat and dissatisfied with the government's handling of the colonial problem.

After Tunisia and Morocco were granted independence in 1956, the controversy over the preservation of the French Empire centered on Algeria, the colony with the largest and most deeply rooted French population. Here France found itself opposed by an enemy fortified rather than weakened by its Indochina effort. Hundreds of the men reeducated by Maarouf and the Vietminh joined the Algerian National Liberation Front. One of these former POWs, Slimane Hoffman, even became director of the Algerian Ministry of Defense. As Hoffman later recalled, it was in Vietnam that the "commitment between the colonial power and the colonized people was broken forever."

The French Foreign Legion

A Czech legionnaire wears the wide-brimmed hat and full beard sported by many legion infantrymen (right).

Cramped inside a French transport plane, foreign legionnaires sing as they head for battle.

Legio Patria Nostra—the legion is our country—was their motto. Fighting France's overseas wars was their job. They were the soldiers of the French Foreign Legion, probably the best fighting group in the French Indochina War and surely the most colorful. The highly disciplined professional mercenary army was composed chiefly of foreign volunteers and led by French officers. The legion asked few questions of enlistees. Those with five years of good conduct qualified for French citizenship and a new identity. Many, like Gary Cooper in the movie *Beau Geste*, took refuge in the legion for romantic reasons. But for every languorous nobleman, jilted lover, or common criminal who wore the white kepi headdress and crimson epaulets, there were many professional soldiers who preferred fighting in the legion to serving in their own country's army. Volunteers from defeated forces and victims

of political persecution have expanded the legion's rolls after every major European conflict since the 1830s.

Founded by King Louis Philippe in 1831 to help control French colonial possessions in Africa, the legion assembled men from fifty-seven countries, replaced their national identity with that of the legion, and endowed them with an almost mystical esprit de corps. The legion has fought innumerable battles on four continents in its 150 years, including an heroic stand at Camerone, Mexico, on April 30, 1863. There, to protect a bullion convoy, a detachment of sixty-three legionnaires held out against the attack of four thousand Mexican troops from dawn to dusk—until the last man had fallen.

No French army unit was more decorated in World War I than was a legion mobile battalion. During World War II, after legion units escaped occupied France, a battalion seized fortified Narvik,

Norway, while others fought with the Free French in North Africa and on the continent. At war's end legion troops, among them many displaced persons (DPs) from central Europe and Germany, streamed through the Suez Canal to fight in Indochina.

Their exploits in the war were legion, but their numbers were not—the legion seldom had more than twenty thousand troops in an army that grew to include several hundred thousand. One of its seven thousand German recruits deserted and became Ho Chi Minh's adopted son, Ho Chi Long. The legion's most valiant hour came at Dien Bien Phu where six legion regiments—one-third of the garrison—formed the core of the defense.

The legionnaires at Dien Bien Phu strong point Eliane had run out of the army-issued condensed wine when it came time to celebrate the legion holiday,

Camerone Day, on April 30. As the Vietminh loudspeakers blared surrender or (as at Camerone) be massacred, they defiantly sang their marching tune, "Here's the Blood Sausage."

The last strong point to fall at Dien Bien Phu was isolated Isabelle, held by fifteen hundred legionnaires under the command of Colonel André Lalande. At 1:15 A.M. on May 8, Colonel Lalande, rather than be crushed by the Vietminh whose troops outnumbered his ten to one, led a charge. Few legionnaires survived. At 1:50 A.M. Isabelle radioed Hanoi, "Breakout failed. We must break communications with you. We are going to blow up everything. *Fini.* Repeat. *Fini.*" Observers noted that the legion, which lost 11,710 men in the war, was never the same after Dien Bien Phu as the following story, recounted by the French writer Bernard Fall, demonstrates.

Shortly after the climactic battle, two

legionnaires—both Rumanian DPs—on a patrol along Route 18 dove to the ground when Vietminh troops fired on them. The younger man, twenty-one-year-old Eliahu Itzkovitz, rose quickly and called out, "Stanescu!" The burly veteran corporal a few paces ahead of him, his uniform black with mud, turned, surprised and frightened to hear the name he had abandoned when he entered the legion.

Eliahu remembered. He had been herded into a concentration camp for Rumanian Jews with his father, mother, and three older brothers in World War II. Not yet ten, he saw his family die in Stanescu's bloody barracks. A mere skeleton when the Russians captured the camp in 1944, Eliahu swore vengeance. Communist authorities allowed him to emigrate to Israel in 1952 after he had served five years for stabbing Stanescu's son. Drafted into the Israeli army in 1953, Eliahu's mission faded into memory until

he heard that Stanescu had escaped Rumania and joined the legion. Within months Eliahu had transferred into the Israeli navy, gone AWOL in Genoa, and enlisted in the legion in France. By early 1954 he had joined the Third Legion Infantry in Tonkin and was on patrol along Route 18.

"You are Stanescu, aren't you?" asked Eliahu as both men picked themselves up.

"Yes, but . . . ."

"Stanescu," Eliahu said evenly, "I'm one of the Jews from Chisinau," and let loose with his MAT–49 submachine gun. A legionnaire did not leave fallen comrades behind, and as Eliahu dragged the body back to the road, a comrade commiserated, "Tough luck. He was a Rumanian just like you, wasn't he?"

"Yes, just like me."

The hunt was over. Honorably discharged in 1958, Eliahu returned to Israel where a military court, made aware of the circumstances, sentenced him to only one year's imprisonment for having gone AWOL.

The legion, like the French Empire it was intended to protect, crumbled slowly. In 1961 a regiment was disbanded in disgrace after it joined the anti–de Gaulle coup attempt by French colonists in Algeria. The following year the remnants of the once mighty French Foreign Legion—one armored, one parachute, and three infantry regiments—moved from Algeria to their present base near Marseilles.

A Moroccan legionnaire, wearing his native turban, serves in a mule artillery unit (above, left). For French colonial subjects, like this Moroccan, service in the legion was a quick route to French citizenship.

A Senegalese legionnaire in naval cap bears the scars made for religious reasons in his African homeland (above, right).

Foreign legionnaires in Indochina prepare their own blood sausages, the inspiration for their hauntingly slow march song: "Here's the blood sausage, the blood sausage, the blood sausage; For the Alsatians, the Swiss, and the Lorrainers; There's none left for the Belgians 'cause they're shirkers" (left).

In the gloomy interior of a U.S.-supplied Dakota, exhausted legionnaires who have just finished one operation are en route to another.

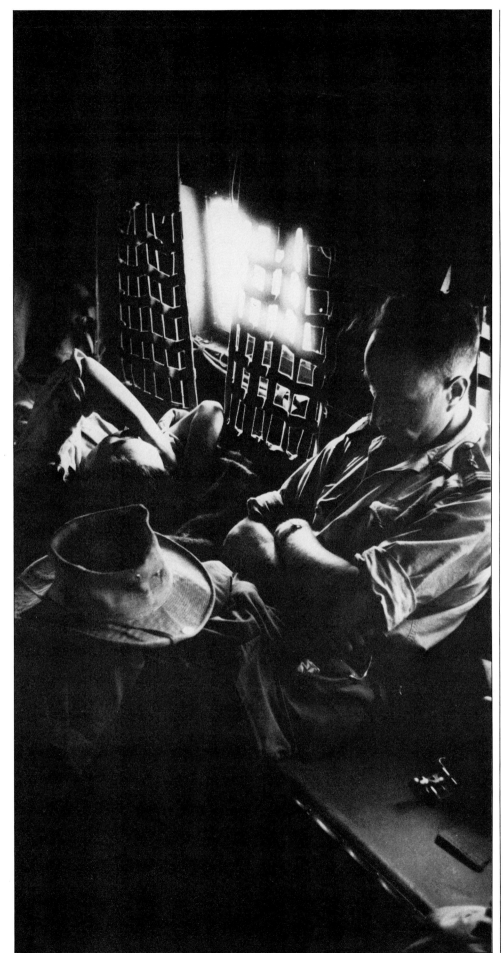

Dien Bien Phu and Geneva

When it was all over, the French War in Indochina, the loss of France's North African colonies; when the French had in desperation begged de Gaulle to return to power in 1958 and approved his constitution for the Fifth Republic; when the Fourth Republic was gone forever, like the first, and the second, and the third, a French historian would write:

The Fourth Republic was born with the war in Indochina. It died with the war in Algeria. Amongst all the errors of the Republic, the most fatal was its failure to establish new relationships with the overseas territories.

With its strong opposition parties the Fourth Republic had little margin for error. The Communists on the left and the Gaullists on the right gnawed at the slender majority of the center. The three parties that formed the centrist coalition—the Socialists, the Christian Democrats (the Popular Republican Movement), and the tiny Radical party in the middle—were forced to find agreement on the issues that separated them or face

the destruction of the republic. Major controversies that could not be settled by compromise were resolved by reshuffling the cabinet. In the nine years from 1945 to 1954 France witnessed a procession of seventeen different governments, the most stable lasting only thirteen months.

On the surface the governing parties were as divided on the war in Indochina as they were on any question. The Socialists preferred a negotiated settlement to the war; the Christian Democrats thought military force was the only way to preserve France's influence in Asia. But the war was one question the parties were not going to allow to divide them. In the end, it was always the Socialists who compromised, supporting the war to avoid antagonizing the Christian Democrats.

As early as 1947 the Socialist minister of overseas territories (formerly, the minister of colonies), Marius Moutet, replaced the stubborn Thierry d'Argenlieu with the more flexible Emile Bollaert as high commissioner to Indochina. Peace feelers had been sent out by Ho in April 1947. Bollaert responded with preconditions for negotiations that were heavily influenced by the Christian Democrat minister of war, Paul Coste-Floret. These conditions called for the virtual surrender of the Vietminh troops; they were asked to give their weapons to the French. Ho responded to the offer with a bit of French-style gallantry: "There is no place for cowards in the French Union. I should be one if I accepted these conditions." When told that Ho would reject the French conditions, a general responded, "I hope so." Moutet was too weak, personally and politically, to quiet the Christian Democrats' war fever.

Hope for negotiated settlement ends

With this intransigence the final hopes for a quickly negotiated settlement passed. The Christian Democrats were simply unwilling to negotiate with "that bandit," Ho Chi Minh. Instead they offered the "Bao Dai solution," the creation of an emperor-led government to compete with Ho's for the loyalty of the Viet-

namese. By 1949, as the war reached its first stalemate prior to the victory of the Communist army in China, the French were ready to impose the Bao Dai solution.

From its beginning the Socialists attacked the policy, arguing that only Ho possessed sufficient popularity and strength to represent the Vietnamese people. Yet, to break with the Christian Democrats over the war was unacceptable. It would bring political chaos to France, perhaps providing the Communists with an opportunity to gain power. In the end, the Socialists suffered the war.

Mao's victory in China in late 1949 provided the Socialists with the means of resolving their dilemma. They could now argue that the war was no longer a colonial venture, but part of France's international commitment to contain communism.

In October 1950, the French National Assembly began a protracted debate on the Indochina War in the aftermath of the disastrous retreat from Route Coloniale 4. The positions of the parties were predictable. The Gaullists urged the government to continue the fight, alone, for France's glory. The Communists called for negotiations with Ho Chi Minh. The Socialists unveiled their new policy: They urged that the United Nations be brought into the conflict, as it had in Korea, thereby internationalizing the war. The Christian Democrats defended their Bao Dai solution.

But it was the leader of the small Radical-Socialist party, Pierre Mendès-France, who offered the most realistic appraisal. He said that France had two choices: a military solution or negotiation. If the choice was a military solution, Mendès-France warned, "We will require three times as many troops and three times as much money, and we will need them quickly." The Radical leader pointed out that such a choice would jeopardize France's economic recovery from World War II, weaken the country's ability to maintain its colonies in North Africa, and deprive France of the strength to determine the future of Germany, still divided between East and West. If this alternative were unacceptable, then France could only negotiate. Few members of the government paid much attention to the leader of this small party. The Christian Democratic premier, René Pleven, had the last word: "When French forces are involved, it is not a question of reason, but of national interest." At France's great peril, Pleven was ignoring Machiavelli's stern warning that "national interest" can only be determined by reason, not by emotion or patriotism.

Preceding page. A wounded foreign legionnaire, Lieutenant Xavier Massénat, rests at the entrance of a crude medical bunker in mid-March 1954, before being evacuated. He was fortunate. After March 31 no one got out.

The dirty war

The frustrations felt by Mendès-France were echoed by the French public. The people were quickly coming to the conclusion that a military solution was impossible. Led by the Communist party, thousands of Frenchmen turned against the war. The brutality of the war—particularly the use of napalm—became a rallying cry. In the face of domestic and international criticism the French eventually restricted the use of napalm.

The soldiers who served in Indochina became targets of France's frustrations. Even the colonists, the very people whose privileges the soldiers were attempting to preserve, treated them as outcasts among Saigon's fashionable population. One soldier complained, "French civilians spat in our face. In Saigon, a beautiful city, we spent the pay that we didn't have to send home .... One Sunday we were three sergeants sitting and the café was full. A party of well-dressed French civilians arrived and we were thrown out. We were grabbed by the waiter."

Much of the French population adopted the Communist slogan: The war in Indochina was France's "dirty war." It has marked the men who fought there to this very day, as was to happen later to American veterans of the second Vietnam War.

French "Vietnamization"

The Bao Dai solution and France's increasing war weariness joined together in 1951 to produce a new policy. The French gave it no name, but fifteen years later Richard Nixon would call the American version of the same policy "Vietnamization." The policy, to create an independent army for the State of Vietnam, was made in the aftermath of the French debacle on RC 4. On October 22, 1950, French and Vietnamese officials agreed to place a Vietnamese army of one hundred and fifteen thousand men in the field by the end of 1951. The army was to be equipped and paid for with American aid.

To French politicians the construction of a Vietnamese army held out the promise that eventually French troops might be slowly withdrawn from the war, making it less unpopular at home. But when de Lattre assumed command he saw it serving a second purpose. De Lattre felt that the chief weakness in the French Expeditionary Force was its lack of mobility. This was due in part to the strategy adopted by French commanders, but was also a necessity if the

Napalm claims the life of a Vietnamese. France's use of the incendiary in Vietnam outraged the French public, as it would Americans fifteen years later.

French forces were to maintain the security of pacified territory. Over one-half of the French forces were assigned static defensive positions (exactly as Mao had forecast in a guerrilla war's second phase). France's ability to seek out the enemy was thus severely limited. De Lattre hoped that the new Vietnamese army would be able to handle these defensive chores, while his men increased their mobility for more aggressive warfare against Giap's forces.

The hopes of both de Lattre and French political leaders were dashed by the indifference of the Vietnamese. By the end of 1951, the Vietnamese National Army had reached at most a total of thirty-eight thousand men, rather than the planned one hundred and fifteen thousand. On the eve of the battle of Dien Bien Phu, Vietnamese National forces numbered one hundred and fifty thousand men, but of these, ninety thousand had merely been transferred from previous positions in the French Union forces. The net increase was only sixty thousand men. This force of one hundred and fifty thousand was commanded by ten thousand officers, but only twenty-six hundred of them were Vietnamese. To fill the holes the French were forced to employ French officers, thus diminishing the sense of independence and nationalism within the army.

The indifference of the Vietnamese to their own army was attacked by de Lattre in a speech delivered at a Vietnamese graduation ceremony in 1951. To a group of middle-class Vietnamese who preferred to see which side would win before committing themselves, de Lattre issued a challenge:

Behave like men. If you are Communists, go and join the Vietminh. There are people there who fight well for a bad cause.... But if you are patriots, fight for your country, because this war is your war.

Indifference was not the only problem to beset the Vietnamese National Army. The French continued to recruit Vietnamese for their own forces, in direct competition with the new army they were attempting to create. In addition, French administrators siphoned off much of the American aid intended for the Vietnamese army, further diminishing its effectiveness.

In fact, the Vietnamese National Army, like the State of Vietnam, was little more than a creature of the French. Its greatest contribution was to the future South Vietnam. The future South Vietnamese leaders Nguyen Cao Ky and Nguyen Van Thieu were both among the few young Vietnamese officers in the Vietnamese National Army.

For young officers like Thieu and Ky there was no turning back; there could be no reconciliation with the Vietminh regime. Others, too, staked their future with Bao Dai, but few did so out of any fondness for his regime or because they had a shared vision of Vietnam's future. Rather they were joined in their common hatred of the Vietminh and the knowledge that they would have no future in a Communist Vietnam. The State of Vietnam became a "coalition of convenience" rather than a social organism animated by shared values and beliefs.

The coalition of convenience

The largest component in the coalition of convenience consisted of the religious sects in the South, the Cao Dai and the Hoa Hao, and the Binh Xuyen bandits. All three began as uneasy allies of the Vietminh but later broke with the front over the heavy-handed tactics of the Vietminh leader in Saigon, Tran Van Giau. The sects were deeply independent and resisted all Vietminh efforts to "discipline" them. The Cao Dai signed a formal military alliance with the French on January 8, 1947, after a Vietminh attack on the Cao Dai holy seat in Tay Ninh. The Hoa Hao followed four months later after their leader, Huynh Phu So, was assassinated by Vietminh soldiers. The Hoa Hao became particularly vicious anti-Vietminh fighters. Their tactics sometimes appalled the French:

The Hoa Hao had the habit of tying Vietminh sympathizers together with ropes and of throwing them into the rivers to drown by packages. They called it 'crab fishing.' One could see those packages of bodies floating down the river like so many trains of junk, at the mercy of the currents and tides.

The French equipped and paid for private armies commanded by the sects. They hoped that these armies would occupy pacified territories, thus freeing French forces for other duties. But the sects' armies were highly unreliable. Leading members refused to cooperate with the former emperor. Nor were the sects pro-French. In March 1948, Hoa Hao troops murdered their French advisers. Both sects were more interested in expanding their own influence, maintaining their independence, and taking from the French what they could than in contributing to the new State of Vietnam. Only their anticommunism made them allies in the coalition of convenience.

The Binh Xuyen, a sort of paramilitary mafia, was commanded by Le Van Vien, alias Bay Vien, a former chauffeur in the French colonial forces. Like the Hoa Hao, the Binh Xuyen formed an early alliance with the Vietminh but parted ways after an assassination attempt on Bay Vien's life. The Binh Xuyen, however, became strong supporters of the Bao Dai regime, and Bay Vien received many favors from Bao Dai in exchange for his support. According to the American journalist Robert Shaplen, Bay Vien, with Bao Dai's backing, became director of the Grande Monde, a famous gambling house in Cholon; his holdings also included the Nouveautes Catinat, Saigon's largest department store, twenty houses, almost a hundred shops, a fleet of river boats, and Asia's biggest brothel, known as "the Hall of Mirrors." In return Bao Dai skimmed a percentage of the sect's profits in the opium trade; the former emperor received as much as 40 million piasters (about $2 million at the time) as a payoff from Bay Vien. Bay Vien eventually became chief of Vietnam's police and security services, a move which dumfounded Americans who did not understand how the Vietnamese Al Capone could become his country's J. Edgar Hoover.

General Henri Navarre, commander of the French Expeditionary Corps (right), and Major General René Cogny (behind), the architects of the Dien Bien Phu operation, inspect the place of battle.

The Catholics change sides

In the early stages Vietnam's Catholic minority was a source of support for Ho Chi Minh. But relations between the Catholics and Ho slowly soured until October 15, 1949, when the Vietminh mounted an armed attack on the episcopal seat at Phat Diem. The Catholics soon swung to Bao Dai's side even though they hated the French colonial presence. Still, they turned their forces effectively against the Vietminh. One French officer said:

These Catholics are swine, even worse than the other Vietnamese—there's not a single trick they don't play on us. But with them, when the crunch comes, when the Viets attack, it's not like with the others: you can rely on the Catholics absolutely then—it's the steadiness of a holy war.

Other groups entered into the coalition of convenience as well. The new civil servants in the State of Vietnam knew that their government positions de-

61

pended upon the survival of Bao Dai's regime. Landlords who fled their lands when guerrilla warfare erupted—only to see their property divided among the peasants by the Vietminh—knew that only with a defeat of the Vietminh could they recover their lands. But as Ngo Dinh Diem was to find out when he assumed power, the coalition of convenience was no basis for a modern state. The loyalties of the various components were to themselves, not to their government. Many Americans, critical of the inability of the French or Bao Dai to create a unified public spirit among the anti-Communists, wondered if there really was any State of Vietnam to save. In 1952, the head of the American economic assistance program to the State of Vietnam concluded, "The Bao Dai government gives little promise of developing competence and winning the loyalty of the population and ... the attainment of American objectives is remote."

France's last general

Soon after General Henri Navarre deplaned from his Constellation in Saigon on May 27, 1953, and took command of the stagnant French war effort, he said, "The Expeditionary Corps lacks aggressiveness and mobility. I am going to do my best to give it back these qualities." Navarre was to be the last commanding French general of the Expeditionary Corps before the Geneva peace talks and, like his predecessors, would have to learn the mysteries of jungle warfare firsthand. By 1953 he recognized that mobility was the key to victory and France's greatest problem. His response was the Navarre plan, whose outlines had been hammered out in March and April by high-level French and American defense planners in Washington.

The first part of the plan posed no problem for the French: The Vietnamese army was to assume a larger role, with the United States assuming the financial burden. But the second aspect of the plan disturbed Paris politicians. The French Expeditionary Force was to be temporarily increased beyond its limit of one hundred and sixty-six thousand men, including Frenchmen, Africans, and legionnaires. The Vietnamese army of one hundred and fifty thousand men would assume responsibility for the static pacification effort, while French forces, with more American equipment, would accent mobility, literally trying to stalk Giap's VPA and engage it in pitched battle.

The Vietnamese army, braced by de Lattre's earlier effort, finally began to grow as expected. Within two months, nine of the fourteen new French battalions requested by Navarre had arrived. But Navarre's attempt to "catch" the VPA never succeeded.

In both July and August 1953, Navarre seemed to have entire VPA divisions surrounded, but in each case Giap sacrificed small units to cover a retreat, while his regulars melted back into the jungle. Having failed to destroy the VPA regular forces, Navarre had to seek out Giap in his own lair—the mountains of Tonkin. Navarre chose to build a hedgehog fortress at Dien Bien Phu as his base of operations.

General Navarre decided to establish his airhead at Dien Bien Phu for three reasons. First, the Vietminh depended on the sale of $1 million worth of opium produced there for cash to buy military equipment and medical supplies. Second, the valley lay on the main route to Laos, which the Vietminh had attacked before and which the French were committed to protect. But most important, Navarre believed that he would lure Giap's elite divisions from the delta into "meat-grinder" battles. French mobile infantry and armored battalions ranging around the huge valley would quickly dispose of them. The French air force would supply and support the ground effort as well as interdict Vietminh supply lines. Navarre doubted that Giap could raise more than two divisions and a few heavy guns. He described suggestions that Giap might raise four full divisions as "utopian."

The French strategy

On November 20, 1953, the French began their 209-day reoccupation of Dien Bien Phu after they had retaken the fort from a small detachment of Vietminh. Spearheaded by Lieutenant Colonel Pierre Langlais and his paratroopers, French mobile units began in early December to conduct the offensive sorties Navarre had envisioned. Giap, meanwhile, encircled the valley, easing two vanguard divisions into place. Not until the battle began some one hundred days later were the French to realize how completely outmanned and outgunned they were.

Soon, French patrols venturing outside the safety of the garrison were in grave danger. By March 12, they had lost 1,037 men on these sorties and had little to show for it. Dien Bien Phu had proven itself useless as a land-air base, and the French presence there had proven to be no obstacle to Vietminh entry into Laos. The European-oriented Navarre failed to see the futility of roadblocks against an enemy that rarely used roads. By late December, it became clear that Giap had begun to build up a huge siege force. The French began to dig in for good.

It would have taken fifty 700-man infantry battalions to secure the fifty-mile perimeter of the valley. The French originally had only seven. They were deployed in eight strongholds in the valley, each given a woman's name (see maps, pp. 74-6). Giap had already forced the French to abandon their attempts to hold the hills even though orthodox military strategy dictated that securing the high points would have been essential to defense of the valley.

But the French never had sufficient air transport capability to bring in the needed construction materials. Instead the French stripped the area of trees, providing themselves with two thousand tons of lumber, a poor substitute for cement. This defoliation provided the Vietminh with an unobstructed view into the fort, and soon the VPA learned the times of French troop rotations and pinpointed the positions of the shiny French artillery.

The French had come to trap Giap but by mid-February they were the entrapped army. Still, not knowing the full extent of the VPA's power, the French high command passed up the last chance to avoid debacle. In early February, Navarre decided against evacuating the 10,500 men garrisoned at Dien Bien Phu because he estimated that to cover the retreat he would have had to send in and sacrifice

eight reserve battalions. In late February, the decision to begin negotiations in Geneva in late April was announced. Dien Bien Phu was rapidly becoming the decisive battle, one that would affect both the balance of forces and the impending negotiations.

To command this ill-fated fortress, Navarre chose a dashing cavalry officer who wore a red cap and scarf and carried a riding crop. Colonel Christian Marie Ferdinand de la Croix de Castries was an aristocrat and world-class horseman. His ancestors had fought for France since the Crusades and included a general, Armand de Castries, who fought with Lafayette in the American Revolution. Equally important to the defense of Dien Bien Phu was the less dashing but more reliable Colonel Pierre Langlais, commander of the paratroopers. Facing the flower of French military leadership was the former history teacher, Vo Nguyen Giap.

Giap's "new look" army

The army that Giap threw into the battle was far different from the one that had battled the French to a standstill for over eight years. Total Vietminh forces, which numbered a little more than one hundred and fifty thousand when Mao's troops appeared on the border in late 1949, had grown to almost three hundred and fifty thousand. More important, Giap's troops were no longer organized into small units. He

In a secret hideaway in the Tonkin mountains, months before the Communist attack was to begin, Commander Vo Nguyen Giap (far right) briefs Ho Chi Minh (center) and his chief lieutenants, Truong Chinh (second from right) and Pham Van Dong (second from left), on the battle strategy.

had moved from battalions to regiments and finally to 12,000-man divisions supplied with increasingly sophisticated Russian and Chinese equipment, including antiaircraft power.

Giap's greatest problem was to supply these large troop concentrations. The French estimated that each VPA division required fifty thousand peasant-porters to carry food and supplies. In the June 1953 offensive into Laos, two Vietminh divisions had been supported by ninety-five thousand porters. On the eve of Dien Bien Phu, Giap could still count on only six hundred operational vehicles, including Russian Molotov trucks and GM trucks captured by the Chinese in Korea. But Giap was still able to win the inglorious battle of supply with little modern equipment. He supplied his nearly fifty thousand men with a stream of peasant-porters carrying materials five hundred miles from the Chinese border. The French were unable to keep their troops supplied via air, three hundred miles from Hanoi. By March Giap had as-

sembled 49,500 combat troops, supported by 31,500 logistical personnel. At the same time Navarre had only 13,200 men, fewer than half of them front-line combatants.

The French believed that the tiny force of seventy-five planes available to them could pinch off Vietminh supply and entrenchment. They were wrong. Improvised bombers—C-119 "Flying Boxcar" transport and Privateer antisubmarine patrol aircraft—as well as B-26s scattered napalm and shrapnel bombs over the entrenching Vietminh army with little effect. American World War II vintage Bearcat, Helldiver, and Hellcat fighter-bombers strafed and bombed VPA supply lines by day. But by night Vietnamese peasants would repair the damage and even tie together tree tops to camouflage their burden.

Most important for the battle was the Vietminh's superiority in artillery and heavy firepower, a jolting surprise to the French. While the guerrillas could count on 200 guns larger than 57 MM, the French had only 40 over 57 MM a week after the battle began. This superiority in artillery, coupled with their superior location in the hills overlooking the valley, insured the Vietminh victory.

A Vietminh bicycle corps. Over a period of years Vietminh agents purchased French-made Peugeot bicycles in Hanoi shops and modified them to carry up to 440 pounds of supplies to the front lines.

French troops patrol across the Laotian border from Dien Bien Phu in December 1953. The French thought their presence at Dien Bien Phu would deter further Vietminh incursion into Laos.

On March 11 the Vietminh completed their final preparations for battle. That evening the chief political commissar at Dien Bien Phu read the order of battle to the assembled troops, the final message from the commander in chief of the VPA, General Vo Nguyen Giap:

Remember this historic battle. Determined to destroy the adversary, keep in mind the motto: 'Always attack, always advance.' Master fear and pain, overcome obstacles, unite your efforts, fight to the very end, annihilate the enemy at Dien Bien Phu, win a great victory!

The Vietminh find the range

March 12, 1954. At dawn the heavy fog of the Tonkin dry season hung over the valley of Dien Bien Phu. But by 9:30 the sun had burned it away. The fine day—clear, dry, and warm—reflected the mood of the French troops dug in there: optimistic, determined, and ready. They had come to do a job they were sure they could do and wanted only to do it. They had waited since January for the Vietminh army massed outside their base to attack. So far the French had been beset more by rumors and alerts than by fighting. That morning, as the regular parachute drop began at 8:00 and a few incoming rounds landed harmlessly, a patrol discovered a half-mile trench reaching toward the French perimeter. More rumors.

French Theater Commander René Cogny, a striking six-foot-four-inch man who limped about with the aid of a cane as a result of Gestapo torture at Buchenwald, landed in his Dakota at about 10:00 A.M. He was the last in a series of notables to view the camp. Some had questioned the sufficiency of French preparations. But General Cogny did not find any serious deficiencies in the French defense and reboarded his Dakota, waving what he thought would be a temporary good-bye to garrison commander Colonel Christian de Castries. Suddenly, 105 MM shells slammed into the airstrip. As everyone hit the ground, Cogny's pilot gunned his engines and headed back to Hanoi. One aircraft parked nearby burst into flames and another lost a wing. It was the first VPA attack on a taxiing plane. The Vietminh had found the range.

The color photographs on these pages are as far as can be determined the only surviving color pictures of the fortress at Dien Bien Phu. Published here for the first time, the photographs were taken by Jean Rondy, M.D., a medical officer at the camp. Dr. Rondy was wounded during the battle, taken prisoner by the Vietminh, and held four months until his release under the Geneva Agreement. He shipped his undeveloped film out of Dien Bien Phu with evacuated wounded soldiers.

At sunset the bugle blows as the French flag is lowered at the Dien Bien Phu encampment of the Thirteenth Demi-Brigade of the French Foreign Legion, a unit that distinguished itself at Narvik in Norway in World War II.

The siege begins

The Vietminh attack on General Cogny's plane on March 12 was merely a calling card. Giap showed his true strength the following day. The weather had turned, and the monsoon rains had come early. It was a hazy, rainy day at Dien Bien Phu. Observers compared the scene to an oversized Boy Scout jamboree. Orderly rows of tents flanked smokey cooking fires, and laundry lay neatly spread out on coils of barbed wire to dry. German, Arabic, and French voices mingled with Vietnamese and montagnard. Suddenly, at 5:00 P.M. the jamboree ended. In man-made lightning and thunder the Vietminh struck. Within a few hours the only fires seen burning were those of the fortress itself, and bodies of Vietminh assault troops were draped over the laundry on the barbed wire.

The Vietminh attacked stronghold Beatrice first. A French sergeant, one of the stronghold's few survivors, remembered that every man in his unit was surprised at their firepower: "Shells rained down on us without stopping like a hailstorm on a fall evening. Bunker after bunker, trench after trench, collapsed burying under them men and weapons." Meanwhile, the men stationed at stronghold Gabrielle witnessed perhaps the most ominous spectacle of the battle: Heavy antiaircraft fire erupted from previously undetected batteries on hills along the airstrip axis,

picking planes off the runway as they scurried to get airborne and turning the airspace into a turkey shoot.

Within the first hours of the battle, the French had all but lost the three northern strongholds. Within forty-eight hours four battalions had been lost. Montagnard units, familiar with the jungle, left en masse for the hills and freedom on March 17, leaving another stronghold defenseless.

The French lost more than the three northern strongholds that day. They also lost the airstrip, all local air support, and any chance of being reliably supplied. The commander of French artillery, Colonel Charles Piroth, personally accepted the blame. On the evening of March 14, he made the rounds of preoccupied officers, confessing his responsibility. At dawn on March 15, he lay down on his cot and with his teeth—he had lost his left arm in World War II—pulled the pin from a grenade that he held against his chest with his right arm.

After the airstrip closed, the garrison had to depend on parachute drops for supplies and reinforcements. The flights became increasingly perilous for the paid volunteer American civilians in Fairchild C-119s and French air force pilots, mostly in C-47s. In order to improve accuracy and to avoid the monsoon cloud cover, the pilots were forced to fly lower and lower—and slower and slower. The World War II veteran American pilots, whom French soldiers at Dien Bien Phu said took more chances than their

Parachute drops of supplies and troops became the only source of reinforcement for the beleaguered French fortress. For many volunteers inexperienced at airborne battle, the first drop was their last.

French counterparts, reported that the Vietminh threw worse flak over the valley than the Nazis had over their industrial cities a decade earlier. After the battle the remnants of 82,926 parachutes covered the battlefield, some said like a monstrous shroud.

Operation Vulture: America on the brink

While the battle was underway, on March 20 General Paul Ely, French chief of staff, flew from Paris to Washington. As concern for Indochina had grown in the U.S., American aid had grown to represent 80 percent of France's war costs. Ely hoped for more, but his request was small: He wanted the U.S. to respond if the Chinese intervened with air power. On March 25 he was assured that the U.S. would respond immediately with American air power if the Chinese involved themselves.

Already reduced to cold meals by February, the French could still count on aerial food drops like this one. One month later, deliveries were reduced to increasingly limited drops, and as the end drew near the French were virtually without food and water.

As Ely prepared to return to Paris, Admiral Arthur W. Radford, chairman of the Joint Chiefs of Staff, urged him to stay another day. Radford unveiled a new proposition conceived by joint American-French military staffs in Vietnam and named Operation Vulture. The plan called for American bombers to conduct one or several raids around the perimeter of Dien Bien Phu, cutting Vietminh communications and artillery installations, to relieve the siege. Radford told Ely that he was only making an offer; Paris would have to approve, and then the U.S. government would consider the proposal. Radford led Ely to believe that he was speaking for President Eisenhower, but Eisenhower had not yet made up his mind about the venture.

The president's private attitude toward Operation Vulture was somewhat different than his public statements would suggest. He has generally been viewed as an opponent of this last ditch effort to use American troops to extricate the French. On March 31 he told the American people that he "could conceive of no greater tragedy than for the United States to become involved in an all-out war in Indochina." And yet in private he placed only one condition on approval of Operation Vulture: He would authorize the

A North African gunner mans an American-built 155MM medium howitzer, the largest field piece available to the French in Asia.

strike around Dien Bien Phu, but only with congressional approval. The year 1954 was an election year, and Ike wanted to avoid Truman's action in Korea: a unilateral commitment of American forces by executive decree.

On April 3 Eisenhower called a meeting of eight congressional leaders—five Democrats, including Senate Minority Leader Lyndon Johnson, and three Republicans—to brief them on Operation Vulture. Eisenhower wasn't present at the meeting, so Secretary of State John Foster Dulles and Radford made the presentation. Dulles carried in his pocket a "sense of Congress resolution" authorizing the strike. It remained in his pocket.

Radford briefed the congressmen on the plan. The French at Dien Bien Phu would be rescued from a strike by two hundred aircraft from the carriers *Essex* and *Boxer* stationed in the South China Sea. The *Essex* carried nuclear as well as conventional bombs, but Radford, many years later, stated that the use of atomic weapons was never discussed. He admitted, however, that their use was not excluded and might have been considered if a first strike had proven ineffective.

The congressmen responded with some tough questions, many of which neither Dulles nor Radford could answer. Would land forces be used if the strike didn't relieve the siege? Would our allies support us? Did the other Joint Chiefs support the operation? To the last question Radford was forced to admit that only he among the Joint Chiefs supported the plan.

His strongest support came from Dulles and Vice President Nixon. At the end of the meeting the eight congressmen were in agreement: The U.S should not support France alone. Only if the strike were part of a multinational effort, either with U.N. approval or at least the support of an ad hoc group of allies, would they give their assent.

On the next day, April 4, General Ely officially requested U.S. intervention on behalf of the French government. Again Eisenhower did not veto the plan. Instead he authorized Dulles to begin discussions to meet the conditions of Congress. Time was too short to go to the U.N., so Dulles began to line up allies. Convincing Australia, New Zealand, Thailand, and the Philippines to support the plan was not difficult. But in the interest of unity in the Western alliance, Eisenhower insisted that the plan have the active support of the French and the tacit approval, at least, of Britain.

Dulles resorted to shuttle diplomacy. Both the French and British governments had come to oppose Operation Vulture, but in his trip to Paris and London Dulles was fortified with a strong warning from Eisenhower. At his press conference on April 7, the president had told the American people and the world:

The loss of Indochina will cause the fall of Southeast Asia like a set of dominoes.

But even this apocalyptic vision could not save Dulles' mission. The French were opposed to the con-

Although these 155 MM howitzers at Dien Bien Phu had a range of ten to twelve miles, they proved no match for the superior position and number of Giap's artillery.

gressional condition—a multinational coalition to stop communism in Indochina. While they had approved a unilateral strike by the U.S., they feared that a coalition would soon take the basic decisions concerning the war out of their hands. France preferred to negotiate a settlement at the upcoming Geneva Conference rather than risk losing control of the war. The British also refused to give even tacit approval to a strike around Dien Bien Phu for fear that it would sabotage the Geneva talks. Dulles returned home on April 14 empty-handed, and Operation Vulture was shelved for the time being.

The noose tightens

Meanwhile the situation at Dien Bien Phu worsened. In early April Giap adopted a new tactic. Instead of costly mass assaults he began to build a series of trenches so that his troops could choke off the outer French strongholds one by one. Every night the Vietminh would move a little farther forward and dig in. The French, by now short on ammunition, were forced to stand back and watch the construction of this deadly network, while they conserved their shells for the final attack. Eventually the defensive perimeter of the French, originally about fifteen miles around, would shrink to the size of Yankee Stadium. All the while, Vietminh loud-speakers blared "sur-

render or die" endlessly in Vietnamese, French, Arabic, and German.

Despite the deteriorating situation, the French government expressed complete confidence in de Castries. On April 16 he was promoted to brigadier general. But his newly won general's stars and congratulatory champagne became a symbol of French frustration. In the first attempt to parachute them into the camp, the stars and champagne fell into Vietminh hands.

In April, the Vietminh were reinforced by an unbeatable ally—the monsoon rains. By grounding French aircraft the rains protected the Vietminh supply system while paralyzing the French. The rains soaked the fortress and mired the men in mud. By the third week in April soldiers on both sides worked in trenches containing, on average, three feet of sticky clay muck. But the French in their low-lying camps along the Nam Yum River suffered more than the Vietminh in their more protected higher positions.

The defenders endured these conditions on stomachs often empty. On April 14 enemy shells blew up the food reserves and, to add insult to injury, most of the camp's tobacco supply. After April 29 the French were on half rations. Men were fighting around the clock, knee-deep in mud and soaked by rain, nourished only by instant coffee and cigarettes. During the last days of the battle the camp physician reported cases of men who simply dropped dead at their posts.

They died of chronic exhaustion, the certificate would say—eight weeks with little food and no sleep.

But there was no thought of surrender. De Castries had already instructed his men: "I expect all the troops to die at the positions assigned to them rather than retreat an inch." The French soldiers, especially the legionnaires, followed these orders to the letter. One legionnaire told of bringing a young comrade back to a first-aid post:

He'd a piece of lead as big as my fist in his thigh. My attention was drawn to one of my friends who was dying and I went over to have a word with him. When I turned round the youngster had vanished. I found him next morning. He'd slapped on a rough dressing then gone off to rejoin his section in an attack. His body was riddled with bullets.

One night this same young soldier experienced the pounding of the Russian-made rocket launchers. He crossed himself. "Funny how pious one gets when death's just around the corner," he said. The next morning the Vietminh attacked in human waves. "A shell burst right in our trench," he remembered, "and the legionary next to me disintegrated. Nothing left of him except odd bits of raw meat. Death was spitting all round, and men falling like flies."

Medical miracles

With air evacuation of the wounded an impossibility, the conditions under which the medical staff worked became increasingly hopeless. A simple mud shelter served as the infirmary. Patients pleaded for water in several languages. The foul odor of dead and dying men fouled the air. Flasks of plasma and saline solution that kept others—their heads and bellies bandaged, arms and legs splintered or amputated—on the near side of the grave were everywhere. In the crude operating room orderlies and nurses performed miracles. And somehow the French carried out de Castries' orders. There was no retreat.

Then in late April, during a brief lull in the fighting, de Castries decided to abandon the embattled northwest outposts since he had been unable to drive the Vietminh off the northern end of the airstrip. The French established a new, and what proved to be final, perimeter only one and a half miles across, leaving only one stronghold standing—Isabelle—three miles to the south. But de Castries professed confidence. "I'm going to kick General Giap's teeth in, one by one," he said.

French political and military leaders had by now lost all such esprit. On April 21 General Ely renewed his request for American intervention to break the

A Fairchild C-119 "Flying Boxcar" burns on the Dien Bien Phu airfield on March 12. The plane was hit in mid-air and landed only to be finished off by Vietminh fire.

A paratrooper dies defending Eliane 2. Although the perimeter to the north became increasingly insecure during the month of April, the French held on to this position until the bitter end.

siege. The next day French Foreign Minister Georges Bidault told Dulles that only massive air intervention by the U.S. could save the fortress. His government was withdrawing its opposition to multinational action. Again, with the alliance strongly in mind, Eisenhower gave Dulles the green light to gain British approval. This was the last obstacle to meeting the congressional condition. Again, the British flatly refused. Churchill told the House of Commons that he "was not prepared to give any undertakings about United Kingdom military action in Indochina in advance of the results of Geneva." Thus faded France's last chance for help.

The final days

The Geneva Conference convened in late April 1954. But the first two weeks of the conference were devoted to the Korean question. Giap still had time before the "Indochina phase" began to make one final crushing lunge at the fortress. After building his army back to fifty thousand troops with new recruits, Giap launched a dual attack on May 1 against the central sector and the isolated southern stronghold. The Vietminh now outnumbered the French ten to one and many of the defenders were wounded.

On May 6 Giap opened fire with mighty eight-tube Russian rocket launchers—"Stalin's organs," the French named them. Russian aid to the Vietminh was always substantially less than Chinese. But at Dien Bien Phu heavy Soviet weaponry—the rocket launchers and artillery—provided Giap with his surprising superiority in firepower.

On May 6 the French fortress measured only one thousand yards wide and de Castries told headquarters in Hanoi, "This may finish us." At 10:00 P.M. bugles blared in the night and four Vietminh regiments attacked the eastern positions. By dawn the French had only two field guns, little ammunition, and no tanks left. De Castries' only hope was that the fortress could hold out until dark so that the able-bodied survivors could try to make a break for the jungle. But it soon became obvious that the fortress would not last until dark.

At 4:00 P.M. de Castries radioed his wife in Hanoi. "Have faith for our wounded," he said. "Au revoir." Forty-five minutes later de Castries spoke with General Cogny: "Our resistance is going to be overwhelmed. The Viets are within a few meters of the radio transmitter where I am speaking. I have given orders to carry out maximum destruction. We will not surrender."

Planted far inside French lines under cover of night, Vietminh propaganda posters like this one warn soldiers of the doom they face at Dien Bien Phu and urge them to desert their French officers and return home.

General Cogny, fighting back tears, reaffirmed the French pride that had led them to Dien Bien Phu: "You will fight to the end. There is no question of raising the white flag after your historic resistance."

"*Entendu*," radioed back de Castries. "We will fight to the end. *Au revoir, mon général. Au revoir mes camarades. Vive la France!*" Then de Castries ordered that the outpost Isabelle turn its artillery fire against his surrounded central command post.

Within minutes the command post was overrun by the Vietminh. De Castries and his staff were taken prisoner. What was left of his office was taken to Hanoi where it remains on display in a museum. De Castries returned to France after the conclusion of the Geneva peace negotiations a hero, the man who refused to surrender at Dien Bien Phu.

A French helicopter pilot who flew into the valley in mid-May to evacuate wounded prisoners recalled, "The whole place was as silent as a graveyard, and when the wind kicked up, we could smell the death around us." One wounded French soldier said that he lay on the ground for three days before the Vietminh doctors and orderlies, who had no medicine or disinfectants and operated without anesthesia, reached him. Others remembered that they were not medically mistreated, but that the Vietminh propagandized the prisoners of war with a vengeance. In all, the French suffered 2,242 killed; 6,463 wounded; 2,711 missing; and 10,754 taken prisoner, over 6,500 of them captured on the last day.

The Battle Scene

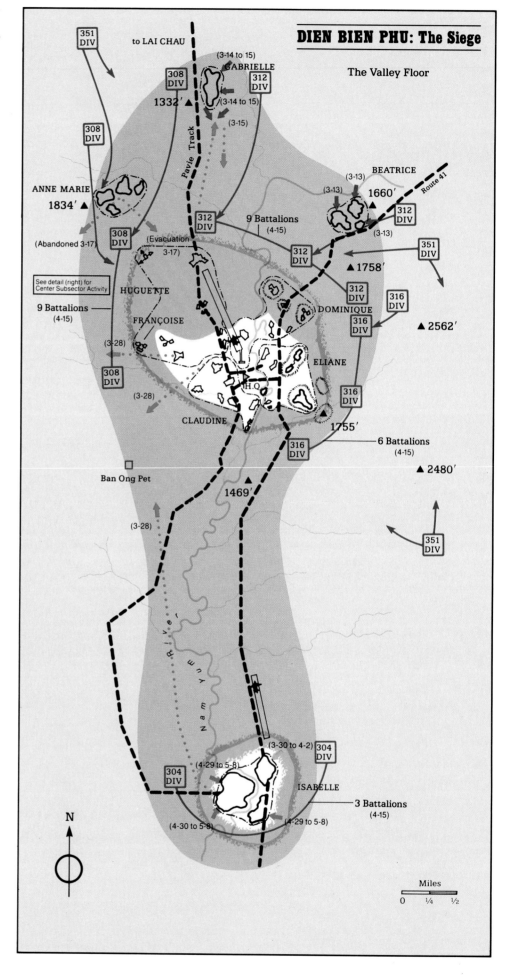

DIEN BIEN PHU: The Siege

The Valley Floor

to LAI CHAU

351 DIV

308 DIV

312 DIV
(3-14 to 15)
GABRIELLE

1332' ▲

(3-14 to 15)

(3-15)

308 DIV

Pavie Track

ANNE MARIE

1834' ▲

(3-13) BEATRICE

(3-13) 1660' ▲ Route 41

312 DIV

308 DIV

(Abandoned 3-17)

312 DIV

9 Battalions (4-15)

(3-13)

312 DIV

351 DIV

(Evacuation 3-17)

312 DIV

▲1758'

See detail (right) for Center Subsector Activity

312 DIV

316 DIV

HUGUETTE

316 DIV

DOMINIQUE

9 Battalions (4-15)

FRANÇOISE

316 DIV

▲ 2562'

(3-28)

ELIANE

308 DIV

316 DIV

(3-28)

H.Q.

CLAUDINE

1755'

6 Battalions (4-15)

316 DIV

▲ 2480'

Ban Ong Pet

1469' ▲

(3-28)

351 DIV

N a m Y u m River

(3-30 to 4-2)

304 DIV

(4-29 to 5-8)

304 DIV

ISABELLE

3 Battalions (4-15)

N

(4-30 to 5-8)

(4-29 to 5-8)

Miles

0 ¼ ½

The French contemplated their installation at Dien Bien Phu as an offensive base. Its placement astride the lush upland valley on the Laotian frontier was meant to tempt General Giap to attack and expose his forces to swift decimation by highly mobile French units. This was not to be. French forces and equipment were insufficient, the terrain proved hostile to mobile units, and the outpost quickly proved practically inaccessible to supply.

The French established eight strongholds, each subdivided into several positions (*Beatrice*, for instance, consisted of B1, B2, and B3) and fortified with widely varying manpower and weaponry. The battle for their control passed through three phases.

Phase One began at 5 P.M. on March 13, when the fire of American-built 105MM howitzers captured by the Chinese in Korea and pot-bellied 120MM mortars began to smother French batteries. By midnight, assault units from VPA Division 312 had captured Stronghold *Beatrice*. VPA artillery began to pound *Gabrielle* at dusk the following day. French 105MM and 155MM howitzers helped offset the eight-to-one VPA manpower edge, but an armored relief column sent out from the central sector foundered, and by 8:30 the next morning two VPA regiments from the 308th Division held *Gabrielle*. Propagandized by local tribesmen, the montagnard riflemen at *Anne Marie* abandoned their position on March 17. By the twenty-ninth, the first phase was over.

In *Phase One* the French lost heavily: the three crucial northern hill positions, a third of their infantry and artillery, all observation posts, and most important, dozens of aircraft and, especially troubling, the use of the airstrip. Supplies would now have to be delivered by inefficient parachute drops, the wounded could not be evacuated, and close aerial support of ground operations would be curtailed. The Vietminh had won a great victory, but their

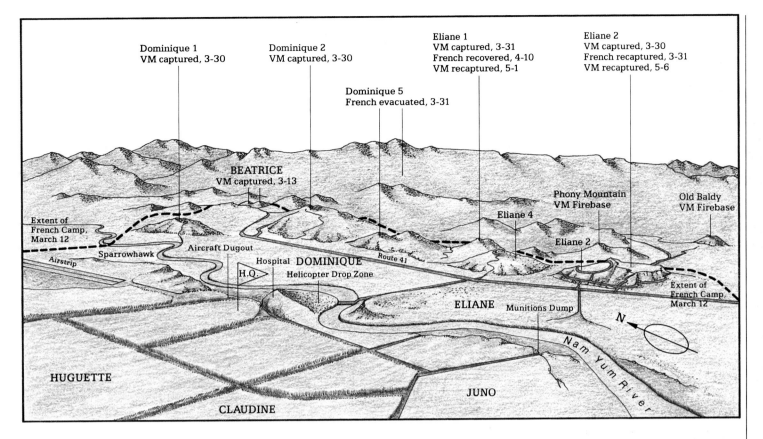

Dominique 1
VM captured, 3-30

Dominique 2
VM captured, 3-30

Dominique 5
French evacuated, 3-31

Eliane 1
VM captured, 3-31
French recovered, 4-10
VM recaptured, 5-1

Eliane 2
VM captured, 3-30
French recaptured, 3-31
VM recaptured, 5-6

BEATRICE
VM captured, 3-13

Phony Mountain
VM Firebase

Old Baldy
VM Firebase

Eliane 4

Eliane 2

Extent of
French Camp,
March 12

Sparrowhawk

Airstrip

Airstrip

Aircraft Dugout

Hospital   DOMINIQUE

Route 41

H.Q.

Helicopter Drop Zone

ELIANE

Munitions Dump

Extent of
French Camp,
March 12

N

HUGUETTE

Nam Yum River

JUNO

CLAUDINE

Panorama of the Dien Bien Phu Valley, looking east across the French command post and the Nam Yum River. The eastern hills (rear) were the scene of the siege's fiercest and largest combat. The Vietminh erected a memorial to their battle dead on the hillock the French called Eliane 2.

Legend for Dien Bien Phu: The Siege and Center Subsector

Vietnam People's Army (VPA)-Controlled
Area at Beginning of

▭	Phase One, March 13, 1954
▭	Phase Two, March 30
▭	Phase Three, April 24
–·–·–	French Stronghold Perimeters
⋈	French Positions
E2	Name of French Positions (Eliane 2)

VPA   French
Attacks   Counterattacks

⬅ ➡	Phase One, March 13–March 29
⬅ ➡	Phase Two, (a) March 30–April 9
⬅ ➡	(b) April 10–April 23
⬅ ➡	Phase Three, April 24–May 7

(3-13) Dates: March 13, 1954

312 DIV	Placement and Infantry Strength of VPA Divisions as of April 15, 1954

351 DIV	Placement of VPA Artillery Division

‐ ‐ ‐	Roads
▲	Elevation
4740'	(Feet)
⠿	Hills in Center Subsector

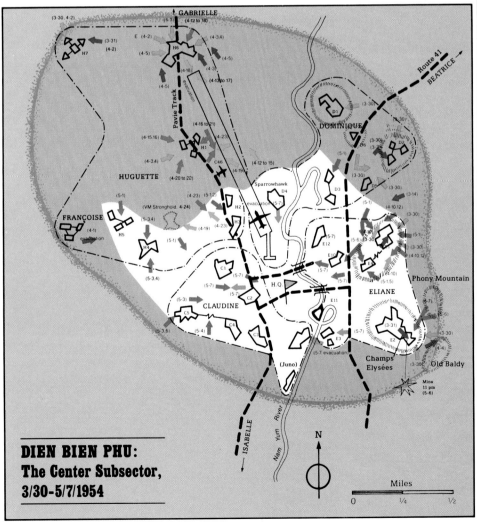

GABRIELLE

Route 41

BEATRICE

DOMINIQUE

HUGUETTE

Pavie Track

FRANÇOISE

Sparrowhawk

ELIANE

Phony Mountain

H.Q.

CLAUDINE

Champs
Elysées

Old Baldy

(Juno)

ISABELLE

Nam Yum River

N

Mine
11 pm
(5-6)

DIEN BIEN PHU:
The Center Subsector,
3/30-5/7/1954

Miles

0   ¼   ½

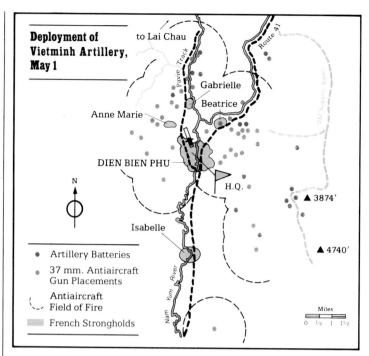

Deployment of Vietminh Artillery, May 1

to Lai Chau

Route 41

Pavie Track

Gabrielle

Beatrice

Anne Marie

DIEN BIEN PHU

H.Q.

N

▲ 3874'

Isabelle

▲ 4740'

Nam Yum River

VM Supply Road

- Artillery Batteries
- 37 mm. Antiaircraft Gun Placements
- ⌐⌐ Antiaircraft Field of Fire
- French Strongholds

Miles
0 ½ 1 1½

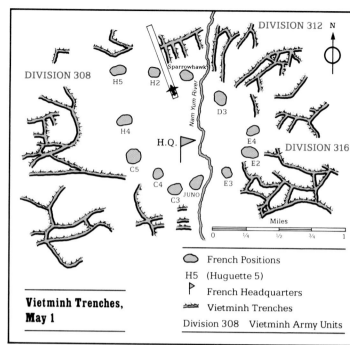

DIVISION 312 N

DIVISION 308

H5 H2 Sparrowhawk

H4 D3

H.Q.

C5 E4 DIVISION 316

C4 E2

C3 JUNO E3

Nam Yum River

Miles
0 ¼ ½ ¾ 1

Vietminh Trenches, May 1

- ⬭ French Positions
- H5 (Huguette 5)
- ⴖ French Headquarters
- ⵌ Vietminh Trenches
- Division 308 Vietminh Army Units

losses were unexpectedly heavy: nearly twenty-five hundred killed and perhaps three times that wounded. This postponed further attack until reinforcements—some extremely young, according to the French—could reach the front.

The patterns established in the first phase persisted throughout the battle. As with *Gabrielle* and *Beatrice*, the French fell back when resupply and reinforcement failed. They counterattacked with artillery shelling of a limited area—usually one that the VPA had seized only recently. This was coordinated with commando-like reinfiltration of the area by paratroop bands such as the 6th Colonial Parachute.

The unexpected strength and secure placement of VPA artillery had proved decisive in *Phase One*, as they would throughout the battle. Of particular importance was the 351st "Heavy" Division, which VPA commander Vo Nguyen Giap modeled after those the Soviets had used successfully against the Germans in World War II. Composed entirely of heavy guns and support teams and assisted by Chinese advisers, the 351st provided firepower unparalleled in Indochina. Some three-quarters of French losses were the result of VPA artillery fire.

Phase Two, the longest and the most violent of the battle, began at dusk on March 30. The VPA simultaneously attacked five French positions. Assault units soon seized positions *Dominique* 1 and 2, but failed to crush the embattled force at the key *Dominique* 3 (D3) position before French guns at *Sparrowhawk* and D3 drove them back. To the south, VPA recoilless rifle and machine-gunfire from *Phony Mountain* as well as artillery fire from distant hills leveled fortifications on both *Eliane* 1 (E1) and the wide plateau on E2 nicknamed the "Champs Elysées." Units from VPA Division 316 scrambled up the two hills. *Huguette* 7 (H7) also fell by midnight but was soon retaken. French paratroopers seized back E1 and D2 the next day but, without promised reinforcements, they had to retreat. The French counterattacked E2 with their M-24 tanks the following day, and on April 4 VPA units finally pulled back. The French reclaimed E1 on April 10 and two days later turned aside a concerted VPA attack. But, once

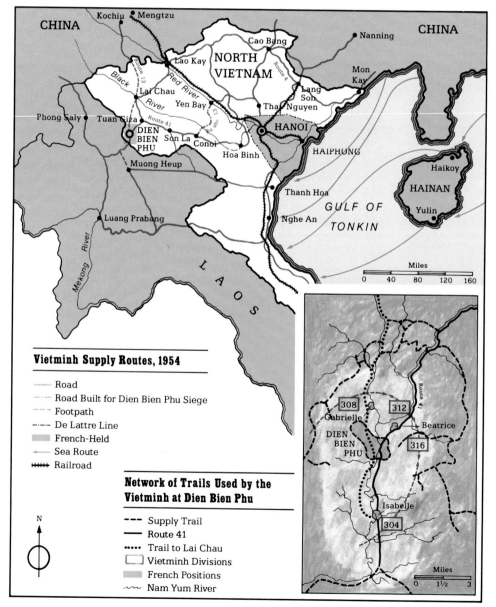

CHINA

Kochiu Mengtzu

Cao Bang

Nanning CHINA

Lao Kay

NORTH VIETNAM

Black River

Lai Chau

Yen Bay

Lang Son

Mon Kay

Phong Saly Tuan Giao

Route 41

DIEN BIEN PHU

Son La

Conoi

Thai Nguyen

HANOI

HAIPHONG

Hoa Binh

Muong Heup

Thanh Hoa

GULF OF TONKIN

Haikoy

HAINAN

Yulin

Luang Prabang

Nghe An

Mekong River

LAOS

Miles
0 40 80 120 160

Vietminh Supply Routes, 1954

- —— Road
- —·—· Road Built for Dien Bien Phu Siege
- ----- Footpath
- —··— De Lattre Line
- French-Held
- —— Sea Route
- ⱵⱵ Railroad

Network of Trails Used by the Vietminh at Dien Bien Phu

N

- --- Supply Trail
- —— Route 41
- ···· Trail to Lai Chau
- ⬜ Vietminh Divisions
- French Positions
- ⵈ Nam Yum River

308 312

Gabrielle Beatrice

DIEN BIEN PHU

316

Isabelle

304

Route 41

Miles
0 1½ 3

Tale of Two Sieges

	Dien Bien Phu	Khe Sanh
Length of siege:	56 days March 13 to May 8, 1954	77 days January 21 to April 4, 1968
Size of position:	33 square miles	8 square miles
Size of forces —combatants:	49,500 Vietminh and 13,200 French	20,000 North Vietnamese and Vietcong and 5,800 Americans and South Vietnamese
—ratio:	4:1 (VM:F)	4:1 (NV&VC:US&SV)
Ratio of artillery strength:	4:1 (VM:F)	1:4 (NV&VC:US&SV)
Defenders' artillery pieces destroyed:	all	3
Artillery fire —average incoming rounds (per day/total):	1,840/103,000	150/11,550
—average outgoing rounds (per day/total):	1,690/93,000	2,080/160,000
Internal deserters:	3,000 to 4,000	none
Daily supply tonnage:	100	200
Day of siege airfield lost:	day 1	airfield not lost
Air time from primary airfield:	75 minutes, Hanoi	30 minutes, Da Nang
Number of aircraft available:	100	1,500/fixed-wing
Daily missions average:	189	320
Bomb tonnage:	175 (estimate)	1,282/(average per day)
Helicopters available:	no	yes/(3,300)
Aircraft lost:	62	24
Relief expedition:	"Condor"—stalled in Laotian jungle	"Pegasus" met little resistance relieving garrison
Casualties:	French: 7,693 (2,080 killed in action; 5,613 wounded, only about 350 evacuated; also 1,606 missing in action to 5/5/54; 6,500 taken as prisoners of war 5/7/54 to 5/8/54) Vietminh: 22,900 (estimated) (7,900 killed in action; 15,000 wounded)	Americans and South Vietnamese: 1,057 (205 killed in action; 852 wounded and evacuated) North Vietnamese and Vietcong: 10,000

When North Vietnamese and Vietcong units cut off a detachment of U.S. Marines and South Vietnamese Rangers at Khe Sanh in January 1968, a haunting name from the earlier Indochina War echoed through the American press. Would Khe Sanh be "another Dien Bien Phu"? Fearful of such a repetition, President Johnson asked to see reports on the spring 1954 battle. It was said that the wily General Giap was personally directing the assault at Khe Sanh. The similarities, as the following chart shows, were unnerving. In each battle a large force had surrounded a smaller one deep in the jungle, and airlifts were the only means of supporting the entrapped garrison. But Khe Sanh did not prove to be another Dien Bien Phu. Khe Sanh's defenders were positioned on a hill rather than in a valley as were the French at Dien Bien Phu, the defenders maintained good fields of fire throughout the battle, and their artillery power far exceeded that of the attackers. Most important, air supply was never interrupted. At Khe Sanh, the defenders' bombing was massive and close aerial support of ground operations effective. Support and manpower levels did not fall precipitously as they did at Dien Bien Phu and in some cases increased. Although the American and South Vietnamese defenders took many casualties, most of them made it out of Khe Sanh alive.

the commanding eastern hills of D3, E1, and E2 fell in early May, the camp's fate was sealed. For now, the battle for the five hills was over.

Giap's army also attacked the more vulnerable low positions at *Huguette* in the west. By April 2, the French had abandoned both H7 and *Françoise*. VPA trenches encircled *Huguette* 6 (H6), but the embattled position held out through another series of attacks in mid-April until supplies ran short; it was evacuated, just before it was overrun, on the eighteenth. *Huguette* 1 (H1) was similarly asphyxiated. And in Colonel Marcel Biegeard's April 23 counterattack on H1, near the burned-out shell of a C-46 Curtiss Commando in which hid a VPA machine-gun nest, the last paratroop reinforcements were decimated. It was as big a loss as that of the *Dominiques* three weeks before. By April 24, the battle for the *Huguettes* and the second phase were over.

The French had lost all of *Dominique* save D3, and the VPA had installed batteries of recoilless rifles on the newly won hills, making life inside the perimeter relentless hell. The loss of the key northwestern positions (H1, H6, H7, and *Françoise*) near the airstrip was equally ominous, for not only did the sites offer good gun placements, but their loss meant that resupply on a large scale had become impossible. The

garrison had lost 40 percent of its territory and five hundred more men. By May 1, only three thousand bone-weary French and Vietnamese paratroopers, foreign legionnaires, and African cannoneers were left fighting.

The lack of shelter and maneuvering room that dogged French troops in the center subsection was far worse at the isolated southern stronghold *Isabelle*. *Isabelle* was situated on a quarter-mile square of flat marshland with no hills nearby for protection. VPA Division 304 immobilized *Isabelle*'s offensive threat by early April but could not silence her guns.

Phase Three began at dusk on May 1 with concerted shelling of the entire camp. By 8:05 P.M., H5 had fallen. Communist units fanned out from a newly established VPA stronghold and by midnight were assaulting H2, H3, and H4. D3 and E1 succumbed the next morning. By May 3, *Claudine* 5 (C5) was under the constant bombardment and attack that E2 and E4 had endured for forty-eight hours. The next day H4 fell.

The VPA unleashed newly delivered Russian-built Katuysha six-tube field rockets at noon on May 6, and by evening everything not under a solid roof was destroyed. French artillery spent its last shells at dusk beating back a crack battalion on the slopes of E2. The VPA responded with a counterbarrage that disabled

the last of the French big guns. At 11:00 that night a bomb that had been tunneled beneath E2 was detonated and ripped apart the hill position. By 5:00 A.M. on May 7, E2 fell. C5 had been conquered early that morning, and just after dawn E4 and E10 went down. The French abandoned *Sparrowhawk* at 10:30. By noon, after thousands of VPA troops from the 308th, 312th, and 316th Divisions had moved in from east and west, the French command found that new enemy trenches outside *Juno* precluded all hope of a breakout.

They contacted the VPA command, indicating that all resistance would end at 5:30 that afternoon. By 4:00 Giap's troops had crushed all positions east of the river. French troops destroyed their weapons and at 5:30 resistance ceased, though without any flying of white flags. By 2:00 the next morning, after bitter hand-to-hand fighting, *Isabelle* too fell silent. The heroic, bloody battle of Dien Bien Phu was over.

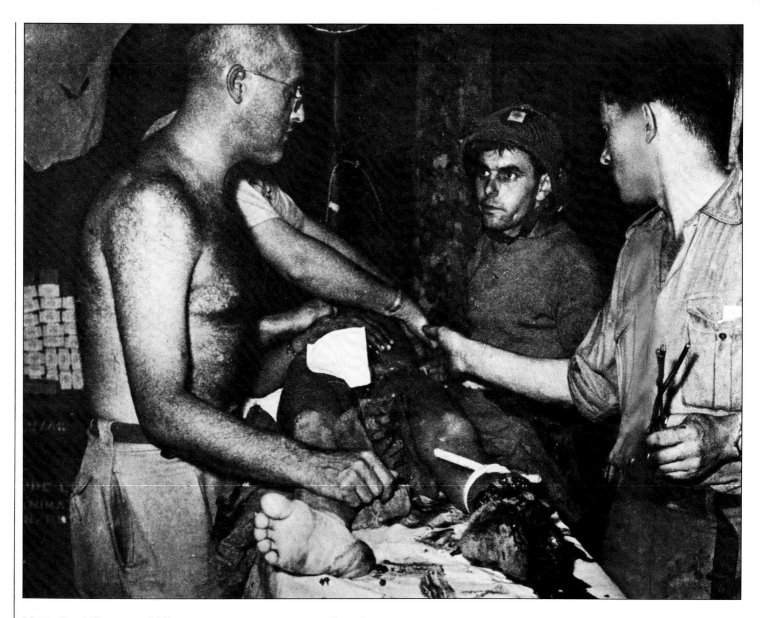

Major Paul Grauwin, M.D., prepares to operate on a French soldier's wounded foot in one of Dien Bien Phu's dark, over-crowded medical bunkers. A career army surgeon, Major Grauwin headed a staff of eighteen doctors who cared for more than three thousand seriously wounded soldiers, many of them suffering multiple injuries.

Although the loss of these forces was a serious blow to the French cause, it was not a statistical disaster. Only 5 percent of the fighting strength of the combined French Union and Vietnamese forces had been lost. French and Vietnamese reinforcements could make up for the manpower loss, and American assistance could replace equipment. Giap suffered over twenty-two thousand casualties, including an estimated eight thousand killed. He was seriously weakened for the drive he would soon mount against the real target of the war, the Red River Delta. In strict military terms, the battle of Dien Bien Phu was neither decisive nor disastrous.

But the outcome, like that of the Tet offensive fourteen years later, could not be considered on military grounds alone. One of the last French strongholds was commanded by Major Jean Nicolas. Sometime after 6:30 P.M. on May 7, he saw a white flag on top of a rifle appear over his trench, followed by a Vietminh soldier.

"You're not going to shoot anymore?" asked the guerrilla in French.

"No, I am not going to shoot anymore," responded the Frenchman.

"C'est fini?" said the Vietnamese soldier.

"Oui, c'est fini," Nicolas said.

Yes, it was the end. The next afternoon, May 8, 1954, at 4:00 P.M. the representatives of nine delegations took their places around a horseshoe-shaped table in Geneva, Switzerland. The only item on the agenda: the future of Indochina.

One month to make peace

On June 17, 1954, Pierre Mendès-France, a Radical-Socialist deputy, ascended the rostrum in the Palais Bourbon to ask the Chamber of Deputies to replace Prime Minister Joseph Laniel's government with one under his premiership. His plea to the chamber electrified the deputies:

I promise to resign if, one month from now, on July 20, I have failed to obtain a cease-fire in Indochina.

The next day the Chamber of Deputies overwhelmingly endorsed Mendès-France, 419 votes to 47 with 143 abstentions.

Mendès-France had been a persistent critic of French government policy in Vietnam, even more so after the Indochina phase of the Geneva Conference had opened on May 8, 1954. He charged that the foreign minister, Georges Bidault, was using Geneva not to make peace but in preparation to continue the war. Bidault had insisted that if Geneva did not produce an end to the conflict, France would continue the war, this time with direct American involvement. Mendès-France charged that this was not Bidault's threat, but his desire.

On June 8 U.S. Secretary of State Dulles pulled the rug from underneath Bidault. Yes, he said, the U.S. would intervene if the Geneva talks failed, but only if seven very strict conditions were met. Most troublesome to France were American demands for a unified Franco-American command structure in Vietnam, thus taking sole control of the conduct of the war out of French hands, and an insistence that the French Chamber of Deputies officially approve U.S. involvement. The demands were too much for Bidault and the Laniel government. A few days later the government resigned, and Mendès-France became the thirteenth prime minister of the Fourth Republic.

Mendès-France, too, threatened to continue the war if peace accords were not signed in Geneva. But unlike Bidault, he did not rely on the Americans. If there were no peace treaty within one month, said Mendès-France, his last act as prime minister would be to dispatch draftees to Indochina. To back up his threat, Mendès-France ordered all conscripts stationed in Germany and at France's major base in Marseilles to be inoculated for yellow fever. With that, Mendès-France, acting as his own foreign minister, headed for Geneva to make peace.

A badly burned legionnaire, his eyes mercifully undamaged.

Stalemate in Geneva, crisis in Hanoi

The situation inherited by Mendès-France, both in Geneva and in Vietnam, made his gamble to bring peace in thirty days seem very unwise. In Geneva, Bidault had refused to speak with Pham Van Dong, head of the Vietminh delegation. Dulles had left Geneva shortly after May 8, leaving the American delegation in the hands of Undersecretary of State Bedell Smith. Shortly thereafter Smith departed, further downgrading the American mission. Both Smith and Dulles acted as if China's representative, Chou En-lai, were invisible. The Americans and the French

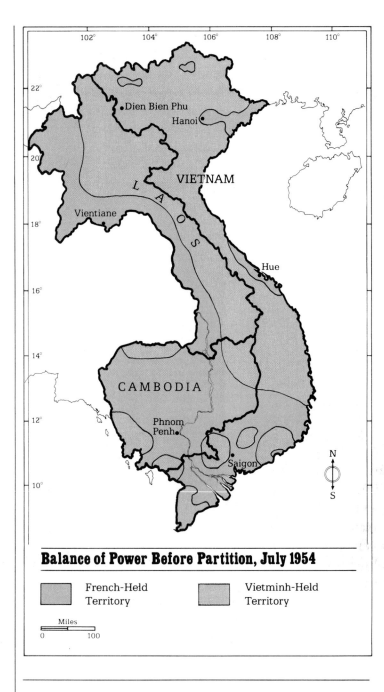

Balance of Power Before Partition, July 1954

| | French-Held Territory | | Vietminh-Held Territory |

Miles
0   100

Geneviève de Galard-Terraube, a twenty-nine-year-old French Air Force nurse, was the only woman to stay through the battle and after the surrender of Dien Bien Phu, tending the wounded and earning in news accounts the sobriquet "Angel of Dien Bien Phu." Back in France and in full dress uniform she wears a smile with her many medals, which include the Croix de Guerre and Legion of Honor awarded her during the battle by General de Castries.

ignored all Communist proposals and depended upon England's Anthony Eden and the Soviet Union's Vyacheslav Molotov to act as intermediaries with the Vietminh and Communist China.

Dulles could envision only one outcome from the conference. The Communist delegations would use the talks to legitimize their takeover of all of Vietnam, and Dulles seriously doubted whether the French had the will to turn them down. He had already written off Eden as a "defeatist" and busied himself largely with plans to contain communism after the "fall of Indochina."

In Indochina the situation had, indeed, become critical. General Giap quickly replaced his losses from Dien Bien Phu and began to threaten the Red River Delta and Hanoi itself. The French high command decided that preservation of the Expeditionary Force and the capability for a Dunkirk-style evacuation receive top priority. In late May and early June the French retreated from the perimeter of the delta to a small enclave around Hanoi, devoting their forces to keeping the road to Haiphong and the open sea clear. Hanoi was in a noose as Pierre Mendès-France took office.

Early public sessions of the Geneva Conference seemed to accomplish little. Bidault read a prepared statement which cast all blame for the war on Ho Chi Minh, calling it a "conflict that was imposed on us." One French journalist remarked that Bidault's statement "bore only an incidental resemblance to histori-

C'est fini. A VPA soldier waves the DRV flag over General de Castries' bunker.

Barefoot Vietminh assault troops storm one of strongpoint Eliane's hills past fallen troops and toward the French command post on May 7, as the battle nears its end.

cal truth" and "was convincing only to the converted." Pham Van Dong described the evils of nearly a century of French colonial rule that, even if correct, were largely irrelevant to finding an agreement to end the conflict.

Behind the scenes the situation was a little more propitious. The Communists truly wanted to end the conflict. Russia was emerging from the Stalin era and was hoping to ease international tensions, if only to provide more consumer goods for a restless population. China was anxious to make a good impression at its debut in international diplomacy, to seem reasonable, to act moderately in rebuttal to U.S. charges that theirs was an "outlaw" government. With China and Russia applying the pressure, the Democratic Republic of Vietnam would have to compromise. Even the Vietminh had reason to seek peace. After eight years of warfare it was time to consolidate gains and continue the revolution.

Alone among the Western statesmen, Eden seemed to understand this dynamic. Already, before Mendès-France took office, he had facilitated compromises on two key issues. First, Pham Van Dong had repeatedly stated that his government would accept a military cease-fire only as part of a comprehensive political settlement. When Eden convinced French and Vietminh military officers to begin secret discussions of military matters, the Vietminh agreed that a cease-fire might be possible without deciding all of the outstanding political questions.

The military talks led to the second compromise by the Vietminh. All parties to the dispute, France, Bao Dai's State of Vietnam, and Ho's Democratic Republic, were opposed to partition. Both Vietnamese governments opposed partition because it would deter Vietnamese unity. But a cease-fire could be effective only if there were a disengagement of opposing forces. France had proposed a "leopard skin" approach, with the opposing sides regrouping in a variety of areas around the country, suggestive of spots on a leopard.

At 10:00 P.M. on June 9, French and Vietminh military experts met at an isolated villa on the outskirts of Geneva. Colonel Ha Van Lau, representing the Vietminh, unfolded a map of Indochina and pointed to the Red River Delta and said, "We need this. We need a state; we need a capital for our state; we need a port for our capital." Lau would say no more, but surely he meant: We need North Vietnam; we need Hanoi; we need Haiphong. It was a clear acceptance of partition. When Mendès-France as-

sumed power the following week, the outstanding questions to be settled before July 20 were the line of demarcation for partition and the timing of elections that might reunite the country.

The pressure to compromise

It quickly became apparent to Mendès-France that the Communists would make the most of his self-imposed deadline of one month. They would refuse to compromise further until the last minute to force the French prime minister to accept their proposals. The Vietminh had originally asked for partition at the fourteenth parallel, roughly halfway between Da Nang and Cam Ranh Bay. But on July 13 Chou En-lai persuaded Dong to offer the sixteenth parallel, just south of Hue. The French insisted that Hue be included in the South, and there the matter stood. No compromises were forthcoming on the question of elections. Pham Van Dong insisted on elections within six months. The French, under American pressure, asked that no specific date be set. The situation was exactly reversed from the stalemate over Korea. There the United States wanted quick elections, sure that the non-Communists would win. The Russians said no. But in Vietnam, the U.S. government recognized the near-certainty of Ho's victory in any election.

July 20 arrived. Mendès-France had only until midnight to conclude peace. As expected the final Communist compromises were forthcoming. Under heavy pressure from Molotov, Dong accepted partition at the seventeenth parallel. At a time when the Vietminh controlled three-quarters of Vietnam, they had settled for less than half. Now only the question of elections needed to be resolved. Mendès-France still held out for not naming a specific date, but when Molotov said, "Two years?" Mendès-France glowed with satisfaction. Pham Van Dong wasn't even asked. It was 5:15 P.M.

News of the agreement spread quickly. Arrangements were made in the Palais des Nations for the signing of the armistice and final declaration. The ceremony was set for 9:00 P.M. But at 8:00 P.M. Mendès-France received a phone call from a furious Molotov. The Cambodians refused to sign. They argued that the provisions calling for Cambodian neutrality violated their sovereignty. The Cambodians wanted to be free to make alliances with any country they chose.

"Earthquake McGoon"

A burly man with a hearty laugh, he was known far and wide as "Earthquake McGoon." On the afternoon of May 6, 1954, Earthquake shoehorned his six-foot, 250-pound frame into the modified pilot's seat of a Fairchild C-119 "Flying Boxcar" at Hanoi's airfield as he had twice daily for weeks. It was the day before Dien Bien Phu fell.

Responding to a French request to help airlift supplies to Dien Bien Phu in March 1954, the United States Air Force had loaned the French a squadron of C-119s, whose white eagle wings were hastily covered with a single coat of gray paint. Some two dozen American civilian flyers employed by Major General Claire Chennault's Civil Air Transport (CAT) had manned the garrison's aerial life line beginning in late March. For the past six weeks, they had flown the perilous ninety-minute shuttle from Hanoi to the beleaguered outpost thirty times a day, weather permitting, and dropped over eighty-five hundred tons of ammunition and food. The antiaircraft fire over the valley was intense.

For this dangerous job the pilots earned good pay: $35 for each flying hour, plus their regular salary—a total of about $3,000 a month. But Earthquake for one, to the hoots of his CAT buddies, would admit that he was not there only for the money or the adventure. "Way I figure it," he said, "we either got to fight the bastards at home or fight them over here."

In the copilot's seat sat Wallace A. Buford, twenty-eight, of Ogden, Utah, a veteran of World War II and the Korean War, who had coaxed a disabled Boxcar back to base ten days before. Heavy antiaircraft fire over the Dien Bien Phu valley had crippled the plane and wounded pilot Paul R. Holdens—the first American combat casualty of the French Indochina War. Both Buford and Earthquake had braved the flak many times, circling

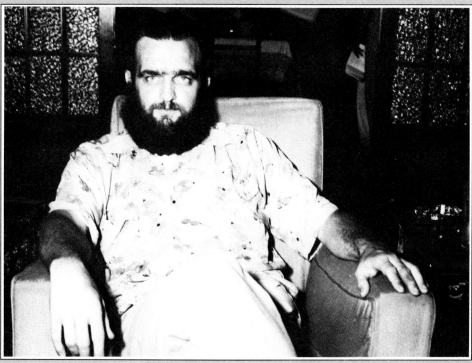

down to fifteen hundred feet or so and slowing the plane almost to a stall so that the "kickers" could shove out the seven-ton load and perhaps hit the ever-shrinking drop zone. McGoon's plane had been hit four times, but "when you are invited to a war," he said, "you expect to get shot at."

Earthquake, who was actually James B. McGovern, thirty-two, of Elizabeth, New Jersey, was no stranger to hazardous duty. A powerful man with a usually gentle manner, he had piloted P-40s and Mustangs for Chennault's famed "Flying Tigers" in China before and during World War II. In 1948, a year after he joined Chennault's new CAT, Chinese Communist fighter planes attacked his transport over Shantung Peninsula; "They missed," a terse Earthquake liked to say. Some six months after he was forced to ditch his plane on a river sandbar behind Communist lines in December 1949, a bearded McGoon emerged from the jungle. "The Communists," he said, "went out of their way to treat me good." But his CAT friends quipped that his captors had freed him because they could not afford to feed him.

Waiting his turn in Hanoi that May afternoon, McGoon had guzzled bad coffee and tossed darts in the sultry air base mess with the other flyers. Then he and Buford strapped themselves into "Bird Two." Once the six-plane convoy

James B. McGovern was a personable man and so huge that he was nicknamed "Earthquake McGoon" after the character in the Li'l Abner comic strip. He and copilot Wallace A. Buford, flying for Chennault's Civil Air Transport, were the only Americans to die in combat during the French Indochina War.

reached the valley, McGoon eased the control stick forward and watched his altimeter indicate a descent to 3,000 feet. They were ready for their run; it was Earthquake's forty-fifth.

Suddenly McGoon radioed, "I've got a direct hit." A shell had crashed into one of the two wing-mounted engines which began to throw oil. Just as he began to regain control, another shell hit, knocking out a critical tail support. The plane was sent reeling toward a narrow four thousand-foot valley. Earthquake radioed the pilot of the plane following his, asking which ridge was lower. The pilot responded, "Turn right!" But it was too late. The controls were crippled, and the big plane could not hold a turn. As his buddies watched and listened helplessly, Earthquake cooly said, "Looks like this is it, son." The left wing tip struck first. The plane tumbled down the hill and burst into flames.

James B. McGovern and Wallace A. Buford were the only Americans to die in combat in the French Indochina War.

Miracle in Geneva

Slowly the clock moved toward midnight. And then came the "miracle" of Geneva. The Swiss clocks—world famous for their reliability—suddenly stopped in the Palais des Nations, precisely at midnight! To give Mendès-France a little more time to meet his deadline, the clocks had been made to stand still.

It was "midnight" for three more hours until the Cambodians finally won their point. Molotov gave in and granted the Cambodians (and Laotians) the right to call on America to help fight communism. But South Vietnam was prohibited from entering any military alliance that would violate its neutrality. It was permitted to receive military assistance from western countries, but only at specified levels.

The cease-fire was signed by the French and Vietminh at 3:20 A.M. The Vietminh delegate asked the head of the French military commission in Geneva, who had the painful duty of signing the document, to have some champagne with him. The French general, ghostly pale, replied, "You will understand that I cannot accept."

The cease-fire agreement turned out to be the only document signed. The next day, July 21, the Final Declaration was read. But when the U.S. and the new South Vietnam refused to sign, so did the Communist nations. Bedell Smith said that while the U.S. would not sign them, it would "refrain from the threat or use of force to disturb them" and would "view any renewal of aggression in violation of the aforesaid agreements with grave concern and as seriously threatening international peace and security."

The Geneva accords: an assessment

The only real accomplishment of the Geneva Conference was the military cease-fire, the end to hostilities between France and the Democratic Republic of Vietnam. Pham Van Dong had repeatedly sought a political settlement to decide what the future State of Vietnam would be. The most he got was the promise of elections in two years: The elections, it was assumed, would determine the political settlement.

After Geneva, Vietnam was neither united nor fully independent. The French would regroup below the seventeenth parallel, expecting to continue to exert their influence on South Vietnam in the context of the French Union.

Vietminh regular forces were also forced by the Geneva accords to regroup. Guerrillas whose homes lay south of the seventeenth parallel were forced to move to the North and thereby earned the name "regroupees." Many of them were bitter about Ho's compromises which forced them to leave their homes in the South. They were pacified only with the knowledge that a victory by Ho in elections scheduled for July 1956 would permit them to return home.

The Geneva accords also provided that, during the 300 days allotted for the regroupment of troops, "any civilians residing in a district controlled by one party who wish to go and live in the zone assigned to the other party shall be permitted and helped to do so by the authorities in that district." All of these provisions were to be enforced by a three-country International Control Commission (ICC) consisting of representatives from one Communist nation, Poland; one neutral nation, India; and one western state, Canada.

The position of the United States toward the agreements might be termed ingenuous if it had not turned out so tragically. The United States had been among the fiercest opponents of a political settlement at Geneva. But now with the negotiations complete the U.S. embarked on a course designed to make the purely military arrangements serve as the basis of a de facto political settlement. The U.S. pledge not to upset the accords by "threat or use of force" already suggested this direction in policy. The U.S. did not promise to abide by the agreements, rather it promised not to use force to break them. By vetoing the elections—and the U.S. had already hinted that it would do so—the American government sought to make permanent the division of Vietnam. The line against Chinese expansion was drawn at the seventeenth parallel. In the new prime minister of the State of Vietnam, Ngo Dinh Diem, who assumed office on July 7, 1954, the United States found a willing ally.

The Geneva accords, thought the Eisenhower administration, offered the United States a new opportunity in Indochina. Long frustrated by what the Americans considered France's lack of will, poor military planning, and identification with colonialism, the U.S. government thought it could make a fresh start with the new Diem government. But an unnamed American diplomat in Paris (probably Ambassador C. Douglas Dillon) had already issued a warning—of sorts—to the American government. In November of 1953 the American diplomat told the French newspaper Le Monde, "We [Americans] are the last French colonialists in Indochina."

French Veterans in War and Peace

Vietnam veteran Charles Daniels knew how French Indochina veterans must have felt. He had been back in his native Boston for thirteen years before he saw a sign saying, "Welcome Home Vietnam Vets." French soldiers experienced many of the same problems in battle and on the home front that dogged Americans later. Like the American soldiers after them, French soldiers were in a divisive and often brutal war lacking in rules, and like the Americans, they often felt misunderstood and maligned, branded by some as fiends for having fought in the war and by others as failures for having "lost" it.

"It is true that we are here to defend human values," a young French officer said carefully, discussing the morality of war. A graduate of the French West Point, St. Cyr, he added, "We must degrade ourselves to inhumanity. For we are dealing with the Vietminh for whom such things are simple and logical. ... The Viets push us into atrocities and our

absurdity helps too. Yet we kill less than the Viets."

In 1950 an American reporter listened to French troops gripe about the conduct of the war. "We could clean them up in three months if the government would let us," an infantry sergeant said bitterly. "But we can't fight. We can only wait for them to fight us."

"Yes, but now we can fight better," a pilot said. "Now we can use American guns and trucks. And the Air-Cobra! Ah, monsieur! What a wonderful plane!"

"Our government in France is weak," a corporal chipped in. "The Communists and Socialists won't let us do anything here."

"It's the United Nations too," the sergeant said. "We used to use flame throwers. Now the UN says they're uncivilized weapons and we can't use them. ... Well," the pilot concluded with scorn, "they're politicians. Pah!"

The comments of a Madame Van der Merce at an army ministry Christmas party some twenty years ago still rankle at least one French veteran. "The best gift that one could send to the troops in Indochina was a bullet in the hide of each," he recalled her saying. "None of us ever forgot that."

The central problem of command in both the French and American wars was that very often it was the skill and experience of platoon leaders more than that of generals that determined success or failure. And a man could learn to lead a platoon only in the bush, where even a small error in judgment could mean the loss of the entire unit. Another young St. Cyr graduate said, "In this Indochina War, everything is based on the officer; he has to master himself, to be a hero all the time, even in everyday life. He is not entitled to make the smallest slip."

Despite the privations and humiliation, many French vets still felt some satisfaction. As one put it, "We are happy to have suffered together. There was in the army at that time a spirit that no longer exists. One was involved. If someone who had a higher rank than yours gave you an order you carried it out. I'm sure that was stupidity. But why wouldn't one do it?"

One French soldier who volunteered

for assignment to Indochina as "a solution to the lack of employment and dignity" recalled, "We had the impression not of being on the other side of the world, but of being on Mars." Returning from this Mars to France was, for many, not a pleasant homecoming. "We were considered pariahs, criminals," recalled one vet. "Three days after I came home I was wearing my uniform because that was all I had to wear. I got on a bus. When I passed in front of the driver he said to the ticket taker, 'Hey, an assassin just got on.' I hit him and spent the rest of the day at the police station."

French Communists stoned hospital trains stopping to unload wounded men in their home towns, provoking outcries in the Chamber of Deputies. Another soldier, taking leave in Paris during 1954, found he "was very let down by France at that time. There were already committees supporting Ho Chi Minh everywhere." Disappointed, he said, "I no longer felt that I was in my country. I had only one wish, that was to go back to Vietnam."

A sergeant who survived both Cao Bang and Dien Bien Phu recalled:

We were rejected when we returned, we were covered with blood, so that I no longer want to think about it. I never collected any of my pension. We were like immigrants in France. It was only after two years that I could begin to talk about it. I stuck with the society of Dien Bien Phu veterans. I rediscovered some comrades. Now I collect my pension. One still can't be sure.

Although the French are erecting a memorial to their war dead now, a tribute long delayed in the United States as well, the treatment of Indochina veterans in the Fifth Republic remains problematic. "What still surprises me today," said a vet in 1981, "is that you see in the paper that a man kills his wife, and they put above it, 'Veteran of Indochina.' I don't understand the reason. There are many civilians who kill their wives because they are jealous, but the papers don't add, 'Former Employee of the Railroad.' That's what is surprising and that's the reason why I don't like to say that I'm a former soldier."

Two Vietnams

Thursday, July 22, 1954. On this, the day after the signing of the Geneva accords, a strangely somber mood settled on Hanoi. The accords marked an end to the violence that had ravaged Vietnam, especially the North, during nearly eight years of bloody warfare against the French. At last Vietnam appeared on the verge of national independence after its long resistance to French colonial rule. Still, there were no victory celebrations, no cheering rallies. Henry Liebermann, a *New York Times* correspondent, described Hanoi as "outwardly calm" with "neither general jubilation or [sic] public wailing." The day passed almost like any other summer weekday in Tonkin's sun-baked capital. The bars, perhaps, were less crowded than usual, but life went on at a fairly normal pace.

The people of Hanoi had good reason for their mixed emotions. Supporters of the Vietminh were cautious and even suspicious about the political settlement reached at Geneva. Once before,

in September 1945, the Vietminh had formed a government and declared independence from France. Yet their hopes for freedom were quickly dashed as the French, with Allied approval and support, had reimposed colonial rule. Since French troops still controlled the Hanoi area, many Vietminh there adopted a wait-and-see attitude toward the independence promised by Geneva.

For the French establishment in Hanoi and those Vietnamese associated with it, the future looked uncertain. French businessmen who held a powerful stake in the economy of the North feared the eventual loss of their investments to the Communist Vietminh. Through their colonial enterprises, these French entrepreneurs had transformed Hanoi into a thriving metropolis. Even behind barbed wire and barricades during the darkest days of the war, Hanoi, with its broad, tree-lined boulevards, stately French architecture, and cozy cafés, had not lost its charm. Many French shopkeepers and small businessmen shared the concern about what was coming. Would the Vietminh drive them out and confiscate their property? Or would it be possible somehow to work out a means of peaceful coexistence with the Communist regime? A French restaurateur echoed the determination of many French citizens to stay in Hanoi and face the consequences: "I came to Hanoi in 1945 as a sergeant-cook. I now have $30,000 invested in my restaurant, and I'm staying until I have to leave."

To many Vietnamese, as well, the Vietminh takeover of the North posed a serious threat. Those who had served in the French colonial government expected reprisals by the Vietminh. Others who had sympathized with the nationalist cause but refused to take an active part in the Communist-led resistance were also worried. During the Geneva negotiations, several thousand of them had gathered in front of the Hanoi Opera House to protest the ceding of the North to the Communists. But theirs was a feeble demonstration against the inevitable.

For these Vietnamese the choice was imminent: to stay, sacrificing their property and facing "reeducation camps," or to flee to the South, a free zone pending reunification elections scheduled for July 1956. Thousands of Vietnamese anxiously weighed the

gamble, some despaired. A barefoot refugee from the battle-scarred countryside, crowded into a three-room house with twenty-three people, lamented: "I left my village two years ago because there was shooting every day. Now there is no place left for me to go."

"Long live a peaceful Vietnam"—
Ho Chi Minh

While the people of the French enclave at Hanoi pondered their dilemma, in the days following Geneva Ho Chi Minh and his lieutenants, Giap, Pham Van Dong, and Le Duan, maintained a low profile, a habit of decades of intrigue against French authorities and secret police. Ho had not been seen for years. Many, including French and American intelligence experts, speculated that he was seriously ill or even dead.

On July 22, the Vietminh did issue a formal message in Ho's name, celebrating independence:

For the sake of peace, unity, independence, and democracy of the Fatherland, our peoples, armymen, cadres, and government have, during these eight years or so, joined in a monolithic bloc, endured hardship and overcome all difficulties to resolutely carry out the Resistance and have won many many brilliant victories. On this occasion, on behalf of our government, I cordially congratulate you, from North to South.

Although the message praised the "people's" victory and underplayed Ho's role in overcoming the French, it represented the supreme moment of triumph for the old revolutionary. Over the years, Ho's personal commitment to defeating the French and his resolute leadership of the resistance had made him a legendary figure, his very name synonymous with the independence movement.

His beginnings had certainly not been auspicious. Born in 1890 in Nghe An Province, the son of a wandering scholar, Ho entered the National Academy at Hue in 1906 to prepare for a career in the French colonial administration. After a year he dropped out and began a life of wandering. In 1912, hoping to see the West, Ho sailed from Saigon as a cook on a steamship line. His travels took him to London and then to Paris. It is rumored that he even visited the United States, and Boston mythology holds that he worked as a hotel cook there. In Paris Ho fell into the circle of Phan Chu Trinh, an influential Vietnamese nationalist, who taught him the trade of photo retouching and encouraged his patriotic spirit.

Preceding page. In front of the French governor general's palace in Hanoi, Vietminh troops raise helmets in celebration of their reoccupation of the former colonial capital. The city was surrendered by the French in accord with the Geneva Agreement of July 1954.

88

Ho Chi Minh briefs his cadres on the politics of revolutionary warfare in preparation for the "borderline campaign"—guerrilla forays against the French from across the Chinese border in 1950.

Ho was a man of action and destined for greater things. In 1919 he boldly appeared at the Versailles Peace Conference where he presented a petition for Vietnam's independence. By taking the initiative, Ho earned himself a lasting reputation among his fellow Vietnamese as a leading spokesman for Vietnamese political interests. In 1920, at Tours, he participated in founding the French Communist party.

The Soviets were impressed by Ho and invited him to Moscow to represent Third World peasants. Ho accepted eagerly and remained in Moscow to study at the Lenin School of Oriental Peoples. There his budding nationalism was channeled, through contact with Leninist theory and Soviet-style politics, in the direction of communism. The Russian Revolution was still in its infancy, and Ho admired the revolutionary fervor of Soviet leaders.

But it was Lenin's "Thesis on the National and Colonial Questions" calling for an international Communist liberation of oppressed peoples from colonialism that radically changed Ho's thinking. He later recalled how the thesis inspired him: "What emotion, enthusiasm, clear-sightedness and confidence it instilled in me! I was overjoyed to tears. Though sitting alone in my room, I shouted aloud as if addressing large crowds: 'Dead martyrs, compatriots! This is what we need, this is the path to liberation!' "

Lenin's political ideology did more than inspire Ho. Soviet training and Leninist teachings equipped him with the organizational principles and tactics to form a revolutionary party in Vietnam. In 1924, Ho returned to Asia with instructions to organize a Vietnamese Communist association. Arriving in Canton, China, Ho met with Phan Boi Chau, Vietnam's most revered nationalist. Phan had been active in the unsuccessful Scholars' Revolt of the 1890s and subsequent diplomatic efforts to gain Chinese and Japanese support for Vietnamese independence. Through talks with Phan and other revolutionaries, Ho founded in 1925 the Revolutionary Youth League of Vietnam, the country's first Communist organization. Its members, after training in China, returned to Vietnam and found their way to factories and plantations, wherever they could agitate among the masses. Five years later, in 1930, Ho formed the Indochinese Communist party. He solidified his unchallenged leadership of Vietnamese Communists by convincing numerous competing factions to cooperate in sowing the seeds of revolution in the Vietnamese countryside.

Over the next twenty-five years, the name and framework of Ho's party changed, but its goals, Vietnamese independence and socialist reform, remained constant. Ho's control of the nationalist movement extended even to non-Communist parties. He courted, negotiated with, and, when necessary, double-crossed his political rivals to keep them working within the fold of the party or not at all.

Ho strictly applied Lenin's principle that opposition to the party constituted subversion. His leadership style was authoritarian, not democratic, but it reflected traditional Vietnamese values. Vietnam's emperors governed by their authority as "Sons of Heaven"; power emanated from them, not the people. They acted on the Confucian principle that their authority, like a father's in the family, held society together. While Ho believed that political power ultimately rested with the peasant masses, in some ways he cultivated the paternal aura that had surrounded the emperors. "Uncle Ho" to his followers, he confidently relied on his ability to hold Vietnam's "revolutionary family" together and to unleash it against the French.

Now, on July 22, 1954, Ho's lifelong vision seemed accomplished. Vietnam was finally free, and apparently the country would soon be united. Still, many people in the North wondered if the struggle was really over. Would the Vietminh initiate a new revolution, the socialist reorganization of society? Would Ho emerge once more to lead it? The fates of many seemed to hang in the balance: Vietnam's Catholics, anti-Communists, and landlords. Most experienced a sense of foreboding, asking over and over the same nagging question: "Was peace really at hand?"

A final adieu

Hanoi, October 9, 1954. A steady rain fell from dismal gray clouds as a small group of French legionnaires and Moroccan troops hauled down the Tricolor for the last time. The soldiers presented arms, bidding a martial adieu to the beautiful old city of Hanoi. There was no fanfare, no songs, just the mournful sound of a bugle. Only a handful of reporters and photographers gathered in Hanoi's Mangin Athletic Stadium to witness the simple ceremony that wrote an inglorious finish to nearly a century of French colonialism in North Vietnam.

While the soldiers solemnly folded the Tricolor, their thoughts must have turned to their fallen comrades who had sacrificed so much for a lost cause. The statistics were grim: 44,967 dead and 79,560 wounded. An irony the statistics obscured was that a majority of the French casualties were not actually Frenchmen. Losses among the Foreign Legion, composed mostly of Germans, the African contingents—

Moroccans and Senegalese, and indigenous Vietnamese regulars outnumbered those of the French by three to one. The casualty toll seemed to overshadow the memories of valor expended in a futile effort to keep Vietnam within the French empire. René Cogny, commander of French ground forces in the South, summed up France's frustrating Vietnam experience this way: "Many deaths for few results, many deaths for nothing."

The downward spiral of events in Vietnam struck a blow at the morale of the French people and their national prestige. The cream of France's fighting forces—superior to their opponents in manpower, arms, and technology—had been humbled by peasant insurgents. The French evacuation of Hanoi and the North, the region of strongest French cultural influence in Vietnam, also symbolized the total failure of the Empire's *mission civilisatrice*, or civilizing mission. By civilization the French had meant their own. Their goal had been to turn the Vietnamese into Frenchmen. But their mission had failed. Gone forever from French control was stately Hanoi with its French university, Pasteur Institute, and magnificent Catholic cathedrals.

A hero's welcome

While the French quietly made their exit, Vietnamese throughout Hanoi were preparing to greet the victorious Vietminh troops massed outside the city. For days the Vietminh political cadres had been busy setting up a welcome. They drew up lists of households and directed the population to contact political committees established in each of the city's wards. Their function was clear: to maximize popular enthusiasm for the incoming troops of liberation.

The soldiers had also been instructed in behavior suitable for the occasion. A proclamation, ostensibly from Ho, was issued to the troops warning them to behave in the manner appropriate to "heroes of the resistance":

Throughout eight years of resistance, you had set examples of heroism, and thereby we won victory. Today returning to the capital you must also set good examples to win victory in peacetime. Urban life is complicated, many

At French headquarters in Hanoi, eight Foreign Legion bugles sound a mournful farewell as the French Tricolor is lowered for the last time, after nearly a century of colonial rule.

In October 1954, the first detachments of thirty thousand triumphant Vietminh troops enter Hanoi by the Doumer Bridge, named after a colonial governor.

temptations can lead to stupidity, debauchery, and degradation.

Finally, on October 10, the triumphant procession arrived. Thirty thousand Vietminh soldiers, including many veterans of Dien Bien Phu, marched into Hanoi amid the cheers of flag-waving crowds. A delegation composed of representatives of various Hanoi civilian associations led the parade. An infantry regiment followed, the soldiers sporting helmets of latania leaves and wearing loose green uniforms and tennis shoes. This regiment included surviving "death volunteers," whose members would strap explosives to their bodies and throw themselves at the barbed-wire defenses of French strongholds. Next came the

Women's Auxiliary Corps, young, smiling girls with their hair in plaits. Behind them, closing out the parade, rolled fifty Molotov trucks, towing French 150 мм guns captured at Dien Bien Phu.

The arrival of the advance units was the signal for Vietnamese to take to the streets by the thousands. A *New York Times* reporter was in the surging crowds along the parade route as the Vietnamese announced to the world that they were free:

Everywhere along the route hundreds of golden-starred Vietminh flags were broken out from windows, doorways, and roofs of the one-story dwellings of the Vietnamese quarter.... Seemingly from nowhere scores of slogans and banners of welcome burst forth proclaiming 'Long Live President Ho Chi Minh' and 'Long Live Chinese-Soviet Friendship.'

The elated troops and their civilian onlookers proceeded to Hanoi's Mangin Stadium, where only the day before the French had said their last ceremonial good-bye. The assembly was addressed by General Vuong Thua Vu, commander of the Vietminh Division—the "Iron Division"—that had been given the honor of occupying the city in recognition of its outstanding service at Dien Bien Phu. Still, none of the giants of the resistance—Ho Chi Minh, Giap, or Pham Van Dong—made an appearance. Ho's absence on this important occasion seemed to some to confirm speculation that he was dead.

"Long Live Uncle Ho"

Later in October, without fuss or fanfare, a captured French army truck rolled into Hanoi bearing the Vietminh's missing leader. Ho Chi Minh had emerged from his forest hideout to reenter Hanoi in the wake of his troops. Robert Shaplen, then a *Newsweek* correspondent, remembers Ho, at this, his moment of glory:

[He is] the same frail, stooped wisp of a man whose classic endurance of body and soul were almost visible aspects of his being, in contrast to the submerged shrewdness and guile that had also marked his long career as one of the cleverest performers on the stage of world revolution.

Ho's demeanor was subdued. With customary humility, he avoided a gala public welcome. He met briefly with an informal gathering of coworkers and friends. Afterwards, shyly stepping out from behind a curtain in a large reception hall, Ho smiled and reminded his audience, "I am an old guerrilla fighter, you know."

While festivities continued in Hanoi the French withdrew toward the port city of Haiphong. The Geneva Agreement gave them until May 1955 to conclude their withdrawal, and it seemed likely to be completed on schedule.

The International Control Commission of Poles, Indians, and Canadians supervised the withdrawal. The commission designated Hanoi, Hai Duong, and Haiphong as regroupment areas for the transfer of some one hundred and ninety thousand Franco-Vietnamese troops south of the seventeenth parallel. At the same time, the commission assisted in the repatriation of around eighty thousand Vietminh soldiers and their dependents being shipped north from regroupment areas in the South.

The transfer of power from the French to the Vietminh, begun several days before the Vietminh victory

parade, went smoothly enough, although it sometimes resembled an eerie mock battle. On October 3, when the French command transferred its headquarters from Hanoi to Haiphong, parties of Vietminh civil servants, soldiers, and police began arriving in the city to accept control. French troops withdrew slowly, almost building by building. After a building was surrendered, one could see the red Vietminh flag with its yellow star unfurled on the roof top. It was as if the eight-year war was being symbolically replayed as French soldiers, bitter at the way the North had been "bartered" to the Vietminh, stubbornly, grudgingly gave way. On occasion armed Vietminh units deployed in battle formation, as if ready to resume combat. The few Vietnamese who gathered to watch stared silently without hostility but without warmth as French forces marched beside their tanks and trucks. No one shouted "au revoir."

"Psywar" and sabotage

While French forces were evacuating the North in the final tragic chapter of the First Indochina War, many thought another war was inevitable. A cold war team of Central Intelligence Agency (CIA) agents, operating under cover of the U.S. military mission in Saigon, was busy at other work. The clandestine operations of the cold war team were under the command of Colonel Edward Lansdale of the U.S. Air Force. Lansdale, who had served with the Office of Strategic Services (OSS) during World War II, had recently helped reorganize the Philippine Intelligence Service to combat the Communist insurgency of the Huks. In mid-1954, U.S. Secretary of State John Foster Dulles, at the request of his brother Allen, director of the CIA, sent Lansdale an urgent message to go to Saigon and learn as much as possible about the chaotic state of Vietnamese affairs. His message closed with "God Bless You."

In addition to his intelligence-gathering activities, Lansdale sent an espionage team to Hanoi to disrupt the Vietminh takeover. One of its major assignments was to conduct psychological warfare, or "psywar," campaigns to arouse opposition to the incoming Vietminh regime. The team's first tactic was to organize rumor campaigns to inflame Vietnamese fears of a Chinese occupation under Vietminh rule. One rumor was based on a story about a Communist Chinese regiment in the North that raped all the girls in a Vietnamese village, recalling the brutal behavior of Chinese Nationalist troops who occupied the North in

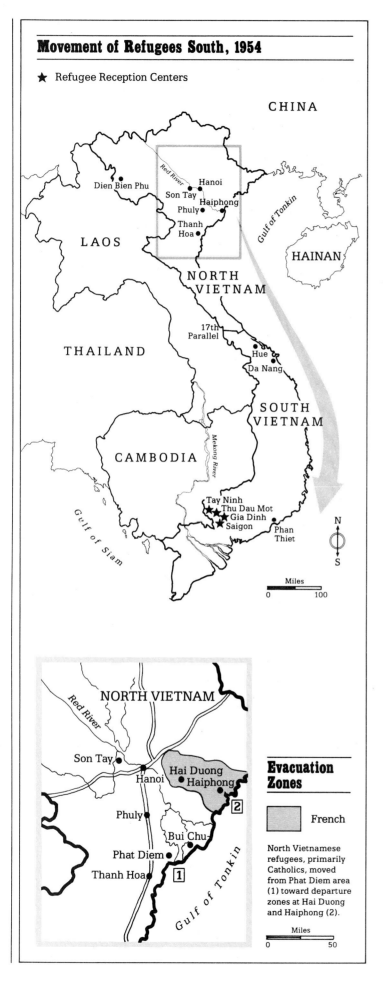

Movement of Refugees South, 1954

★ Refugee Reception Centers

CHINA

Dien Bien Phu

Red River

Hanoi
Son Tay
Phuly
Haiphong
Thanh Hoa

Gulf of Tonkin

HAINAN

LAOS

NORTH VIETNAM

THAILAND

17th Parallel

Hue
Da Nang

SOUTH VIETNAM

CAMBODIA

Mekong River

Gulf of Siam

Tay Ninh
Thu Dau Mot
Gia Dinh
Saigon
Phan Thiet

N

S

Miles
0   100

NORTH VIETNAM

Red River

Son Tay
Hanoi
Hai Duong
Haiphong
Phuly
Bui Chu
Phat Diem
Thanh Hoa

1

2

Gulf of Tonkin

Evacuation Zones

☐ French

North Vietnamese refugees, primarily Catholics, moved from Phat Diem area (1) toward departure zones at Hai Duong and Haiphong (2).

Miles
0   50

1945. Lansdale arranged for soldiers of the Vietnamese Armed Psywar Company, dressed as civilians, to spread the story. But the plan backfired. The psywar company received its instructions, went north on its mission, and never returned. All of its members deserted to the Vietminh.

Other CIA missions proved more successful. In September the team engineered a "black psywar strike" in Hanoi. It distributed leaflets, supposedly signed by the Vietminh, that instructed residents about property confiscation, monetary changes, and the treatment of workers under the new Communist regime. The leaflets had their intended effect: Many frightened Hanoi residents fled south, and North Vietnamese currency dropped in value by 50 percent. Vietminh authorities denounced the leaflets as a French trick but could not stem the panic among property owners, workers, and businessmen.

In October, the team contaminated the oil supply of the Hanoi bus company. The objective: the gradual wreckage of the bus engines. Lansdale in his report on the mission recalled an unexpected hitch:

The team had a bad moment when contaminating the oil. They had to work quickly at night, in an enclosed storage room. Fumes from the contaminant came close to knocking them out. Dizzy and weak-kneed, they masked their faces with handkerchiefs and completed the job.

Lansdale's agents also devised more ambitious projects. A special technical team gathered detailed notes on potential Hanoi targets for future paramilitary operations. The team wanted to sabotage the city's power plant, water facilities, harbor, and bridge but were prevented from doing so by the Geneva regulations. The CIA's "coup de grace," in Lansdale's opinion, was the infiltration of a U.S.-trained Vietnamese paramilitary team into the North. For months agents cached eight and a half tons of arms and equipment in northern areas not yet taken over by the Vietminh. The paramilitary team infiltrated through the port at Haiphong, then jammed with French evacuees and refugees. Lansdale praised the U.S. Air Force pilots who smuggled shipments of arms secretly into Vietnam, where CIA officers "did coolie labor in manhandling tons of cargo, at times working throughout the night." By January, Lansdale proudly surveyed the results. The paramilitary team was in place in the North, had adopted civilian covers, and was ready for a general uprising against the Vietminh regime. It never came.

Colonel Edward Lansdale of the USAF and CIA (center) receives the Distinguished Service Medal on January 8, 1957. Lansdale directed various psychological warfare projects in Vietnam during the mid–1950s. To Lansdale's right is CIA Director Allen Dulles.

The exodus begins

When negotiations at Geneva provided for 300 days of free movement between the zones of the North and South, the negotiators probably did not foresee the ramifications. Their action sparked an exodus from the Vietminh zone of nearly 1 million Vietnamese refugees, most of them destitute. Men, women, children, entire families, and even whole villages pulled up roots from ancestral homes in the North to seek new lives in the "free zone" of the South.

This vast movement of people, unprecedented at the time, received worldwide attention. There was an international outpouring of sympathy for the hundreds of thousands of refugees trying to escape the "bamboo curtain" of the seventeenth parallel. The flight of the refugees, hailed as a massive popular rejection of Communist rule in the North, had its strongest impact in the United States. Newspapers and magazines across the country carried such headlines as "Pilgrims of the East," "Slow Boat to Freedom," and "Tragic Flight." The sheer magnitude of the refugee problem, more than any other event of the Indochina War, focused the attention of the American public on the crisis in Vietnam. It also awakened Americans in an emotional way to the issue of Communist expansion in Southeast Asia and the uncertain future of a divided Vietnam.

The number of refugees shocked the French. They had offered transportation south to any Vietnamese requesting assistance but had estimated that no more than thirty thousand, mostly landlords and businessmen, would take up their offer. From the beginning,

French air and naval resources were stretched to the limit by the thousands of refugees flowing daily into the port at Haiphong. The city quickly became swamped with people unable to find shelter. Food and medicine could be had only at a premium. Every day the situation deteriorated.

Other nations also stepped in to help: Great Britain, Nationalist China, and the United States. Ships of the U.S. Seventh Fleet arrived in Haiphong with tons of medical and food supplies. Private relief agencies also took part in dispensing aid and assistance to the refugees. Behind American aid, there was clearly an anti-Communist motivation. Harold Stassen, director of the Foreign Operations Administration, emphatically stated the American position: "We are glad to give assistance in this voluntary movement of people who wish to escape being forced to live in an area under Communist domination."

"The Blessed Virgin is moving south"

The refugees were primarily Catholic. It is estimated that 60 percent of North Vietnam's 1.5 million Catholics joined the throng of refugees. Many of the Catholics came from the bishoprics of Phat Diem and Bui Chu fifty miles from Haiphong. They represented a legacy of French colonial rule and energetic missionary work by the Catholic church. Most Catholics were militant anti-Communists who had allied themselves with the French during the war. Now that the French were leaving for good, the bishops and priests, leaders of their congregations, were all too

Exodus to the South

Catholic peasants from the Red River Delta scramble through the window of a crowded refugee train headed for Haiphong, where they expect to board ships for Saigon (left).

The United States Navy supplied food, medical care, and transportation for hundreds of thousands of North Vietnamese refugees in 1954. Here crew members apply DDT to refugees exposed to lice in over crowded refugee camps (right).

Dr. Tom Dooley, who became something of an American hero for his role in helping tens of thousands of refugees attempting to flee North Vietnam in 1954 (far right). A U.S. naval officer, Dooley spent two years in Vietnam and three in Laos providing medical care to peasants in cities and remote villages. He died of cancer in 1961 at the age of thirty-four.

Along roads in the Red River Delta, anxious refugees, their few possessions in tow, hurry toward embarkation points on the coast.

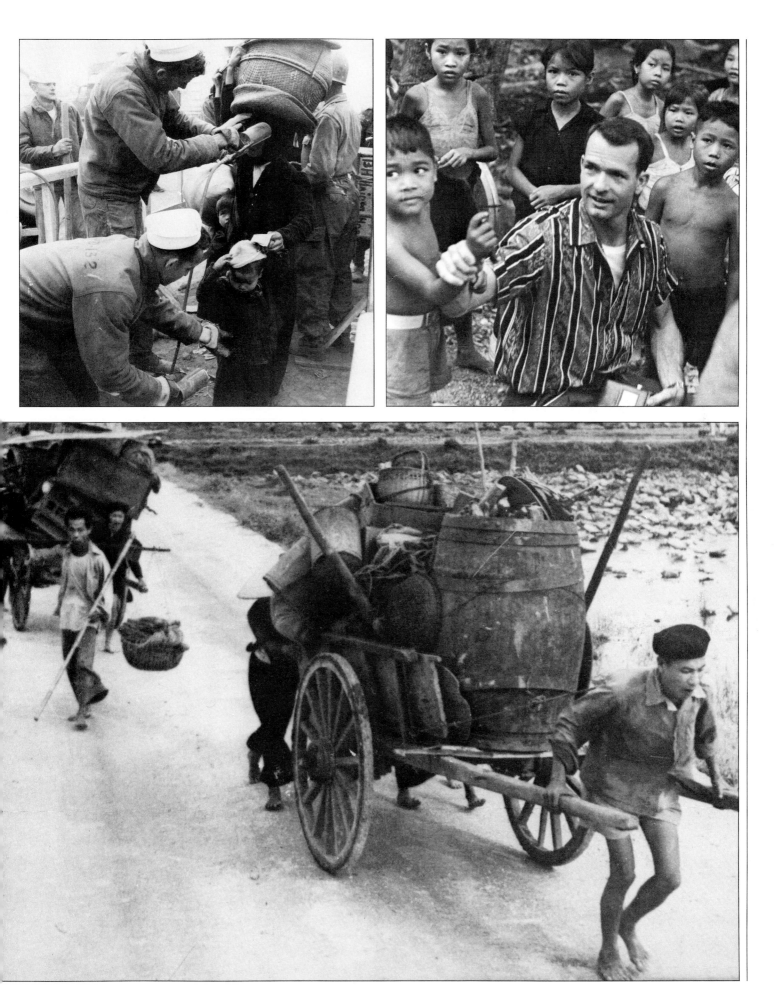

aware of the possibilities of life under Communist rule: lack of religious freedom and reprisals for collaborating with the French. Gruesome tales circulated among Catholics about Vietminh persecutions during the war. Father Denis Paquette, a French priest expelled from North Vietnam, recounted ugly incidents of Vietminh retaliation against church leaders:

Some [priests] were hanged by their thumbs or feet and flogged with a thorned twig. More than one hundred thorns were taken from the body of one priest after he was whipped this way. Some were put in a stable with pigs ... or chained for weeks or months.

The high proportion of Catholics among the refugees increased the American public's already substantial interest in the refugees' welfare. No American more poignantly described the refugees than Dr. Tom Dooley, a young U.S. naval officer. Dooley's experiences in Vietnam administering aid to the refugees, told in his book *Deliver Us From Evil*, transformed him in the eyes of many Americans into a champion of religious freedom and democracy. Dooley, an ardent Christian and vigorous anti-Communist, wrote impassioned accounts of the arrival in Haiphong of weary Catholic refugees from Phat Diem:

They hoisted, on a broken spar, their own drenched flag; a flag they had hidden for years.... Their symbol, their emblem, their heraldry ... a yellow and gold flag displaying the Pope's tiara and the keys of St. Peter.

Dooley, one of the ten most admired Americans in a 1960 Gallup poll, also depicted the tide of refugees as a spontaneous break for freedom:

It is impossible not to respect their driving compulsion for freedom, impossible not to admire the story of such a valiant people.... [The] difference between them and us is that we have our freedom and our hearts command us to keep it. The Vietnamese does not possess it and his heart's command is to struggle against all odds to achieve it.

Others, like Bernard Fall, a French writer, maintained that the exodus was not so spontaneous after all. He accused the U.S. of promoting the mass flight through "an extremely intensive, well-conducted, and, in terms of its objective, very successful psychological warfare operation." For example, American propaganda appealed to the Catholics with such

themes as "Christ has gone to the South" and the "Virgin Mary has departed from the North."

The U.S. rationale for encouraging the refugees was twofold: to offset the North's population edge in the projected reunification elections and to provide Ngo Dinh Diem's shaky Catholic regime in the South with anti-Communist Catholic support. Diem himself went to Hanoi in the summer of 1954 to whip up Catholic sentiment for resettling in the South. U.S. Information Agency (USIA) propaganda was not subtle. Psywar teams distributed posters showing Communists closing a cathedral and forcing the congregation to pray under a picture of Ho Chi Minh. The caption read: "Make Your Choice."

Haiphong: escape route to freedom

When refugees surged into Haiphong, they encountered the chaos of an overcrowded and hostile city. By August 10, 1954, an estimated two hundred thousand refugees were encamped at Hanoi and Haiphong awaiting evacuation. Most had sold all their possessions and were making the best of life in the streets. Refugees were often subjected to catcalls and even physical abuse by Vietminh cadres. However, they patiently waited their turn to board an evacuation ship. The memories of war and terror they were putting behind them gave them courage to bear any affront. Ngo Yan Hoi was typical in expressing no regret about leaving: "Some of my family were killed by the French bombings and by the Vietminh. And then we were forbidden to go to church."

Day after day, until the free movement period ended in May 1955, French and U.S. ships made trips, nearly five hundred in all, carrying refugees south to Saigon. Often, smaller shuttle boats landed on beaches to pick up refugees for transfer to larger vessels standing by off the coast. Howard R. Simpson, a press officer with the USIA, witnessed one such operation on a beach near Haiphong. Tired refugees piled out of trucks, eagerly watching for the French landing craft moving toward the beach. A contingent of U.S. Marines moved among the refugees to assist in loading. The marines searched the refugees' few belongings, making sure no weapons or explosives would be smuggled on board. Finally, the long-awaited moment came: The boat was ready for boarding. A stream of refugees eased up the metal ramp onto the cramped, steaming deck of the vessel.

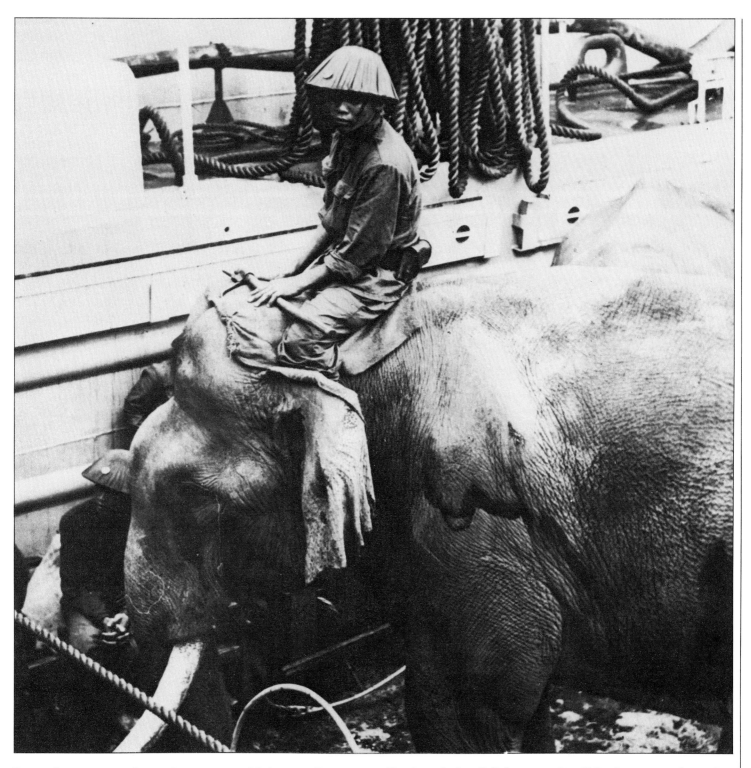

On board the Polish steamship Kilinski, a member of a Vietminh unit of elephant-mounted soldiers on his way to North Vietnam. The Vietminh used elephants to bear supplies and weapons, especially in the rugged jungle terrain in Laos.

In a day or so, the refugees would be in Saigon. There, their dramatic story, resettlement in a new land, would continue. Simpson, as he watched this small episode of the greatest exodus Southeast Asia had ever seen, breathed a sigh of relief:

The LSM [landing craft] filled with refugees. Its tongue-like ramp withdrew into its bow as the bow doors swung to. The whole beach seemed to vibrate under the strain of the LSM's engine as the stern swung out and the bow grated free of the beach. One hundred and sev-

enty-eight more refugees were leaving the Communist zone. As the loaded LSM headed downstream, an empty one headed in for shore and another load. . . . The Communists were one day closer.

The Revolution Continues

The dramatic story of North Vietnam's emer-
gence from the wreckage of the First Indochina
War into one of the most powerful states in
Southeast Asia contains elements that would appeal to Americans, much as they might abhor the
methods employed. Within five years after Geneva, Ho Chi Minh's war-ravaged zone, with 55
percent of Vietnam's population but only 30 percent of its agricultural land, achieved a rate of economic recovery and industrial growth that took
other nations in similar circumstances decades to
reach. The North Vietnamese, starting with almost
nothing, exhibited initiative, drive, and ingenuity,
qualities Americans generally admire.

Here, in some ways, was a success story. But
few Americans ever read or heard about it. In the
cold war 1950s, Americans were too preoccupied
with crises in other less remote areas of the
world: Cuba, Berlin, the Suez Canal, and Algeria.
For a time in 1954, the shocking events of the

refugee crisis had filled the front pages of newspapers across the nation. Yet this was not 1975. The refugees were not bound for the United States but for South Vietnam.

As the flow of refugees slowed to a trickle in the spring of 1955, scant attention was paid to the continuing problems and "revolutionary" transformation of North Vietnam. The architects of that revolution—Ho Chi Minh, Pham Van Dong, Le Duan, and Vo Nguyen Giap—remained equally unfamiliar to the world beyond the seventeenth parallel. But in little more than ten years the achievements and goals of the leaders of that once seemingly far-off Asian land would impress themselves upon Americans in a most compelling way: in the form of the longest, most expensive, and most destructive conflict in American history.

A call for solidarity

As Ho Chi Minh contemplated the problems facing the North, he never wavered in his long-held conviction that a revolution, guided by Communist principles of political, social, and economic reorganization, was the key to building a vigorous, independent Vietnam. It never occurred to him to try to turn back the clock to Vietnam's "romantic" imperial past, when emperors from the sacred precincts of a "forbidden city" governed a country of peasant-farmers and tradition-bound villages. For better or worse, French colonialism forced upon the Vietnamese an irrevocable break with their traditional past.

Ho chose the festive occasion of the New Year's Day celebrations on January 1, 1955, to proclaim the beginning of North Vietnam's war reconstruction and to outline the revolutionary tasks of the party and the people. He delivered his address on a sixty-foot-high parade reviewing stand in front of a gigantic portrait of "Uncle Ho." Flanked by other party leaders, Ho proudly watched as military units and civilian organizations filed by waving flags and carrying bigger-than-life pictures of Marx, Lenin, Stalin, Mao, and other Communist heroes. Encouraged by the enthusiasm of the crowds, Ho announced a two-point program for rebuilding the North and realizing the objectives of the revolution.

We shall endeavor to restore our economy, agriculture, commerce, industry, and transport, gradually to raise our people's living standards. We shall continue our work of mobilizing the masses for land rent reduction and land reform in order to put the slogan 'land to the tillers' into practice.

Ho's optimistic assessment of the country's prospects found a receptive audience. With the characteristic determination that had carried them through the war against the French, the North Vietnamese were ready to shoulder the burden of economic recovery and the revitalization of a devastated countryside. But difficult times lay ahead. Repairing what the war had destroyed would require great effort and sacrifice. A still heavier price was being asked of the people. According to Ho's Communist blueprint, it would be necessary to postpone political freedom for the masses in favor of the party's chief concern: an economically self-sufficient Socialist state.

Heroes of the revolution

Politically, the Vietminh established the type of government their supporters had expected and the refugees had feared: an authoritarian, Communist regime. After the August Revolution of 1945, Ho had instituted numerous features of representative government, such as a National Assembly of popularly elected officials, in part to counter French charges that the Vietminh represented a Communist-inspired insurrection and not a broad-based nationalist movement.

Now that the French were evicted, Ho established an authoritarian government that shared no power with non-Communists, tolerated no opposition parties, and made no pretense about securing a popular democratic mandate for its policies. Truong Chinh, secretary of the North Vietnamese Communist party, went so far as to identify communism with patriotism, denying the claims of non-Communist opposition parties to a legitimate share of political power:

Patriotism cannot be separated from internationalism. The Communist doctrine is indeed the synonym of patriotism . . . sincere patriots are militant Communists.

In the Democratic Republic of North Vietnam, the National Assembly continued to exist, but its members soon recognized that their function was pro forma. In vain they complained that the "executive branch," Ho and high-level party leaders, displayed a "lack of respect" by not implementing laws passed by the assembly.

Preceding page. At an agricultural cooperative in Ha Tay, North Vietnam's President Ho Chi Minh helps peasants prepare farm land for irrigation.

Genuine political power was wielded only by members of the Communist party. Members of the party, called cadres, represented in number a fraction of the population, but their control of government was absolute. At every decision-making level, in every administrative area, political, economic, or social, the cadres held sway. The party hierarchy consisted of cadres organized in "cells." Every factory, village, school, city, borough, or army company had its own party cell. In addition to the regular party machinery, cadres set up new organizations to assume direction of the general populace. In urban areas, cadres formed Street and Inhabitant Protection Committees to announce and popularize government decisions dealing with city affairs. Hanoi alone had forty-six hundred block chiefs and deputy chiefs, plus three thousand committee members, all responsible to the cadres for their performance.

Under the supervision of the cadres, North Vietnamese society gradually assumed a collective aspect in almost every sphere of activity. Yet, collectivization was not exactly foreign to the people. Communal obligations and social and religious groupings had always been an important characteristic of village life. In effect, the cadres were developing to an extreme degree, even in urban areas, the traditionally collective tendencies of village peasants.

Outside the cities, the cadres fanned out among thousands of villages to manage reconstruction and to bring the revolution to the peasants. They served in many ways like those mandarins once honored as "heroes of the state," who had entered the countryside with the sometimes frustrating task of adapting the ways of Confucianism, Vietnam's ruling ideology, to the circumstances of everyday life. Confucius once wrote, "He who is magnanimous wins the multitude, he who is of good faith is trusted by the people, he who is diligent attains his objective, and he who is kind can get service from the people." But French colonial rule ended the supremacy of the mandarins, casting the peasants adrift without leadership, direction, or spokesmen for their interests.

The cadres' mission was indeed revolutionary. Peasants, victims of oppression and corrupt colonial officials, were suspicious of outsiders. Yet by their moral behavior and dedication to the resistance, the cadres gradually acquired the peasants' confidence. During the Indochina War, French reports noted the remarkable honesty and loyalty of the cadres in their dealings with peasants. French soldiers told of capturing one cadre, a resistance tax collector, in a "state of extreme malnutrition." To the amazement of his captors, his pockets were stuffed with tax receipts, money he refused to spend despite his dire condition. Such stories are reminiscent of those peasants once passed on about the virtue of the mandarins.

To establish rapport with the peasants, the cadres diligently practiced the "three withs": to eat with the peasants, live with the peasants, and work with the peasants. According to Ho Chi Minh, "only by so

On January 1, 1955, a parade of over one hundred thousand people wound slowly through Hanoi to celebrate the return to Hanoi of President Ho Chi Minh and other leaders of the Democratic Republic of Vietnam. Here, as part of the parade, Vietminh veterans of the Indochina War pass Ho's reviewing stand at Ba Dinh Square.

doing can we get acquainted with their living conditions and understand their difficulties ... their aspirations." The cadres, like the mandarins, were not above using coercion to obtain peasant cooperation, but they succeeded primarily by their self-discipline and devotion to values the peasants esteemed: family, community, and hard work. In return, many peasants respected the cadres, so unlike their former colonial masters, as "heroes of the revolution."

The toil of the masses

In 1955 Ho's cadres organized battalions of peasant workers to reconstruct the French-built railway line linking Hanoi with the Chinese border at Lang Son. The French had spent millions of francs to develop an efficient railroad, canal, and roadway network, but the war had battered it to ruin. Most of the steel from the rails and trains had been stripped to supply the Vietminh war industry. A third of the permanent way had been incorporated into the surrounding rice fields or had been cut by deep trenches.

With the cadres relentlessly driving them, eighty thousand workers rebuilt in six months a railroad that had taken the French ten years to construct. The hectic pace of the project demanded that the workers labor around the clock to repair roadbeds, dams, and hundreds of demolished bridges. The toll in deaths and injuries was high. Exhaustion and malnutrition were common among the workers, and medical care was insufficient. Still, the railroad proved a valuable investment. It linked North Vietnam not only with the Chinese rail system but also with overland routes to the Soviet Union and Eastern Europe. Over these rails in the next two decades, billions of dollars worth of Communist bloc military hardware and industrial equipment would reach North Vietnam, fueling its recovery and later its war against the South.

Vietminh leaders learned an important lesson from the massive Lang Son railroad project. Although peasant workers were readily available, only limited accomplishments were possible using masses of unskilled labor. Technicians, equipment, and railroad stock were in critically short supply, and North Vietnam's crippled economy could not fill the void left by the exodus of French technicians, industrialists, and trained managers. Since South Vietnam refused all economic and trade connections with the North, Ho's regime turned to Communist China and the Soviet Union for help.

Close ties with China seemed a logical move. China had recently expelled colonial influence and had experienced a Communist revolution of its own. After Mao's victory over Chiang Kai-shek in 1949, his regime offered valuable assistance to Vietminh insurgents in the North, a turning point in their war against the French. China, with its large peasant population and war-torn countryside, also provided a model for North Vietnam in dealing with problems of modernization and Socialist development.

But North Vietnam's ties to China were much older than those forged by communism. For two thousand years, Vietnam had belonged to China's cultural and political sphere, sharing its Confucian ideology, technology, and institutions. China was Asia's overlord, and Vietnam, like other small countries along China's borders, paid the powerful Middle Kingdom its due in tribute and respect. In turn, Vietnam could look to China for help in countering foreign aggression or recovering from natural disasters.

China responded generously to North Vietnam's requests for economic assistance. In June 1955, Ho arrived in Peking for economic talks and was personally greeted by Mao Tse-tung at the airport—an honor not even extended to Nikita Khrushchev. Accompanied by his ministers of finance, industry, agriculture, education, and health, Ho signed a treaty of friendship by which China pledged $200 million in aid to North Vietnam, including equipment for repairing and constructing roads, railroads, waterworks, and postal services. Soon Chinese technicians were busy supervising all sorts of nonmilitary reconstruction programs throughout the North.

Between 1955 and 1960, Chinese aid to Vietnam would total $225 million, more than that from any other country. China, in addition to fostering "good will" with a fellow Communist regime, had its own motives for nurturing Ho's government. Mao hoped that a Chinese-supported regime in North Vietnam could serve as a buffer to protect China's southern borders and to prevent domination of Southeast Asia by either the Soviet Union or the United States. As for Ho, he accepted Chinese aid graciously but warily. Like Vietnam's independent-minded emperors who unflaggingly resisted Chinese aggressive designs, Ho was not about to compromise Vietnam's freedom of action.

Ho Chi Minh (right) and Mao Tse-tung exchange a friendly toast at a Peking reception in Ho's honor during the summer of 1955, when Ho negotiated a major aid agreement with China.

Ho looks to the Soviet Union

Ho did not confine his pleas for aid to China. He also sought substantial grants of industrial equipment, machinery, and technical advice from his "Socialist brothers" in the Soviet Union. Ho's relations with the people in power in the Soviet Union were personal, cordial, and long lasting. By training and inclination, he had warm feelings for the Soviet Union, the leader of the Socialist camp and the land of Lenin, his idol. During his youthful sojourn in Moscow, Ho had witnessed the beginning of the Soviet Union's metamorphosis from an underdeveloped country of peasants into one of the world's industrial powers. For Ho there was never any question that there was much to learn and gain from close relations with Moscow.

Ho's choice of the Soviet Union as a model for industrial development had far-reaching con-

Workers put the finishing touches on the Long Bien Bridge on the outskirts of Hanoi. Despite long hours, food shortages, disease, and oppressive heat, work teams like these rebuilt North Vietnam's war-damaged bridges and roads in remarkably brief time.

sequences for North Vietnam. He was firmly convinced that the country's future depended not on agriculture but on technological advancement and a solid industrial base. As for the role of industry in the Socialist revolution, Ho followed the teachings of Lenin, who wrote: "The only possible foundation of socialism is large-scale machine industry. Whoever forgets this is no Communist." North Vietnam was already experiencing a severe famine and desperately needed industrial exports to purchase rice and other foods from abroad to compensate for its severely limited agricultural output. Ho was also keenly aware that industrialization on the grand scale he was planning required a radical, revolutionary shift in the North's traditionally agricultural economy. There were relatively few artisans and industries in precolonial Vietnam. Farming Vietnam's fertile rice lands was the primary occupation of peasants, and rice was the nation's chief resource.

After their success in China, Ho and his economic ministers journeyed to Moscow where they were feted by Soviet dignitaries. Curious Muscovite shoppers lined the streets to catch a glimpse of the new Communist celebrity. He rode in a slow-moving open car adorned with flowers, followed by a fleet of black limousines containing Nikita Khrushchev and other party leaders. The Russians, charmed by Ho and his entourage, pledged $100 million in economic aid. They also arranged credit for an emergency purchase of 50,000 tons of Burmese rice to relieve the famine threatening North Vietnam in 1955. This helped to offset the cutoff of 250,000 tons of rice sales to the North by the Diem regime, which hoped that food shortages would lead to political troubles for Ho.

The Soviets shipped a wide array of economic and industrial aid to North Vietnam: mining equipment to tap the North's abundant coal and mineral deposits, machine tools, factory facilities, fish canning and freezing plants. Like the Chinese, the Soviets sent along technicians, engineers, teachers, and managers to instruct the North Vietnamese in operating the machinery and organizing industrial projects.

The Soviet Union had an ulterior motive for its aid to North Vietnam. One Soviet technician was quoted as telling a North Vietnamese official, "Up to now you are the only tropical country of the Socialist camp." For Soviet strategists, North Vietnam could serve as a unique laboratory for the development of Soviet bloc equipment and techniques to be used in other tropical areas. The DRV also represented a Communist wedge into the Southeast Asian mainland.

Although Ho Chi Minh was substantially indebted to his Socialist benefactors, the Soviet Union and China, he never became a puppet of any foreign power, as his critics often suggested. U.S. Secretary of State Dean Acheson once called Ho a "mortal enemy of native independence in Indochina." Yet Ho, like Tito in Yugoslavia, proved that a synthesis of communism and nationalism could provide a workable basis for an independent regime. History has shown that neither Ho nor his government ever slipped into the "hip pocket" of either the Soviet Union or China. Rather, when circumstances permitted, Ho deftly picked their pockets to satisfy the internal needs and goals of North Vietnam. While welcoming foreign aid, Ho and the party sought to develop an economy that could be maintained solely, if necessary, by the North Vietnamese themselves.

The North's determination to avoid a new colonialism, particularly by the ever-threatening Chinese, is best illustrated by the steadily diminishing share of foreign aid in its budget. From 1955 to 1961, the percentage of foreign aid in the total budget dropped from 65.3 percent to 19.9 percent. North Vietnam's increasing independence from foreign economic influence also presented Ho with a made-to-order propaganda weapon against South Vietnam, where the United States was financing a large part of the Diem regime's budget. In the propaganda war between North and South, many Vietnamese found it difficult to refute the charge that South Vietnam was degenerating into complete dependence on U.S. economic and political support.

Mountain tribesmen and socialism

Perhaps the brightest innovation of the DRV's reconstruction and social policies was its enlightened treatment of the mountain tribes in the highlands of northern and central Vietnam. These tribes are for the most part culturally and racially distinct from the Vietnamese. For centuries the Vietnamese simply ignored the tribal peoples of the high country, whom they derogatorily called "moi," or savages. The tribes, left to their own devices, lived in isolation and

Haiphong, North Vietnam's principal port. After the French withdrawal in 1954, Haiphong's silt-laden harbor was cleared with Chinese and Soviet aid, and its docks and shipbuilding yards were modernized.

practiced rudimentary subsistence farming. They were led by fiercely independent chiefs who exercised feudal powers in their highland domains.

The outbreak of hostilities between the French and the Vietminh in 1946 abruptly ended the mountain tribes' isolation. General Giap concluded that "to seize and control the highlands is to solve the whole problem of southern Vietnam." Soon French and Vietminh agents were wooing the mountain tribes whose valor and knowledge of the rugged terrain made them invaluable allies in the guerrilla fighting. Tribal chiefs, often courted by both sides with gifts, weapons, and supplies, were notorious for switching allegiance to the highest bidder. But the Vietminh won significant tribal loyalty by promising to give the stubbornly·independent montagnards regional autonomy and economic assistance after the war.

In 1955 Ho Chi Minh moved to keep that promise by establishing the first of three tribal autonomous zones. Additional legislation eventually guaranteed the right of the tribes to preserve their own customs, languages, and writing systems. Politically, the montagnards acquired the right to representation in the National Assembly and an opportunity to replace their feudal chiefs, whose harsh tactics they resented, with locally elected tribal councils. A member of one tribe gave an example of the excessive powers that many a chief wielded over the people:

We all had to work his land for him. If he wanted anything at all, from building a hencoop to building a house, from plowing his paddy field to threshing the harvest, we had to do it for him. If he sees a nice, strong buffalo he just tells you to drive it over to his house. If he finds a nice pot in your house, just send it over he says, and you send it over, because there's nothing else to do.

Ho also made good on the promise of economic and technical aid to the relatively impoverished tribes. He invited selected tribesmen to Hanoi where they were trained as teachers, medical technicians, and administrators. North Vietnamese military advisers also incorporated specially trained montagnards into regular units of the army.

The DRV's minority policies were genuinely progressive and even revolutionary, considering traditional Vietnamese racial animosity toward the mountain people. The government's intentions, however, were not entirely humanitarian. Their tribal allies during the war against the French had shown their usefulness in enabling the Vietminh to operate freely in the northern highlands, which served as a direct

gateway to the southern highlands and the Mekong Delta. In the event of war or insurrection in South Vietnam, Vietminh strategists were counting on the tribes to support guerrilla bases, defend supply lines, and provide unimpeded passage to troops on their way south. The cadres also recruited agents from northern tribes to propagandize and foment discontent among their tribal cousins in South Vietnam. As early as 1957, American social scientists warned the Diem government of Communist activity in the southern highlands, but little was done. As a result, when war erupted in 1960 well-armed anti-Diem montagnard units were already operating on South Vietnamese territory.

Road building: Construction in 1959 of the Ho Chi Minh Trail, which was used to move troops and supplies from the North to the South, required clearing and cutting through the extensive forests of the Truong Son Mountains.

Land reform: "sky splitting and earthshaking"

Ho Chi Minh intended the keystone of socialism in the North to be his campaign for land reform. With the departure of the French, land reform posed problems for both the North and South. The roots of these problems went far back in Vietnamese history. For the emperors, land reform had been a perennial issue.

Landlords able to buy land from peasants impoverished by poor crops or other catastrophes continually built up large estates. This forced many peasants, dispossessed of their only means of livelihood, to labor as sharecroppers or tenants on land they had once owned. The greatest emperors tried to solve the problem by confiscating all arable land and redistributing it among the entire population. But even such drastic measures proved temporary solutions at best. Inevitably, successful farmers would again exploit their neighbors' misfortunes to expand their estates and to form a new landlord class.

Actually, in North Vietnam in 1954 land reform in the traditional sense did not appear necessary. Unlike South Vietnam, where 2.5 percent of the landlords owned half the cultivated land and many peasants were landless, in the North 98 percent of the farmers owned their farms. In addition, the flight of nearly a million refugees to the South had freed tens of thousands of acres of already developed land for distribution to the landless peasants. But Ho had something else in mind, a socialist twist to traditional land reform. His revolutionary objective was not a peasant class of private landowners but the collectivization of agricultural lands under state ownership. The party knew that the road toward socialized agriculture would be long and that intermediate stages would have to precede it. First on the agenda was the abolition of landlordism. Next, landless and poor peasants were to own the land distributed to them. But the party foresaw that when all the land was divided among the peasant population, most families would not own enough to feed themselves. The party also knew that peasants, hard-pressed and with no other option, would eventually turn to collectivization as the only viable alternative.

Communist party Secretary Truong Chinh directed the land reform campaign. He was assisted not by regular administrative organs but by special land reform committees and battalions of cadres indoctrinated for the purpose. In dispatching the cadres to the countryside, Ho Chi Minh compared their role to that of the soldiers of the resistance:

In the coming mass mobilization drives for land reform, those among you who perform outstanding deeds will be awarded medals, just like soldiers fighting the enemy.

Truong Chinh was a strong advocate of Maoist revolutionary tactics. Mao's technique for land reform was to initiate a cadre-directed, peasant campaign of terror to eradicate landlords through "people's committee" trials, executions, and imprisonment. Since Mao had to contend with entrenched and powerful landlords who, like warlords, commanded their own armies and generally oppressed the peasantry, such extreme methods seem somewhat justifiable. But their application to North Vietnam was totally inappropriate since the number of true landlords was small. Their principal effect was tragic overkill: unrestrained terror, fear, and injustice.

"To right a wrong, one should exceed the limit of the right"
—Mao Tse-tung

To identify landlords, the "enemies of the people," the cadres, many inexperienced in land reform administration, divided the rural population into five categories: landlords, rich peasants, middle peasants, poor peasants, and landless laborers. The cadres collected evidence of landlord crimes by entering villages disguised as poor peasants. According to Hoang Van Chi, a former member of the Vietminh resistance and a firsthand observer of the land reform process, the cadres were meticulously thorough in gathering incriminating details about landlords for presentation to the people's court:

The cadres usually stayed from two to three months, and the peasants were very pleased to have them since they worked without accepting payment. They demanded to know every detail in the lives of their hosts, showing particular interest and sympathy when they heard of any past misfortunes which the peasants had suffered. Before very long their hosts took them completely into their confidence and opened their hearts to them. ... The next step was to make these peasants understand that there was only one way of improving their lives; namely to side with the party and attack the despicable exploiters who were responsible for all the misery in the village.

Once the cadres had enough damning evidence against villagers suspected of landlordism, peasants were mobilized to denounce the accused in a people's court. Chinese advisers, experts in the ways of Mao, assisted the cadres in conducting mass trials in which defendants were denied legal counsel or the right to appeal their sentences. Most defendants faced confiscation of their property or imprisonment, but some paid the penalty of death. An angry mob of peasants would hurl a multitude of charges at them, such as demanding unfair rents, swindling their neighbors, or extorting loan-shark rates on loans and mortgages. If a defendant confessed, he or she might receive clemency, but admission, whether true or not, was no guarantee of a lesser sentence. Sometimes the accusations, published in the party newspaper, approached the improbable, if not the ridiculous:

At Nghia Khe village, in the district of Bac Ninh, landlords urged small children to steal documents and to throw stones at peasant meetings. In Lieu Son, they persuaded a small child to set fire to a peasant's house. More cruelly they gave a poisoned cake to some children in Lieu Ha, almost killing them. In Van Truong, they urged young Suu, aged thirteen, to persuade two other small girls to join her in committing suicide by jumping together into a pond.

It was not unheard of for overzealous cadres, if they could not meet their quota of accused landlords, to try rich or even middle peasants in their place. The paranoia and uncertainty created by these witch hunts intensified the villagers' terror. Irrational fears prompted neighbors to denounce each other or induced family members to testify against one another. Such disloyalty, however, violated the traditional bonds of close-knit peasant families, and many resisted the temptation to save themselves at the expense of a relative.

A more brutal tactic was the practice of isolating villagers believed connected with landlords or implicated in a conspiracy of landlordism. The cadres subjected them to house arrest. Their neighbors treated them as outlaws and lepers, undeserving of sympathy. Families locked in their houses received no allocations of food so that their only alternative to confessing was slow death from starvation. Le Van Giao, a refugee, vividly recalled the misery of such families:

There was nothing worse than the starvation of the children in a family whose parents were under the control of a land reform team. They isolated the house, and the people who lived there would starve. The children were all innocent. Should the father be guilty, he could be executed. The children were all innocent. There was nothing worse than that. They wanted to see the whole family dead.

If, as the Vietnamese proverb says, "eating is the people's heaven," isolation victims experienced a living hell.

"Rectification of errors"

The ferocity of the land reform, with the number of prisoners swelling to perhaps one hundred thousand, continued unabated until the late summer of 1956 when orders from party leaders called a halt to the waves of

Tribespeople (in black headgear) and Vietnamese students attend a course in medicine at a school in the Thai-Meo autonomous region, one of several means by which the Communists wooed the area's numerous ethnic minorities.

trials, imprisonments, and executions. On August 17, 1956, in a letter to his "compatriots in the country," Ho Chi Minh himself admitted errors in implementing the land reform and promised "corrections":

Land reform is a class struggle against the feudalists [landlords], an earth-shaking, fierce, and hard revolution ... a number of our cadres have not thoroughly grasped the land reform policy or correctly followed the mass line. ... All this has caused us to commit errors and meet with shortcomings carrying out land reform. ... The correction of errors should be resolute and planned.

In his later report on land reform to party leaders, General Vo Nguyen Giap was critical of the reckless behavior of many party cadres:

We attacked the landowning families indiscriminately, according no consideration to those who served the Revolution and to those families with sons in the army. We showed no indulgence towards landlords who participated in the resistance, treating their children in the same way as we treated the children of other landlords. We made too many deviations and executed too many honest people. We attacked on too large a front and, seeing enemies everywhere, resorted to terror, which became far too widespread.

Reeducated cadres soon went back into the countryside to undo the damage. In addition, the government announced that twelve thousand people, sentenced by people's courts, would be released from prisons and labor camps. Radio Hanoi also explained that those unjustly condemned would be given back their jobs, possessions, and civil rights. The party, however, acknowledged that it could not erase the agony and deaths of the ten to fifteen thousand men, women, and children isolated or executed. As Ho remarked, "One cannot wake the dead." The government did offer decent graves and public funerals for unfortunate victims of cadre "errors."

In Nghe An Province, however, the government's corrective actions came too slowly and too late. Farmers and small landowners, reeling from the shock of land reform, were not satisfied with the party's excuses. Farmers in the predominantly Catholic Quynh Luu district decided to march on party headquarters to air their grievances and demand immediate redress. Regional troops and party cadres arrived to head them off and "to explain to the compatriots the government's policy." The farmers, furious at the delay, overwhelmed and disarmed the troops on the evening of November 5. They then turned the tables on the cadres, forcing them to admit publicly their crimes and sign written confessions.

Rebellion spreads

Throughout the following week the rebellion spread across the district. By November 14, the government decided that the situation was out of hand. Detachments of battle-hardened troops sealed off the district and moved to crush the uprising with force. Whether the soldiers felt any hesitation at suppressing mostly unarmed peasants is not known, but they acted with ruthless efficiency. Western sources claim that about one thousand peasants were killed or wounded and that several thousand were arrested or deported. A

refugee from the district of Quynh Luu recalls the fighting:

The situation of the night of November 14 was still confused; one still heard gunshots throughout the region. Being old and unable to take part in the fighting, I must bring my children here to take refuge. The other six members of my family remain over there to continue fighting. Before my departure, the revolutionary combatants told me that in case of failure they will withdraw toward the mountainous region, to carry on their guerrilla operations against the Communist Vietminh.

The upheavals of land reform and the violent quelling of the Nghe An revolt took a heavy toll in lives. But despite the apparent sincerity of the rectification of errors campaign, the party was satisfied with the results of its callous scheme to clear the way of peasant opposition to collectivization of agriculture. Almost all landlords, as well as thousands of so-called rich and medium-income peasants, had been ruined and their lands confiscated for distribution. As the party knew from the beginning, however, there was still not enough land, even after redistribution, for peasants to farm at any more than a subsistence

A veteran of the war against the French, with his wife and child, attends a land reform meeting at his home village. His sign identifies him as "Nguyen Van Dinh, landless peasant."

level. Because few westerners had access to North Vietnamese economic data on land distribution, it is difficult to obtain reliable statistics to document the results of the land reform program. And since the land reform program was a controversial political issue both in North Vietnam and among western observers, statistics vary according to the biases of different economic studies. The following statistics based on a Soviet study show that the poor farmer and laborer classes more than any others may have benefited substantially from the redistribution of the land seized from the landlords:

Social Class	Landholdings (in acres)	
	Before redistribution	After redistribution
Rich farmer	.5	.5
Medium farmer	.3	.4
Poor farmer	.2	.3
Laborer	.04	.35

But since the average peasant family needed 2.47 acres of rice land to earn a decent living, farmers of all classes were pushed toward a level at which they could produce barely enough to survive. Collectivization, therefore, became the only alternative to subsistence farming. Laborers and poor farmers, confronting outright hunger, were the first to be collectivized. The cadres banded them together into "work exchange teams," which at first carried out small agricultural projects in their villages. Soon work exchange teams formed small cooperative groups, which the government gradually consolidated into large-scale cooperative farming projects in the early 1960s.

By the end of 1959, 28,775 such cooperatives were in operation. Nearly 60 percent of all farming families had yielded to state ownership the plots of land passed on to them by their ancestors. This represented a significant departure from Vietnamese tradition. Although as much as 50 percent of village land was customarily owned by the village, peasants leased such land for as long as three years and farmed it for themselves. But the traditional dream of every peasant was to own a piece of land. This, like many other traditions in the "new" Vietnam, however, was quickly becoming a thing of the past.

Using rotor-tillers from China, these Vietnamese farmers on an agricultural cooperative prepare the soil for planting. A wide range of Chinese agricultural equipment helped North Vietnam recultivate thousands of acres of rich rice land abandoned during the war.

"We shall achieve unity....
No force in the world can stop us"
—Pham Van Dong, prime minister of North Vietnam

Ho Chi Minh did not allow the North's internal problems to interfere with his efforts to arrange the reunification elections scheduled for July 1956. In his New Year's speech of 1955, Ho expressed unqualified optimism that the elections would take place:

We shall work closely and broadly from North to South and support our southern compatriots in their struggle for freedom and democracy in conformity with the Geneva Agreement. ... All this work must be done to prepare the ground for free general elections for national reunification.

As the months rolled toward the date for elections, however, Ho realized that he had miscalculated in his appraisal of the political situation in Vietnam. In the South, Diem's regime, with the U.S. behind it, was establishing itself as a strong contender for the election. Ho—to his surprise—had underestimated Diem, who had struggled successfully with the chaotic state of affairs in the South after Geneva. Ho had hoped that Diem's government would collapse, leaving the North to pick up the pieces and achieve unity by default. Yet Diem was not only consolidating his government but was also feeling secure enough to express disagreement over the election provisions of the Geneva Agreement, which he had never signed. Here was a new and ominous development that Ho, for all his experience, had not anticipated.

Because of Diem's increasingly anti-election position, Ho decided to play what he believed to be his trump card: the French. As part of its cease-fire agreement with the Vietminh, France had promised to arrange and supervise reunification elections. It is ironic that Ho, who had seen many French promises go unfulfilled in the past, should have trusted their willingness or ability to come through on elections. Yet Ho had seemed firmly persuaded that France would not renege on its responsibilities. At the close of the Geneva Conference, he issued a statement demanding that "the French government should correctly implement the agreements they have signed with us." Later, Premier Pham Van Dong reminded the French that so far as Hanoi was concerned, "It was with you, the French, that we signed the Geneva Agreements and it is up to you to see that they are respected."

Ho was once again mistaken. Under pressure from the U.S. and the intensely anti-French Diem, France was well on its way out of Vietnam by the end of 1955, militarily and politically. By the time the elections were to have taken place, France was no longer in a position to exercise more than token influence in Vietnamese affairs, much less to guarantee elections.

With France out of the election picture, Ho again altered his tactics. Hanoi sent numerous telegrams to South Vietnam repeating the message: "We demand the southern authorities to correctly implement this agreement." Hanoi received no response from Diem. Diem's attitude had hardened: "Nothing constructive ... can be done as long as the Communist regime in the North does not permit each Vietnamese citizen to enjoy the democratic liberties and the fundamental rights of man." Ho's frustrations with Diem exploded in the form of virulent tirades against the United States, which backed Diem's intractable stance. On July 6, 1956, Ho publicly accused the U.S. of violating the Geneva accords and subverting the elections:

The U.S. imperialists and the pro-American authorities in South Vietnam have been plotting to partition our country permanently and prevent the holding of free general elections as provided for by the Geneva Agreements.

Ho's attacks inflamed anti-American sentiment among the North Vietnamese. Eventually, demonstrating public rancor against the U.S. became an annual event in North Vietnam, designated "Hate America Week."

Despite the belligerent tone of Ho's outbursts against the U.S. and Diem, there was little he could do when the "crisis" date for elections arrived. American officials in Washington and Saigon feared the Communists would use Diem's refusal to hold the elections promised by the Geneva accords as a pretext for an attack on the South. But the election deadline of July passed without incident. Last-ditch North Vietnamese diplomatic maneuvers to persuade the Soviet Union to reconvene Geneva and take up the matter of elections were of no avail.

Ho had made a gamble and lost. For a time North Vietnam turned increasingly inward, absorbed by the stresses of economic recovery and caught in the throes of land reform. But for the restless Vietminh cadres who had stayed behind in the South to agitate for elections, it appeared time to take matters into their own hands. While North Vietnam went about its business, the southern cadres' struggle for unity entered a different, more violent phase: armed propaganda and political subversion.

Le Duan: Ho's Southern Connection

Le Duan, first secretary of the Vietnam Worker's party central committee, surrounded by young cadres attending the "Congress of Heroes in Resisting U.S. Aggression for National Salvation" held at Hanoi in 1966.

The name is little known outside of Vietnam. But for the past fifty years, no one except Ho Chi Minh himself has done more to affect the fate of Vietnam than Le Duan. Duan, a native of the South whose overriding concern was to liberate his homeland, made his career in the North. A man of wide political influence, he never held an important post in Vietnamese government but only in the Communist (Lao Dong) party to which he devoted his life. The basic feature of his career, the almost anonymous exercise of power, suggests the large extent to which a vanguard Communist party based in the North controlled the course of the Vietnamese Revolution.

When the Vietminh seized power in August of 1945, they freed Duan from the French prison on Poulo Condore Island where he had been incarcerated for ten of the previous fifteen years. Born in Quang Tri Province in 1908, Duan had joined the outlawed Indochinese Communist party in the early 1930s. He later took command of a short-lived "Committee of the South," which ruled Saigon briefly before the French returned after World War II and drove the Communists underground.

After rebellion against the French broke out in 1946, Duan became the Communist party's chief political commissar in the South. He adhered strictly to the Vietminh belief that a resistance led by any entity other than the party was destined to fail. When the southern Vietminh military commander, Nguyen Binh, was deemed guilty in 1950 of deviating from the party line (by attempting a take-over of Saigon), Duan personally served on him recall orders to the North. Then, as Binh traveled a lonely trail in Cambodia, Duan's agents did away with him. Having rid the southern wing of the Vietminh of other "undesirable" elements, Duan restored party control of the resistance in the South.

When Vietminh troops regrouped to the North in 1954, Duan stayed in the South. Convinced that the elections promised by the Geneva accords would never take place, he felt that the Vietminh should have finished off the "demoralized" French instead of negotiating.

After becoming secretary of the Lao Dong Central Committee for the Southern Region in 1956, Duan grew increasingly impatient with the "political struggle." He recommended to Hanoi in no uncertain terms that it apply "military pressure" to "succeed in gaining control of South Vietnam." Meanwhile, Duan issued a widely distributed and influential pamphlet, "The Path to Revolution in the South." It called on old Vietminh guerrillas and recruits to form a united front under the aegis of the Communist party and to conduct a systematic propaganda and terror campaign against Diem's local administrators and province chiefs.

Returning to the North in 1957, Duan took over many of the responsibilities of party secretary although he was not officially appointed to the post. Two years later, after a second clandestine trip to the South, Duan succeeded in convincing party leaders that the time was ripe for Hanoi to assume direction of the expanding insurgency against Diem's government. Infiltration units were soon headed south on the Ho Chi Minh Trail.

An extremist concerning South Vietnam, Duan was a moderate on the divisive issue of relations with Moscow and Peking. Like Ho, he realized the importance of steering a middle course between the pro-Chinese and pro-Soviet factions within the party, as well as between the North's allies in Moscow and Peking. This pragmatic approach made Duan especially valuable to Ho. In 1960 Ho installed his fifty-two-year-old lieutenant as party first secretary, the second most powerful post in the Communist party. By putting a younger man ahead of older officials, President Ho also assured himself that his second in command would not try to supplant him. When Ho died at the age of seventy-nine in September 1969, the torch passed to Le Duan. He was still party chairman in 1981.

Vietnam in the Movies

In this scene from the film The Quiet American, *pipe bombs set off by Vietnam's Cao Dai sect agitators rock the crowded plaza outside Saigon's Continental Hotel during the stormy first year of the Diem regime. Graham Greene's novel characterized Alden Pyle, the "quiet American," as a meddlesome American adviser, dangerously mixed up in Vietnamese politics and Cao Dai intrigue, and erroneously determined "to do good, to people, to countries, to the whole world." But the film transformed Pyle into a genuine American hero, an impassioned foe of communism in Vietnam.*

Much of the relatively little Americans heard about Vietnam during the 1950s and early 1960s was not through newspapers or television but at the movies. With the release of the films *The Quiet American* in 1958 and *The Ugly American* four years later, for the first time the subject of Vietnam and America's increasing involvement in Southeast Asia reached a mass audience in theaters across the country.

Both films were adaptations of controversial novels, published in the mid-1950s, about America's role in Vietnam: *The Quiet American* by Graham Greene and *The Ugly American* by William Lederer and Eugene Burdick. Greene's novel incurred the wrath of American policy makers by attacking their policy of exporting American ideology and culture to Southeast Asia in an attempt to stop communism. Greene cautioned the United States against following the French in using force in Indochina and predicted that communism would ultimately triumph in Vietnam because it, not western-style democracy and capitalism, offered solutions to the problems affecting millions of peasants. Lederer's and Burdick's book aroused furor by accusing the

United States of providing the Vietnamese with "guns and butter" instead of the means of developing a genuine democratic alternative to communism.

Had Hollywood forcefully carried over the central themes of the novels into its films, perhaps Americans would have questioned American policy in Vietnam long before the antiwar movement of the late 1960s. But Hollywood producers, still influenced by the anti-Communist witch hunt of Senator Joseph McCarthy, were loath to appear critical of America's cold war struggle against communism. As a result, Hollywood's version of *The Quiet American* took off where the book ended, substantially changing the story from criticism of American interference in Vietnamese affairs to an indictment of Communist treachery and aggression in

Pyle and his antagonist Thomas Fowler, a British journalist opposed to American involvement in Vietnam, visit a Cao Dai temple outside Saigon. The Quiet American was shot on location in and around Saigon, even though Greene's book, a dagger-eyed look at American naiveté in the fight against Vietnamese communism, was officially banned by the South Vietnamese government.

Southeast Asia. *The Ugly American* fared no better in its Hollywood version. Lederer and Burdick's blunt and forceful criticism of American involvement in Vietnam underwent a remarkable transformation on the screen, becoming an endorsement of American intentions in Vietnam and in other Asian nations threatened by communism.

The Quiet American

In this passage from Graham Greene's

In this scene from The Ugly American, *Marlon Brando, as Gilbert MacWhite, ambassador to the fictitious Southeast Asian country of Sarkhan, seeks shelter from an angry mob of anti-American protesters.*

novel, *The Quiet American*, Alden Pyle, a naïve American adviser in Vietnam, discusses America's fight against communism with Thomas Fowler, a veteran British journalist hostile to U.S. intervention in Vietnamese affairs.

Fowler: You and your like are trying to make a war with the help of people who just aren't interested.

Pyle: They don't want communism.

Fowler: They want enough rice. They don't want to be shot at. They want one day to be much as another. They don't want our white skins around telling them what they want.

Pyle: If Indochina goes . . .

Fowler: I know the record. Siam goes. Malaya goes. Indonesia goes. What does 'go' mean? If I believed in your God and another life, I'd bet my future harp against your golden crown that in five hundred years there may be no New York or London, but they'll be growing paddy in these fields, they'll be carrying their produce to market on long poles wearing their pointed hats. The small boys will be sitting on the buffaloes. I like the buffaloes, they don't like our smell, the smell of Europeans. And remember—from a buffalo's point of view you are a European too.

Pyle: They'll be forced to believe what they are told, they won't be allowed to think for themselves.

Fowler: Thought's a luxury. Do you think the peasant sits and thinks of God and Democracy when he gets inside his mud hut at night?

Pyle: You talk as if the whole country were peasant. What about the educated? Are they going to be happy?

Fowler: Oh no, we've brought them up in our ideas. We've taught them dangerous games, and that's why we are waiting here, hoping we don't get our throats cut. We deserve to have them cut.

The Ugly American

In this passage from the novel *The Ugly American*, Tex Wolchek, a U.S. military adviser, and Gilbert MacWhite, a U.S. ambassador, discuss the futility of employing conventional political and military strategy against Communist guerrillas fighting to control Vietnam during the French Indochina War.

'Just call me MacWhite,' the tall man said. His voice was crisp and assured.

'Okay, MacWhite. I'll tell you the truth. We don't know why the French are losing. Neither do they. . . .'

'All right. . . .' MacWhite said. 'What are we doing wrong?'

In the next few minutes, Tex discovered that MacWhite understood tactics and fighting. He asked tough questions and expected hard answers. They stood on the side of the road, in the midst of exhaust fumes and dust, talking strategy and tactics.

'There just isn't any simple answer,' Tex finally said. 'We're fighting a kind of war here that I never read about at Command and Staff College. Conventional weapons just don't work out here. Neither do conventional tactics.'

'Well, why don't we start using unconventional tactics?' MacWhite asked. 'Apparently, the Communists have some theory behind what they're doing.'

'Armies change slowly, MacWhite,' Tex said. 'All our tanks and planes and cannons aren't worth a damn out here. We need to fight the way they fight . . . but no one is quite sure how they fight.'

Anti-American protesters attack the limousine of Ambassador MacWhite. The authors of The Ugly American *focused on American "bumbling" as the source of anti-American feelings among Asians; the film version presented an altered interpretation, a reaffirmation of the righteousness of American foreign policy in Southeast Asia.*

Diem

March 29, 1955. All day long tension had been mounting. Rumors raced throughout Saigon, warning of an impending attack by artillery and mortar fire. The South Vietnamese forces stationed in the city were on full alert, awaiting an attack at any time. As was his ritual, Premier Ngo Dinh Diem was working late that night in the presidential palace. Alone in his office, he welcomed the brief respite to ponder the threat to his regime. At midnight, mortar shells rocked the palace grounds. Bursts of rifle and machine-gunfire broke out in the heart of Saigon, and artillery explosions ignited huge fires that lit up the city. A battle for Saigon, neither the first nor the last to wrack that beautiful city, was underway.

The attackers were not Communists, the enemy Diem had always expected to face, but the Binh Xuyen, the mob of gangsters who controlled most of Saigon. Their leader, Bay Vien, wielded more power and influence in Saigon than Diem himself. Like one of the bosses who

ran gang-land Chicago, he also dominated the Saigon police, and his henchmen, five to eight thousand of them, terrorized the citizens. Now it was only too plain that Bay Vien wanted to own one last piece of Saigon, namely Diem and his shaky government.

For three and a half hours into the early morning of the thirtieth, South Vietnamese soldiers battled hundreds of Binh Xuyen mobsters brandishing Tommy guns and assaulting the National Army headquarters. The shooting stopped in a stalemate, with neither side able to encroach upon the other's barricaded territory in the city's streets. Bodies littered the sidewalks. In addition to army and Binh Xuyen casualties, innocent bystanders were killed and scores injured in the crossfire that raked Saigon's busiest streets. General Paul Ely, commander of the remaining French forces in the South, arranged for a truce on March 31. But everyone in Saigon sensed that the truce was temporary.

Preceding page. A South Vietnamese soldier wounded by Binh Xuyen gunfire. Diem had only four battalions of troops (1600 men) to counter an attack by over 6,000 Binh Xuyen rebels.

As for Diem, holed up in the palace, he must have been wondering how he had ever landed himself in such a mess. Three years before, in the seclusion of the Maryknoll Seminary in Lakewood, New Jersey, his dream of governing a new country, an independent Vietnam, had been so appealing. He could not in his wildest nightmares have imagined the chaos, violence, and banditry that now threatened to overwhelm his fledgling administration. Diem had hoped to govern a united Vietnam, but the Geneva accords had left him with half a nation. After nine months in office, his authority over that hardly extended beyond a tiny island of government buildings surrounding the palace. Outside the city, where anarchy prevailed, the troublesome Hoa Hao and Cao Dai sects were masters of several southern and western provinces. What they did not control was in the hands of the Vietminh.

A beleaguered premier

It all must have seemed so ironic to the embattled premier. For twenty-five years he had struggled

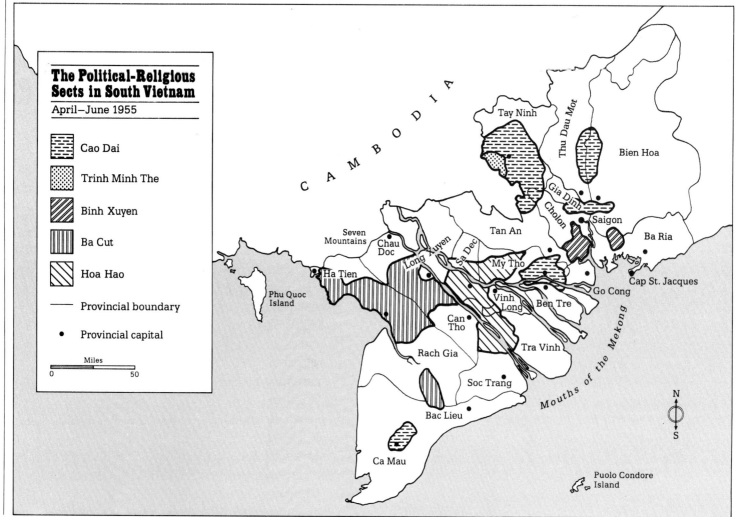

The Political-Religious Sects in South Vietnam
April–June 1955

- Cao Dai
- Trinh Minh The
- Binh Xuyen
- Ba Cut
- Hoa Hao
- —— Provincial boundary
- • Provincial capital

Miles
0   50

against the French and groomed himself for a leadership role in an independent Vietnam. Brought up in a family descended from a long line of mandarins, Diem had refused a French offer of a scholarship in Paris because he wanted to remain a "pure" Vietnamese. Diem later enrolled at the School of Public Administration and Law at Hanoi, where he finished at the top of his class and received a diploma as a ninth-class mandarin. By his early thirties, he was minister of the interior in the government of the Emperor Bao Dai. The French ignored his recommendations for a series of reforms to liberalize the colonial government, so Diem broke with them in disgust.

When the French stripped him of his honors and position, Diem vowed "to work more directly for the independence of my country." However, his strict Catholic upbringing (he had once considered becoming a priest) and his hatred of communism prevented Diem from joining Ho Chi Minh and the Vietminh in 1945 and 1946. Besides, the Communists had killed his older brother Ngo Dinh Khoi, a former member of the French colonial administration. Many

times the Vietminh tried to lure him into their organization, but Diem consistently refused. Under continuous French surveillance, he became a patriot without a movement, a leader without a following, a loner in the struggle for independence. Oddly enough, Diem was proud of that.

During World War II, Diem scouted the Japanese as potential allies against the French, but the Japanese had their own imperial designs on Southeast Asia and were not interested in creating a free Vietnam. After the war, Ho Chi Minh once more attempted to attract Diem to the Vietminh, since he wanted the support of as many non-Communists as possible for his negotiations with the French. When Diem confronted Ho in Hanoi, he immediately asked, "Why did you kill my brother?" Ho said it had been a mistake, suggesting that they forget about the past.

Diem's response, as he later reported it, was emphatic: "I told him [Ho] he was a criminal."

The spring of 1950 was the turning point in Diem's career. After learning that the Vietminh had sentenced him to death in absentia, he went into exile, visiting Europe and then traveling to the United States. There, in the tranquility of the Maryknoll Seminary, he mustered his energies for a new campaign for Vietnam's independence. He sought to raise American awareness of the Vietnam situation by lecturing at universities and talking with political and religious leaders, including Francis Cardinal Spellman. With Spellman's name and influence as his calling card, Diem gained access to important political circles in Washington. There he met Senator Mike Mansfield and Representative John F. Kennedy and other congressional leaders.

By 1954, interest in Vietnam was growing in the capital. The French were in danger of losing to the Vietminh, and the prospect of a Communist takeover disturbed Washington's cold warriors. Diem, one of the few Vietnamese nationalists familiar to Americans and an anti-Communist at that, made a favorable impression that was not forgotten by U.S. officials when the matter of the leadership of South Vietnam came up during the Geneva negotiations.

There is some controversy over whether France or the United States was principally responsible for putting Diem in power. But, according to the *Pentagon Papers*, the Emperor Bao Dai, "urged by America and France," offered Diem the premiership in 1954. Diem was ecstatic. His lifelong dream of leading an independent Vietnam seemed about to come true. Bao Dai, head of Vietnam's French-supported government, had been enjoying the good life in Paris and elsewhere during the Indochina War. Neither the French nor the Americans had much confidence

A weapons carrier hit by Binh Xuyen mortar fire burns outside Saigon police headquarters on April 28, 1955.

124

in his ability to handle the tumultuous state of affairs in the South.

Diem was somewhat puzzled by Bao Dai's choice of him for the post, especially since his relations with the foppish monarch had never been warm. In the excitement of the moment, it perhaps never entered Diem's mind that Bao Dai was perhaps expecting his failure and hoping that the French might then turn to the emperor as their only alternative. Diem, however, was determined to make the most of his opportunity and at least he knew the Americans were on his side.

Double-crosses and intrigue

Things went wrong for Diem from the start. The Geneva accords, which Diem called a "disgrace," left him only half a nation to build. Although politically and economically the South was in a shambles, Diem—independent as always—demanded and received assurances from Bao Dai of a free hand in establishing a new government. Then it happened, the first in a series of crises highlighted by double-crosses, intrigue, and outright sabotage. Bao Dai, not content to wait for Diem to fail, decided to stir up some trouble for his premier. What galled Diem the most was that the French, whose colonial *mission civilisatrice* he had rejected decades ago, were apparently in league with the former emperor. French diplomats were already calling Diem "bloodthirsty" and would later call him "not only incapable but mad." The instrument of Bao Dai's plot to undercut Diem was General Nguyen Van Hinh, chief of staff of the Vietnamese National Army. Hinh, like Diem, was a hardline anti-Communist. He had graduated from the French Air Academy in 1938 and served with French colonial forces in Algeria and Tunisia. Married to a French woman, Hinh had been integrated into the Vietnamese National Army in 1952 with the rank of brigadier general.

As a "to-the-ender" partisan in the struggle against the Communists even after Geneva, Hinh was determined to form a coalition government with the anti-Communist sects and the Binh Xuyen crowd as a "third force" capable of resisting Communist aggression. Like most diplomats and military officers in the French camp, Hinh was contemptuous of Diem's

The fire and smoke of battle envelops Saigon in April 1955, as refugees newly arrived from the North scatter in search of safety.

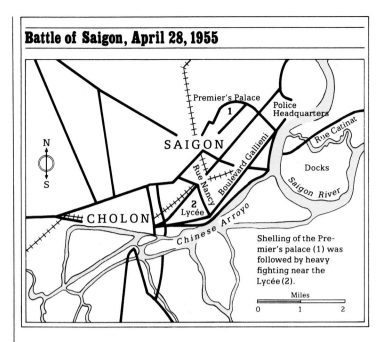

Battle of Saigon, April 28, 1955

Premier's Palace

Police Headquarters

SAIGON

Rue Catinat

Docks

N

S

Rue Nancy

Boulevard Gallieni

Saigon River

2

Lycée

CHOLON

Chinese Arroyo

Shelling of the Premier's palace (1) was followed by heavy fighting near the Lycée (2).

Miles

0   1   2

chances of winning the loyalty of the sects. Diem had other ideas, centering around a relatively democratic regime with a strong central government. For Diem the sects, armed and supplied by the French during the war, posed a threat to orderly government and could lead the South to anarchy.

In September 1954, suspecting the flamboyant general's scheme to unseat him, Diem ordered Hinh to leave the country for a six-month vacation. Hinh refused, and Bao Dai promptly ordered Diem to come to Paris for "consultation." When Diem refused, Hinh set in motion plans for an October coup. The support of the army for his anti-Communist "crusade" was all the muscle Hinh felt he needed to succeed.

With Bao Dai, his army, and his chief of staff ready to betray him, Diem assumed that he was on his own once more, a leader without followers. But he had one friend in intrigue-ridden Saigon, and a shrewd one: Colonel Edward Lansdale, CIA. Diem and Lansdale had met shortly after Diem arrived in Saigon. Lansdale, who went to the palace to greet the new premier personally, remembers the embarrassing moment when he asked "a plump man in a white suit" where he might find Diem. "I'm Diem," the man replied. Nevertheless, the two had a cordial conversation, and Diem listened intently to Lansdale, nodding his head in agreement. "After that," Lansdale said, "the ice was broken. To me he was a man with a terrible burden to carry and in need of friends, and I tried to be an honest friend of his."

Colonel Lansdale was as good as his word. Just as Hinh was poised to pounce on Diem, Lansdale stepped in to save the premier. First Lansdale

whisked most of Hinh's top officers off to Manila to study the counterinsurgency techniques of Philippine President Ramón Magsaysay, whom they greatly admired. Then the United States government dealt the decisive blow to General Hinh's plans. General "Iron Mike" O'Daniel, commander of the U.S. Military Assistance and Advisory Group in South Vietnam, informed Hinh that a coup would provoke a cutoff of U.S. aid. Hinh relented and Bao Dai, persuaded by U.S. representatives, summoned his rebellious general to France. The coup was averted although it had been a close call for Diem. Hinh later boasted that "nothing could have opposed the army.... I had only to lift my telephone and the coup d'etat would have been over."

No sooner was Hinh restrained than the leaders of the Hoa Hao and Cao Dai religious sects made their bid for power. The sects, with their thousands of soldiers, were sorely in need of the kind of funds formerly provided them by the French. This spurred them to discuss with the Diem government the possibility of merging sect troops into Diem's National Army. The Hoa Hao and Cao Dai leaders united in a coalition front, wanted what Diem was unwilling to bargain away: a share of political power. They demanded that Diem recognize the sects' existing territorial autonomy, reserve cabinet posts for them in his government, and provide financial subsidies to their local operations.

When the situation began to heat up, Diem's "American connection" paid off again. Using divide-and-conquer tactics, Diem, with money provided by the U.S., dispensed bribes to key sect leaders to fragment their opposition. According to one estimate, "The total amount of American dollars spent on bribes by Diem may well have gone beyond $12 million." Diem's pièce de résistance was his "persuading" Cao Dai strongman, General Trinh Minh The, to switch sides. The, now more than $1 million richer, rallied to the government with a flourish, marching into Saigon at the head of five thousand black uniformed Cao Dai troops. Meanwhile, other sect leaders, wondering which would desert to the government next, began feuding among themselves, ending the coalition that had aspired to bring Diem to his knees. Though considerably weakened, the sects held one last card. When Diem ignored their final ultimatum, the sects agreed that their allies, the Binh Xuyen, should humble Diem in his own backyard, Saigon. This culminated in the mess that plagued Diem on that riotous evening of March 29.

Trial by fire

April 1, 1955. Surprisingly, General Ely's cease-fire seemed to be holding. In the bustle of Saigon's crowded streets, South Vietnamese soldiers and Binh Xuyen hoodlums glared at each other from behind defensive barricades. For the next few weeks newspapers around the world printed stories about the "war" in Saigon. To many Americans it seemed the only news to come out of Vietnam was bad: war, refugees, and now civil strife. Diem's predicament was worse than ever. Bribes could not buy his way out of this one. The Binh Xuyen, with their monopoly of prostitution, gambling, and drugs, were little in need of bribe money. Blood had been spilled, and the Binh Xuyen were ready to move in for the kill.

As the tension-filled days of April ticked by, Diem found few cohorts to rely on. Ministers and officials deserted his besieged government. His few trusted associates, Foreign Minister Tran Van Don and Minister of Defense Ho Thong Minh, resigned, leaving Diem without even the semblance of a government. Although his two brothers, Nhu and Luyen rallied to his side, another close relative, Nguyen Van Thai, announced his resignation while on a diplomatic mission outside the country. Nguyen and his lot represented the breed of *attentists*, or fence-sitters, who preferred to stay on the sidelines and watch the showdown between Diem and the Binh Xuyen.

While Diem surveyed the seemingly hopeless situation, his courage, or perhaps foolhardiness, tempted him to cast caution aside and come out fighting. The "traitorous" French were predicting imminent disaster for his regime and edging him closer to it. His attempts to move a few reliable battalions to Saigon were frustrated by the French, who refused the requisite means of transportation. Among the Americans, even Lansdale cautioned Diem against tangling further with the Binh Xuyen.

The American most on Diem's mind was U.S. Ambassador Gerald D. Lawton "Lightning Joe" Collins. According to Lansdale, the nickname "Lightning Joe" had been given Collins "for the speed with which he thought problems through and came up with solutions to them." Collins and Diem despised each other. American journalist Robert Shaplen reports that "unlike Lansdale, whom Diem regarded as a friend, Collins, so far as Diem was concerned, was a general who liked to give orders and to lecture. ... A great mimic, Diem used to demonstrate to friends how Collins talked to him, brandishing a finger in his face." But the bad blood between Collins and himself worried Diem. Would Collins turn Washington against him? Would the U.S. withdraw its economic and mili-

Cyclists and pedestrians dive for shelter as mortar shells rock Saigon on April 28, 1955. The Binh Xuyen attack that day cost at least five hundred Saigonese their lives.

tary aid from his struggling government? Diem suspected that Collins, when called back to Washington in mid-April, would advise ending American support for his regime.

"Things are not going well in Vietnam"

Diem's apprehension was justified. Collins told President Eisenhower and Secretary of State Dulles that Diem was unworthy of U.S. support and "had to go" as soon as possible. Collins' negative appraisal of Diem was not unexpected by the secretary. As the sect crises simmered in Saigon, Dulles himself had been toying with the idea of replacing Diem. In a call to one U.S. senator he expressed grave misgivings about Diem as a leader: "Things are not going well in Vietnam. . . . We may have to make some changes. . . . It will be at the top and civilian."

A U.S. national intelligence report for April 1955 complicated the decision-making process in Washington. It not only confirmed reservations about Diem but also emphasized the futility of establishing a stable non-Communist regime in the South, regardless of its leadership:

Even if the present impasse with the sects were resolved, we believe that it would be extremely difficult, at best, for a Vietnamese government, regardless of its composition, to make progress towards developing a strong, stable, anti-Communist government capable of resolving the basic social, economic, and political problems of Vietnam, the special problems arising from the Geneva Agreement and capable of meeting the long-term challenge of the Communists.

The American press was equally as gloomy in its assessment. Joseph Alsop, in a series of articles in the *New York Herald Tribune*, pronounced Diem "virtually impotent" against the sects and concluded that "the Diem experiment has failed." Most American newspapers, even those friendly to Diem, talked resignedly of the inevitability of civil war, the fall of Diem, and the victory of communism. The novelist and journalist, Graham Greene, prophesied that South Vietnam was "about to return behind the Iron Curtain."

Despite such dire predictions, U.S. policy makers were not about to abandon Vietnam even if they entertained second thoughts about Diem. Secretary Dulles and the Vietnam Task Force at the State Department were still resolved to prevent a Communist

takeover in Vietnam, and this attitude dominated discussions about a solution to the Diem problem. Simply pulling out was not a desirable option, yet it would not be easy to get rid of a premier so determined to hang on. Besides, Diem still had powerful friends in Washington, Senator Mike Mansfield being one of his most outspoken supporters. State Department officials finally shaped a feasible compromise formula: Diem would become president of South Vietnam, a symbolic nationalist leader, but real power would be invested in a "general manager," perhaps a premier. At first Dulles opposed the compromise formula, but Mansfield and Assistant Secretary of State Walter Robertson convinced him it was the way to go.

On April 28, when Collins left to return to Vietnam, a cablegram was ready for dispatch to the Saigon embassy, informing Diem that he was being removed in favor of a new premier. But it was too late. Kenneth Young, head of the Vietnam Task Force, describes the event that threw their plans into confusion:

At six o'clock on the afternoon of the twenty-eighth, I took the cable into Secretary Dulles' office. The secretary signed it. After all the long discussions and all the headaches they had provoked, we were once again hopeful that a solution could be reached—we even thought we had signed a new Magna Carta. Then, shortly after Dulles signed the cable, I got a call from him. He had just received a cable from Lansdale. Fighting had broken out again in Saigon, between the Binh Xuyen and the government forces.

Diem comes out fighting

April 28, 1955. Saigon was in an uproar. What everyone had dreaded, a shootout between Diem's forces and the Binh Xuyen, was ravaging the streets of Saigon. The fighting began when the Binh Xuyen launched a mortar attack on the presidential palace, an action not unwelcome to Diem and his adviser, Lansdale. Diem, his back to the wall and with nothing to lose, ordered immediate counterfire. By mid-afternoon a fierce fight was raging for the control of National Police headquarters. Continuous mortar and artillery shelling transformed a square mile of the city into a "free fire" zone. Numerous explosions and house-to-house combat drove thousands of people into the streets. Panic-stricken residents along the Boulevard Gallieni, exposed to waves of crossfire, were wounded or killed. Hospitals quickly filled with casualties, while four battalions of government paratroopers attacked Binh Xuyen defensive positions.

In a Saigon court, the Hoa Hao sect leader, Ba Cut, stands trial in April 1956 for rebellion against the South Vietnamese government. Despite a plea for clemency by the American adviser, Colonel Edward Lansdale, Ba Cut was sentenced to death by a military judge and guillotined on July 13, 1956.

Enormous fires razed buildings and shacks housing thousands of North Vietnamese refugees who, ironically, had fled the North to escape violence and turmoil and instead were greeted by death and destruction. Yet even as the killing went on, there was a bizarre "business as usual" atmosphere in the shops and cafés. A. M. Rosenthal, then a *New York Times* correspondent in Saigon, wrote:

While the mortar cracked and machine guns barked, some people were living their lives as usual. A shoe shine boy did a good business in a café crowded with shelter seekers. And on a balcony an American G.I. pulled at a bottle of beer and watched the show.

By the thirtieth, Diem's paratroopers, overrunning one Binh Xuyen position after another, had the disorganized gangsters in full retreat. Diem's successful counterattack stunned everyone, including the Americans. Although the battle of Saigon had taken five

hundred army, Binh Xuyen, and civilian lives and inflicted nearly two thousand injuries, the once-invincible Binh Xuyen forces were broken, running for refuge in their old lair in the Rung Sat swamps. Over the next few months army battalions pursued the Binh Xuyen into the swamps, destroying or capturing many of them. Bay Vien, Saigon's kingpin of vice, managed with French assistance to escape to Paris.

The rout of the Binh Xuyen drove their allies, the sects, into panic, while Diem, exhilarated by his success, took the offensive against the Hoa Hao and Cao Dai strongholds. Within a few months, again to the surprise of many, Diem gained the upper hand, and

his troops faced little more than mopping-up operations to eradicate sect resistance. The Cao Dai pope fled to Cambodia. Most Hoa Hao leaders, except for the infamous Ba Cut, surrendered. Ba Cut (which means cut finger) earned his nickname when he cut off his finger to prove his determination to crush the French. For almost a year, the fanatical Ba Cut evaded capture. A 1 million piaster price on his head kept him on the move. At last, in April 1956, on Friday the thirteenth, Ba Cut, the "terror of the West," was taken alive by the army. To distract his trackers, he had scattered 100 and 500 piaster bills on the ground. But his pursuers, seeking the bigger reward, ignored the bait. Ba Cut was later guillotined.

Hail the conquering hero

Diem's astonishing victory over the Binh Xuyen and the sects made him into something of an instant hero in South Vietnam. The *attentists* flocked to his side, and a new surge of political activity swept the city. This time, to Diem's relief, it was directed against Emperor Bao Dai and his political agents. On the afternoon of April 30, the day the Binh Xuyen were skulking back to the swamps, some two hundred people gathered at the Saigon Town Hall, calling themselves the "General Assembly of democratic and revolutionary forces of the nation." The assembly claimed to represent almost all political parties in South Vietnam. Its resolutions repudiated Bao Dai and requested Diem to form a new government and elect a national assembly to adopt a constitution. Diem was receptive to the program of the revolutionary assembly, especially since his brother Nhu was in large part responsible for drafting it. Following the revolutionary assembly's mandate, Diem turned over the problem of Bao Dai to an elected National Assembly. Composed of 700 elected counselors from thirty-nine provinces, it drew up a program to transfer all civilian and military power from Bao Dai to Diem pending a constitutional convention to be convened in six months.

The American response to Diem's heroics in whipping the armed opposition was quick and enthusiastic. The Eisenhower administration was now convinced that Diem was the only man to build a new state and that Bao Dai was a "villain" who might stand in the way. Leading Democrats shared this partiality, particularly Senators Mike Mansfield and

Hubert Humphrey. On the Senate floor, Humphrey voiced unrestrained support for Diem:

Premier Diem is the best hope that we have in South Vietnam. He is the leader of his people. He deserves and must have the wholehearted support of the American government and our foreign policy. This is no time for uncertainty or half-hearted measures. . . . If the government of South Vietnam has not room for both of these men, it is Bao Dai who must go.

Secretary of State Dulles, who but a few days before had contemplated Diem's removal, also joined the chorus singing the premier's praises. In a cabled message to a joint meeting of U.S., French, and British representatives in Paris, Dulles insisted that Diem's leadership role be upheld: "Diem is the only means U.S. sees to save South Vietnam and counteract the revolutionary movement underway in Vietnam. U.S. sees no one else who can. Whatever U.S. view has been in the past, today U.S. must support Diem wholeheartedly."

Since the French were still dead set against Diem, they interpreted "wholehearted" U.S. support for him as a rejection of a continuing French presence in South Vietnam. U.S. and French officials differed not only on the suitability of Diem but on France's future military and economic influence in South Vietnam. French Prime Minister Edgar Faure frankly stated his government's position:

Diem is a bad choice, impossible solution, with no chance to succeed and no chance to improve the situation. Without him some solution might be possible, but with him there is none. . . . What would you say if we were to retire entirely from Indochina and call back the French Expeditionary Corps, would the United States be disposed to help protect French civilians and the refugees?

The United States' ultimate answer to Faure's question was yes. Diem's recent display of courage and determination bedazzled U.S. policy makers in Washington and Saigon. The French envisioned a South Vietnamese leader capable of unifying divisive forces and factions through compromise, negotiation, and persuasion. American policy makers in Washington, on the other hand, saw the need for a strong individual who could control factions, impose order, and win the loyalty of the people. They also believed that Diem was able and willing to carry out democratic reform in South Vietnam and to lead a government acceptable to the majority of the South Vietnamese people.

But the now lavish U.S. encouragement had the effect of strengthening Diem's natural bent toward one-man, authoritarian rule. It was not hard for Diem to see what pleased Lansdale and his American advisers most: swift action, the spectacular event, and a take-charge attitude. This translated into a hard line against communism, a tough approach to domestic dissension, and "thinking big" on economic problems. Diem also learned other "negative" lessons which had ominous overtones for the future of his regime. After his experience with Hinh and other untrustworthy officers, Diem developed an almost obsessive fear of strong military officers and army-led coups. And the "betrayal" by his ministers and subordinates strengthened Diem's own compulsion to control everything around him, to avoid ever having to rely on anyone not totally loyal.

The changing of the guard

After subduing the Binh Xuyen and the sects, Diem denounced the French for their "collusion" in a conspiracy to topple his government. In May, his secretary of national defense accused the French of attempting outright sabotage by funneling arms and ammunition to the rebels. Such incidents intensified Diem's bitter dislike for the French and prompted his demand that France withdraw from the South as quickly as possible. The French had tried to keep South Vietnam within the military and economic sphere of the French Union. But as relations with Diem deteriorated, French officials reluctantly agreed to get out. On January 19, 1956, Diem informed the French that further stationing of French troops in Vietnam was pointless since "the presence of foreign troops, no matter how friendly . . . was incompatible with Vietnam's concept of full independence."

Diem was not alone in adamantly pushing for a speedy French withdrawal. American military and civilian advisers felt that the French had become a hindrance to an independent regime. This angered the French and generated hostility between French and American officers. Ill feelings rose to the surface on both sides when French and American advisers participated in a joint program, the Training Relations Instruction Mission, to reorganize the South Vietnamese army. The French command charged an American officer with being the author of leaflets inciting the Vietnamese against the French. An American official, Angier Biddle Duke, accused the French

of providing explosives used in numerous bombing raids against American offices in Saigon. Friction also developed over appropriate training methods. French officers felt their long experience in the Indochina War should count heavily in devising tactics and warfare techniques. American officers, on the other hand, expressed some disdain for the suggestions of French "losers." The Americans exuded confidence which irritated their French colleagues, a sort of "this time we'll do it right" demeanor.

Secretary of State Dulles, after receiving strongly worded arguments for phasing out the French role in Vietnam, generally favored such a course. He did so, however, with hesitation. In November 1954 he had warned that "If we do this, the French will plaster us with the responsibility all over the world and try to sabotage the result—they are still powerful there. If we fail, it will be a terrible blow to our prestige in that area. So far we have been able to say that losses in the area have been French failures." Despite Dulles' doubts, Diem got his way.

In April 1956, the last ten thousand soldiers of the French Expeditionary Corps, which had numbered nearly one hundred and fifty thousand in 1954, bid their final adieu to Vietnam. On April 10, almost a century after the first French units had landed in Saigon, the last parade of French troops took place in South Vietnam's capital. Like the farewell parade from Hanoi nineteen months earlier, it was a solemn event. Paratroop commandos in camouflage uniforms and purple berets led the march, followed by foreign legionnaires with glistening white kepis, and Moroccans wearing turbans. Among the spectators along the parade route were many Vietnamese ex-soldiers displaying medals and citations they had won in the service of France. French observers reported that some of them cried as they watched the troops file by. The soldiers, too, shed a few parting tears for the fallen comrades they were leaving behind after one hundred years of colonial rule.

In the wake of the soldiers a Eurasian airlift transported the often forgotten casualties of the French military presence in Vietnam: orphan children of Vietnamese women and French soldiers killed or missing in action. Every week a special plane landed at Paris-Orly Airport with dozens of anxious passengers, orphans aged one to twelve. Their nationality was French, but their features were partly Oriental. Although they took French names and surnames, these forlorn children remained visible reminders of France's Vietnam War.

"The Alliance That Never Really Was"

September 6, 1954, a hot afternoon in Manila, representatives of eight nations gathered to establish the Southeast Asia Treaty Organization (SEATO). The purpose of the treaty was clear to all involved: to devise an agreement with teeth in it, a powerful deterrent to the expansionist designs of the Communist bloc in Asia. Allied in this crusade against communism were three western powers, the United States, Britain, and France, and several Pacific nations: Australia, New Zealand, Pakistan, Thailand, and the Philippines.

The treaty was the brain child of U.S. Secretary of State John Foster Dulles, who repudiated the Geneva Agreement, ratified two months earlier, as a dangerous concession to the Communist bloc. As the Manila meeting approached, he passionately argued that the "important thing from now on is not to mourn the past but to seize future opportunities to prevent the loss of North Vietnam from leading to the extension of communism throughout Southeast Asia and the Southwest Pacific." When the Geneva Conference concluded, Bedell Smith, the American representative, emphasized Dulles' sense of urgency about the need for a new security arrangement like SEATO: "We must get that pact."

Dulles, with his fervent anti-communism, was destined to be disappointed by the outcome of the Manila conference. Dulles began optimistically enough, declaring in his opening address to the delegates that he expected SEATO to serve as a warning to Communist aggressors that "an attack upon the treaty area would occasion a reaction so united, so strong, and so well placed that the aggressor would lose more than it could hope to obtain." While the delegates may have agreed in spirit with the secretary's proposal, except for France and Britain they represented countries with little capacity for mobile striking power or the ambitious defense plans espoused by Dulles. In addition, the U.S. Joint Chiefs of Staff were not very enthusiastic about earmarking specific troop commitments to maintain SEATO. In addition the U.S. Senate was generally opposed to the kind of military precommitment, based on the NATO model, that would empower the president to employ armed forces in an emergency without consulting Congress.

Other SEATO participants harbored similar reservations.

Hesitation among delegates led to a series of awkward compromises that produced, to Dulles' chagrin, a weak and hybrid treaty. The treaty committed each member, in the event of armed attack on another member, to do no more than "meet the common danger in accordance with its constitutional processes." In effect, each member retained the right to decide under what conditions it would abide by its treaty obligations—the very antithesis of what Dulles originally had in mind. A similar compromise applied to more subtle forms of aggression: subversion, infiltration, and guerrilla warfare. Members adopted a provision only to hold immediate consultations if any territory covered by the treaty were "affected or threatened by any fact or situation which might endanger the peace of the area...."

Dulles was in for more frustration. The secretary vigorously lobbied to include France's former Indochinese territories—South Vietnam, Laos, and Cambodia—as members of the treaty organization. However, France vetoed such a move on the grounds that it would violate the Geneva accords, whose provisions specifically prohibited these three "neutralized" states from joining military alliances. Still, Dulles persuaded SEATO at least to "throw a mantle of protection" over South Vietnam, Laos, and Cambodia through a protocol bringing them within the jurisdiction of the treaty. A compromise provision to this effect was incorporated into the treaty.

While SEATO supplied an excuse for a variety of U.S. interventions in Indochina, the vagueness of its provisions to trigger a joint response to Communist aggression made it an unwieldy weapon. In fact, the reluctance of treaty members to commit themselves to the risks of America's anti-Communist containment policy in Asia should have warned Dulles that the United States might have to go it alone someday in Asia, particularly in Vietnam. The treaty itself was not even systematically invoked until 1966 by Secretary of State Dean Rusk and then without great conviction. Three years after Dulles died, C. L. Sulzberger of the *New York Times* called SEATO "the alliance that never really was."

Twilight of Peace

During France's Indochina War and the brief period of Bao Dai's French-dominated regime, the United States poured more than $1 billion in aid into Vietnam. Now, with the French gone, the U.S. was the only foreign military presence in the country.

In the late spring of 1956, the Americans reorganized their military advisory program, the Military Assistance Advisory Group (MAAG). Under the command of General Samuel T. "Hanging Sam" Williams, MAAG's new mission was to streamline the Vietnamese army of 250,000 men into a smaller conventional force of 150,000 capable of repelling an invasion from the North. The U.S. equipped and trained this army while paying for its entire payroll as well as most of the wages of 40,000 men in the newly established local militia, the Self-Defense Corps. The U.S. now dispensed its funds for the armed forces directly through Diem, strengthening Diem's formerly tenuous authority over the military

The Americans emphasized conventional training techniques. They established a military school system and sent hundreds of young officers to study American military tactics at schools in Korea, Okinawa, Taiwan, and the United States. In August 1960, on the eve of his retirement as commander of MAAG, a proud General Williams said, "In 1954 the Communist army of North Vietnam could have crossed the seventeenth parallel and walked into Saigon standing up. Today if they tried it, they would have one nasty fight on their hands."

MAAG, however, prepared the Vietnamese army for the wrong kind of war. Following the analogy of the Korean conflict, the type of conventional forces that the American commanders designed were inappropriate for a guerrilla conflict. The result was what the French observer Bernard Fall has termed a "road-bound, over-motorized, hard-to-supply battle force totally incapable of besting the real enemy [that is, the elusive guerrilla] on his own ground."

At the same time U.S. advisers embarked on a program to mobilize a fifty-thousand-man Civil Guard. In charge of this task was the Michigan State University (MSU) advisory group. The head of the group, Professor Wesley Fishel, was a close friend of Diem, who admired the work of Michigan State's unique School of Police Administration. Since the MSU group envisioned the Civil Guard as a rural police force, they left the training for this operation, according to one observer, in the hands of "retired American sheriffs and police captains—as if Vietnam's main security problem was catching speeding motorists or controlling juvenile delinquency." Not until 1960, when the Civil Guard was transferred to the U.S. military mission, was it trained in antiguerrilla tactics.

Enter the Americans

The professors of the MSU group and other U.S. advisers—engineers, social scientists, public administrators, doctors—carried out one of the most ambitious experiments ever undertaken by Americans abroad: the building of a nation. To guarantee their success, the U.S. initiated a program of aid totaling $320 million for fiscal 1955 alone and almost $2 billion between 1955 and 1960. Since the French left the South Vietnamese government bankrupt and the pullout of

Preceding page. The people of Hanoi welcome Vietminh troops from South Vietnam, regrouped to the North in accordance with the Geneva Agreement.

French soldiers created a shortfall in tax revenues, generated almost totally by army purchases, U.S. economic aid was used to pay almost all government salaries as well as Diem's other operating expenses. In addition, the U.S. provided military equipment at an average cost of $85 million per year. Nearly three-quarters of the $2 billion of aid during this period went to South Vietnam's military budget. Only 25 percent of that total was allocated to projects such as transportation, education, health and sanitation, community development, and social welfare.

The U.S. purchased consumer goods for import by South Vietnam with foreign aid dollars, which went directly to exporters. In South Vietnam, importers paid for these goods with piasters, which went into a counterpart fund from which Diem's administration drew to pay salaries and operating expenses. However, while the import program was designed to benefit consumers by increasing the availability of scarce commodities and thereby forestalling inordinate price increases, it was ill suited to Vietnamese economic conditions. Most South Vietnamese lived in rural areas, farming rice at a subsistence level. Those few farmers who could even afford the imported goods were hampered by inefficient transportation and shipping facilities linking the cities with rural communities. As a result, imported commodities tended to accumulate in urban areas where they benefited only a small group of wealthy consumers.

The commercial import program severely hampered the development of substantial industrialization in the South. Although an industrial development center was created in 1957 with American financial support, the commercial import program discouraged investment in local industrial projects to produce the goods that the Diem regime was already receiving in such great quantities. In addition, the flood of imported goods actually forced many of the few existing local industries into bankruptcy. For instance, at the end of January 1958, South Vietnam for a population of 12 million had 7.6 million yards of imported textiles on the market, expected another 22.4 million yards for the first three months of 1958, and had approved orders for 12.2 million additional yards. Even though the total yardage then available was considered adequate to meet consumer needs for at least two and one-half years, warehouses continued to amass huge stocks. As a result, in February 1958, textile prices plummeted to an all-time low. A staggered retailers' association asked the government to halt all textile imports, but the damage to the solvency of many South Vietnamese textile businesses was already irreparable.

In the opinion of many economic experts, an industrial base in South Vietnam was the prerequisite to political independence. Yet because the middle class, which formed the core of Diem's support, wanted the types of goods comprising the bulk of commercial imports—textiles, radios, appliances, automobiles—the Diem regime was unwilling to use import funds for the purchase of capital goods such as machinery and construction equipment. In the words of one high American official, "The Vietnamese government seems to prefer Chevrolets to dredges."

"President Diem, you have exemplified patriotism of the highest order"

—*President Dwight Eisenhower*

Perhaps no accomplishment of Ngo Dinh Diem's aroused more admiration among Americans than his attempts to install a seemingly democratic form of government in South Vietnam. Diem not only held elections in late 1955 to allow the people to choose between himself and Bao Dai but also formed a popularly elected legislature and drafted a constitution. To Americans who hold such democratic institutions sacred, it seemed that South Vietnam's president had indeed performed a miracle. However, these sacred symbols of a democratic society in many ways remained exactly that in South Vietnam—symbols.

In his campaign to transform Bao Dai's monarchy into a republic, Diem used every trick in the book to deprive Bao Dai of a fair chance in the election. There was no doubt that Diem's popularity was enough to insure him victory, but recent strife with the sects had heightened his already intense insecurity and distrust. Diem swept the election with 98.2 percent of all votes cast (5,721,735) to Bao Dai's 1.1 percent (63,017). His incredible margin of victory, however, was hardly indicative of an election free of corruption and the stuffing of ballot boxes. In fact, *LIFE* Magazine noted in 1957 that American advisers had told Diem that a 60 percent margin would have been sufficient and "would look better," but Diem insisted on 98 percent.

The constitution, which Diem himself participated in drafting, gave the new president executive powers that were more authoritarian than democratic. Although the constitution established a legislature, intended to be independent of the executive branch so as to achieve separation of powers, Diem as president was empowered to override its decisions in most important areas of legislation. With its functions severely restricted the legislature degenerated into a rubber-stamp body, disparagingly referred to as "the government's garage."

An additional authoritarian feature of the con-

Lieutenant Thomas Moore, an American military adviser, instructs a South Vietnamese officer in military tactics during training exercises in 1955. The U.S. military advisory program stressed conventional strategy to prepare the South Vietnamese army against a Korean-style invasion from the North.

stitution was the power it vested in Diem to rule solely by decree when the legislature was not in session and to suspend any law in any part of the country even when the legislature was in session. The constitution stated: "The president of the republic may decree a temporary suspension of the right of freedom of circulation and residence, of speech and the press, of assembly and association, and the formation of labor unions and strikes, to meet the legitimate demands of public security and order and national defense." Such unilateral power to deprive citizens of civil rights under the umbrella of "national security" inhibited the development of substantial democratic freedom in South Vietnam.

The last Confucian

Ngo Dinh Diem's mandarin background has sometimes been cited as an example of his deep roots in traditional Vietnamese society and of his understanding of the problems facing the people of his country. Diem's "immense nostalgia for the Vietnamese past," however, smacked more of an elitist yearning for a time when, according to his biographer, Vietnam's political ideology was "based not on the concept of the management of the public affairs by the people or their representatives, but rather by an enlightened sovereign and an enlightened government." Having denied the legislature an equal partnership in governing, Diem was in the position of Vietnam's ancient emperors who relied on an elite class of mandarins to administer the government.

Diem's Confucian perspective manifested itself in the form of a new ruling ideology, Personalism. Personalism was based on the 1930s philosophical movement of young French Catholic intellectuals critical of western-style democracies. Diem himself described Personalism as "a system based on the divine, therefore, spiritual law, which ... extols man's transcendent value. ... The practice of Personalism is symbolic of good citizenship with a highly developed civic spirit." In his interpretation of Personalist doctrine Diem argued that these spiritual goals require government leaders to provide a suitable moral example so that each person may individually achieve his true value as a citizen. The result, not unlike that engineered by Ho in the North, was that individual liberty would have to take second place to the collective moral and social betterment of society as a whole. Here was Confucianism in another guise.

Since Diem believed that "society functions through personal relations among men at the top," the very basis of the old Confucian government, he cultivated his own elite of Personalist mandarins to govern the state. At the top, Diem surrounded himself with his "mandarin" family, whose devotion and loyalty he could count on.

South Vietnam's new mandarins

No group of individuals created more controversy and indignation in South Vietnam than the Ngo family. For the time Diem served as president, his four brothers, Can, Luyen, Thuc, and Nhu, and his sister-in-law, Madame Nhu, formed a powerful, tightly knit political circle. Diem's brother Can became the virtual overlord of central Vietnam, the ancestral home of the Ngo family, although he held no government position. Thuc, the archbishop of Hue and primate of Vietnam, also held no official position but functioned as a presidential adviser and garnered Catholic support, both in Vietnam and in the United States, on Diem's behalf. Another brother, Luyen, became an ambassador and an international spokesman for the policies of the Diem regime.

The most influential of Diem's brothers, Nhu, whom many called a Vietnamese Rasputin, was Diem's closest adviser. Nine years younger than Diem, Nhu was educated in Paris. He first came into prominence in 1952 when he organized the Catholic trade union movement, which had as one of its chief objectives the advancement of Diem's political ambitions. John Mecklin, a former American reporter and official in Saigon, once described Nhu as a "small man, slight of build even for a Vietnamese. He spoke softly with a permanently fixed smile (earning him the nickname 'Smiley' in the American community). It was a professorial smile, implying generous tolerance for the listener's stupidity." Added to Nhu's arrogance was a generous portion of anti-American sentiment, which alienated many in the American community.

Nhu, with Machiavellian slyness, organized and controlled the semicovert Personalist Labor Revolutionary party. Members of this party, like the Communist cadres in the North, functioned as a parallel hierarchy within the government and wielded real power at all decision-making levels. With its secret membership and five-man cells, it was able to maintain surveillance throughout the government. Nhu's political action cells also quietly eliminated bothersome opposition and exercised a virtual monopoly of power both in the bureaucracy and in the army.

Nhu's political activities, while solidifying Diem's control of the government, also alienated much of the public. The growing awareness among opposition parties, and even among average citizens, that the legislature, the courts, and the bureaucracy were not the "real" government bred skepticism about the possibility of achieving a democratic regime. Doctor Pham Quang Dan, a political rival of Diem, expressed the frustration of many South Vietnamese at Diem's "you're either with me or against me" attitude when he said, "We do not consider the government our enemy, for we have a common enemy, communism, and a common purpose, the strengthening of the republican regime."

Through the efforts of the Personalist revolutionaries, the tentacles of Diem's authoritarian power reached down even to village peasants. The cadres' attempt to inculcate in the villages the Personalist cult of Diem's "superior" morality, however, elicited more resentment than admiration.

For instance, Diem's popularity among the peasants of Duc Lap fell abruptly after his Personalist cult was installed in the village. When asked if Diem had won his support, one Duc Lap villager frankly responded, "No! Imagine that he required every house to buy one photo of him and to hang it up in his house as if to worship him. He did it as if he were the father of the people, and each portrait cost from 50 to 80 piasters. How much money did they get from all the houses of this village?"

Diem's biggest mistake in seeking absolute control of government was in arbitrarily replacing all previously elected village chiefs and village councils with outsiders hand-picked by his bureaucracy. By centuries-old tradition, honored even by the French, Vietnam's villages were autonomous units with their

An effigy of Bao Dai, the "playboy emperor." During the 1955 presidential campaign between Diem and Bao Dai, Diem's supporters used this and similar propaganda tactics to highlight the emperor's luxurious lifestyle—note the moneybag and the woman in Bao Dai's lap—and to publicly discredit him.

own elected officials—hence the saying "the emperor's law stops at the village gate." Thus, the peasants naturally reacted bitterly to the elimination of this surviving remnant of village autonomy.

In urban areas, Diem's attempts to impose conservative morality upon intellectuals and the middle classes, as if by royal edict, earned him further public enmity. The antivice campaign launched in late 1955 and championed by Diem's arrogant sister-in-law, Madame Nhu, was characterized by heavy-handed tactics to prevent such abuses as opium smoking, alcoholism, and prostitution. Madame Nhu was known for her good looks, vanity, and contempt for the masses. The columnist Joseph Alsop once called her a tigress. Others lampooned her as the "dragon lady" and the "Queen of Saigon."

Madame Nhu used poster exhibits and dramatic skits to portray the evils of vice. Public bonfires were lit to burn such "wicked" things as playing cards. Youths were arrested for wearing "cowboy clothing" and loud shirts. Harsh penalties, including imprisonment at hard labor and death, were prescribed for "white collar" crimes such as embezzlement.

To enhance their commitment to morality, government employees and other citizen groups were also required to hold meetings to study the president's life and "his revolutionary virtues." The compulsory playing in theaters of a song entitled "Venerate President Ngo," which came to be called the second national anthem, induced such a negative reaction that the practice was stopped.

Land reform: the "revolutionary solution"

The keystone of Diem's "revolutionary policy" to win the hearts and minds of peasants, the majority of the population, was land reform. Land reform had bedeviled Vietnamese governments for centuries. It confronted the Diem regime as one of the primary social and economic problems in the countryside. Diem's American advisers never stopped informing him, frequently to his irritation, that the solvency of his government depended to a large extent on his success in implementing sweeping land reform measures. In fact, again to Diem's signal displeasure, the United States government made land reform one of the chief conditions for continuing aid to his regime. President Eisenhower's personal letter to Diem of October 1, 1954, pledging assistance to South Vietnam, sought "assurance as to the standards of performance in the undertaking of these reforms."

Land reform in South Vietnam involved two processes: land clearing to settle landless peasants and redistribution of huge tracts of land under the control of powerful landlords. Almost from the beginning, Diem was faced with a flood of refugees coming south escaping Communist rule and seeking the promise of a new life in the rich agricultural land of the Mekong Delta. Temporarily, the government settled the refugees in camps surrounding Saigon and in areas like Bien Hoa and Rach Bap. An American

Ngo Dinh Nhu, Diem's brother and closest adviser, meets with President Eisenhower in Washington on March 27, 1957. Shortly after the meeting Nhu, or "Smiley" as some Americans satirically called him, told reporters that "Communist subversion" would intensify in South Vietnam.

Madame Nhu, Diem's activist sister-in-law, enters the National Assembly building in Saigon in March 1956. Although a member of the assembly, she seldom attended its sessions. But the extensive power of the Diem family enabled her to control legislation affecting women and refugees.

writer, Gertrude Samuels, visited a camp in Rach Bap and was shocked by the harsh conditions encountered by refugees crowded into tents and shacks:

Thousands of the tents covered the ground as far as the eye could see . . . filled with people. They huddled on their rice mats on the soggy earth under the canvas; or, standing ankle deep in mud, dumbly watched us as we drove up; or struggled to get a sack of rice in from the rain. . . . Some people said they have been without food and medicine and water for days. Some were catching rain in tins outside their tents. Others simply sat with their babies in a seeming state of shock. The whole area reflected such helplessness that you could only pray that their prayers were being heard somewhere.

To deal with the enormous task of resettling hundreds of thousands of refugees, the U.S. and South Vietnam cooperated in joint land-clearing projects. The most ambitious of these was at Cai San. This project, financed with $37 million in U.S. funds, required peasants to provide much of the labor. Each family head received $800 for building a home and $4 per day per family member for subsistence until the first harvest. Eight thousand houses were built on an expansive swamp, while refugees labored daily at the arduous tasks of digging nearly fourteen miles of canals, draining thirty thousand acres of land, and preparing the soil for planting a rice crop. The U.S. supplied more than one hundred tractors to Cai San, making it one of the largest concentrations of motorized agricultural implements ever used on a single project in Asia.

Cai San was hailed by the U.S. as a "symbol of South Vietnam's determination to shelter people who linked their future with that of the free government." However, a serious hitch developed. The peasants expected that the property they cleared was to be their own. Diem's government thought otherwise. In the late summer of 1956, the Cai San project director, the nephew of the minister of agrarian reform, insisted that refugees sign tenancy contracts for the land, promising payment over time in return for title to the land. Spokesmen for the farmers claimed that the land belonged to the farmers, citing the revolutionary slogan they had learned in the North, "land to the tillers." The obdurate project director spurned their complaints and cut off daily payments to refugees who balked at signing the tenancy contracts. Thus was dissipated much of the good will that Diem had hoped to acquire from the project.

One other problem afflicted the refugee resettlement plans. Many southerners, who considered northerners to be pushy, too aggressive, and selfish, resented what they considered to be government favoritism toward these unwelcome newcomers. Diem's own actions exacerbated the situation. Since most of the refugees were Catholics, and most southerners were Buddhists, Diem's partiality toward his fellow Catholics, who often received the choicest plots of land and most lucrative government posts, caused resentment in many communities. So, many peasants held yet another grudge against Diem and the government.

Resettlement in the highlands

"Resettlement blues" were not confined to refugees. Diem, like Ho Chi Minh in the North, was aware of the strategic importance of the highlands as a gateway to the South. So he decided to resettle landless Vietnamese in the highlands and thereby establish a line of strategic settlements to prevent Communist infiltration from the North. Because of the government's tactless and insensitive approach, the project created more problems than it solved. The intensely independent highland tribes felt threatened by incursions of Vietnamese lowlanders into their traditionally autonomous domain. They reacted angrily to proposals that they share their land with Vietnamese who in the past had shown nothing but contempt for them.

While Ho Chi Minh won the cooperation of tribes in the North by promising continued autonomy; by respecting their languages, customs, and traditions; and by assuring them a role in the central government, the South Vietnamese regime did precisely the opposite. Diem's officials not only tried to compel the tribes to move off ancient tribal lands to resettlement camps but also attempted to force upon the reluctant tribesmen an assimilation policy that offered them the chance to become full Vietnamese citizens. The tribesmen, however, interpreted assimilation as another word for extermination. As Frederick Wickert, an American knowledgeable in tribal affairs, wrote,

"The Vietnamese are settling on their lands, with the best lands going first, and the tribesmen see themselves starved to death. They feel that the Vietnamese are letting diseases, such as smallpox [carried by the lowlanders], kill them off. Too, they feel that the Vietnamese are trying to force them to give up their culture." In the end, with these fears uppermost in mind, the tribes grew increasingly restive and proved dangerously receptive to North Vietnamese propaganda promising them an autonomous and prosperous existence under a Communist regime.

The biggest challenge on Diem's land reform agenda was to redistribute land under the control of wealthy landlords to the peasants. Atrocious conditions, created by the landlords' stranglehold on landownership, were an unfortunate inheritance from the days of the French colonial administration. In South Vietnam, particularly in the fertile areas of the Mekong Delta, fifty-three hundred (mostly absentee landlords) of the two hundred and fifty thousand landowners in all possessed 45 percent of the total arable land. The fact that 2 percent of the landowners held 45 percent of the land and 72 percent only 15 percent presented an obvious field for thorough reform. Ho Chi Minh took the brutal but direct path: He eliminated the landlords and divided the land into small parcels. Diem's land reform, on the other hand, operated on the supposition that "agrarian reform does not mean spoliation. It operates with justice and equality and with respect for private property." Since a substantial number of South Vietnam's farmers were tenants working for landlords, in 1955 Diem attempted to limit land rents to 25 percent of the farmers' crops. Landlords in the past had often charged as much as half the crop in rent. Unfortunately, Diem's measure contained no easily workable mechanism to guarantee compliance. In 1956 Diem also announced a measure limiting individual landholdings to 247 acres with another 70 or so allowed if the owner farmed the land himself.

Here again the purpose of the laws was contravened by Diem's officials. Implementation was often blocked by officials who were either landlords themselves or members of landlord families. The minister of agrarian reform was accused of sabotaging the program because "he is certainly not interested in land distribution which would divest him of much of his property." Moreover, the government in its "respect for private property" enforced the rights of many absentee landlords to land they had abandoned during the war years. In many cases, the

Vietminh had already carried out land reform in these same areas, and the peasants to whom they had distributed the landlords' holdings now considered the property their own.

The issue of Diem's preferential treatment of Catholics also clouded the prospect of land reform. Critics attacked Diem's refusal to transfer 370,500 acres of land owned by the Catholic church to the government for distribution. In the final analysis, the land reform program, intended to be the showpiece of U.S.-Vietnamese cooperation, became a serious disappointment. Denis Warner, an Australian journalist, summed it up this way: "The much vaunted rural help program did not exist. Land reform was a flop."

The Vietminh cadres in the South

While Diem was wrestling with the problem of the Binh Xuyen and the sects in the fall of 1954, the southern Vietminh forces, as prescribed by the Geneva accords, were preparing to regroup to the North. It is estimated that about one hundred and twenty thousand Vietminh troops and dependents chose regroupment. Vietminh commanders had strict orders concerning who was to assemble for regroupment and military training and who was to remain in the South as a civilian. They endeavored to select soldiers who possessed combat experience or skills in communications, medical aid, and artillery.

Who were these tough southern soldiers who had fought amid their homes and villages to defeat the French and now, by a treaty decision, had to uproot and leave behind the land of their ancestors?

Vo Van Tan was typical of them. Tan, a twenty-seven-year-old guerrilla, had never been far from his birthplace, a Mekong Delta hamlet, even during the war. The son of a prosperous peasant, Tan had received little formal education before he began tending his aunt's water buffaloes in Hang Doi hamlet. At age eighteen he went to work in his father's rice fields and became a carpenter's apprentice in a nearby village. Then, in 1946, like so many other young men swept into the nationalist struggle against the French, Tan made the biggest decision of his life. He joined the Vietminh. For the next nine years, first as a youth commando and later as a regular in a hamlet guerrilla unit, Tan took part in attacks on scattered French outposts in the delta.

In the first week of October 1954, Tan said good-bye to many relatives and friends and with

At this relocation camp near Saigon, refugees endured overcrowding, poor sanitation, food shortages, and disease. Discontent with conditions in the camps sometimes led to protests and riots.

143

A Vietminh soldier, awaiting regroupment north of the seventeenth parallel, says good-bye to friends and relatives in the South.

three thousand of his comrades boarded a Russian steamer bound for Hanoi. The Vietminh political leaders in Hanoi had issued regroupment orders and Tan, like thousands of other soldiers, resigned himself to his fate.

Unlike the northern refugees who sought permanent homes in the South, most regroupees expected to return from the North within two years. Vietminh leaders had carefully explained to them that national elections would take place in July 1956, after which the soldiers could return to their homes in a united Vietnam under Vietminh control. Nguyen Huu Tho, appointed president of the National Liberation Front in 1961, later said, "There were mixed feelings about the two years delay over reunification, but the general sentiment was that this was a small price to pay for the return to peace and a normal life, free of foreign rule." Their dream, however, did not come true.

The "stay-behinds"

The Vietminh were also highly selective in choosing soldiers to stay in the South and represent their interests there. In 1954, the Vietminh controlled over two-thirds of the South's villages and over one-third of its territory. Its military control in the South was strongest in remote regions like the U Minh forest on the Ca Mau Peninsula or along the Cambodian frontier. Vietminh political influence was pervasive. Cadres maintained a complete parallel, or "shadow," government from village resistance committees through district and province levels. In some areas, Quang Ngai Province for example, the Vietminh provided the only effective government. Joseph Alsop, the columnist, visited a Vietminh zone in the Mekong Delta and was surprised at not finding the bleak, totalitarian atmosphere he expected:

The very face of the countryside told its own story. This is no easy region to defend, with natural strong points and places of refuge. Yet the Vietminh had successfully defended it, with no more elaborate artificial defenses than guerrilla traps around the villages and blockades on the canals to stop the passage of French armed launches. And there, after the long war and the hasty rebuilding of the bombed-out villages, the country looked perceptively more prosperous—with larger palm huts, better vegetable gardens, and more pigs and chickens running in the village streets—than the French-controlled territory.

The Vietminh, forced to demobilize their most reliable cadres for regroupment, recruited youths—often by coercive means—to replace them. To supervise and discipline them, the Vietminh left behind three thousand political and five thousand armed cadres. Although the Vietminh represented a broad coalition of nationalists—non-Communists as well as Communists—Communist party cadres monopolized decision-making authority. According to a ranking party source, the cadres organized young supporters into party committees and youth groups, similar to social and political collectives in North Vietnam. Party and youth group members "were extremely well armed and their main activity was in preserving the secret of their existence. ... They maintained no bases, no camps. ... Each soldier had a hammock which was his home."

The "stay-behinds," however, did not resort to violence or sabotage against the Diem regime. In anticipation of the elections scheduled for July 1956, they conducted organizational and propaganda activities. A cadre recounted that "We were given training about the Geneva Treaty. We were instructed to work normally with the peasants, to earn a living and to explain to them the clauses of the treaty. We pointed out that general elections would be held in 1956." A captured party document explained the rationale for restricting efforts to a political rather than a military struggle: "If, immediately after peace was restored, we had advocated the use of armed forces for struggling, the people would not have listened to us." In urban areas, cadres formed legal and semi-legal societies and political groups to criticize Diem's policies and mobilize support for elections.

Diem tightens the screws

In response to Vietminh propaganda in 1955, Diem initiated the Anti-Communist Denunciation Cam-

paign. Eager to strip the Vietminh of the nationalist claim of representing Communist and non-Communists of all political persuasions, Diem's government no longer called the cadres Vietminh but used the derogatory term "Vietcong," or "Vietnamese Communist." Diem's own corps of cadres, members of the National Revolutionary Movement dominated by his brothers Nhu and Can, organized mass meetings in the countryside to incite peasants to expose and condemn Communists. A Vietminh cadre described these meetings as a "solemn ceremony of denunciation of Communist crimes [at which] the Vietminh flag was publicly torn." At a denunciation rally in 1956, tens of thousands of Saigonese witnessed two thousand former Vietminh cadres "convert" to the government. A Saigon newspaper was immediately shut down by the government for calling it a "puppet show."

The denunciation campaign was largely the work of Diem's Department of Information, which was headed by Tran Chanh Thanh. The fact that Tran was a former Vietminh himself and an administrator of justice in Ho Chi Minh's government explains the obvious resemblance of his denunciation methods to the "people's courts" of North Vietnam. His repressive

Psywar Strikes Again

During the 300-day regroupment period provided by the Geneva accords, Colonel Edward Lansdale's CIA psychological war—"psywar"—teams were active in the South as well as the North. While the Vietminh were using every

means to encourage regroupment, Lansdale's teams schemed to discourage southern soldiers from obeying orders to go North. In a classified report for the period 1954 to 1955 entitled "Highlights of the Year," Lansdale described one of his psywar operations:

Polish and Russian ships had arrived in the South to transport southern Vietminh to Tonkin under the Geneva Agreement. This offered the opportunity for another black psywar strike. A leaflet was developed ... attributed to the Vietminh Resistance Committee [in charge of regroupment]. Among other items, it reassured the Vietminh they would be kept safe below decks from imperialist air and submarine attacks, and requested that warm clothing be brought; the warm clothing item would be coupled with a verbal rumor campaign that the Vietminh were being sent into China as railroad laborers.

The First Armed Propaganda Company printed the leaflets and distributed them by disguising soldiers in civilian clothes and sending them into southern Vietminh zones on foot. Lansdale was more than satisfied with his strategem's

effectiveness: "Intelligence reports ... revealed that [Vietminh] village and delegation committees complained about 'deportation' to the North after distribution of the leaflet. ..."

Lansdale and his CIA teams also played a role in rooting out suspected Vietminh agitators and Communist sympathizers who remained in the South. Various CIA front organizations, ostensibly engaged in construction and community aid projects, cooperated with South Vietnamese government agents on the trail of Vietminh Communists operating in the villages. The Eastern Construction Company, headed by a Filipino named "Frisco" Johnny San Juan, furnished five hundred trained Filipino technicians to South Vietnam and Laos. Their mission was to carry out "unconventional" warfare operations under the cover of a public service group. Another private Filipino public service corporation, Operation Brotherhood, supplied medical services to rural farmers in South Vietnam while closely coordinating with army operations to "clean up" Vietminh stay-behinds.

techniques, which invited neighbors to inform on each other, were evaluated this way by an American observer: "All he knows are the methods that he saw work with the Vietminh. And they do work. He has been terrifically successful, you have to give him that."

A 1956 presidential ordinance authorizing the arrest and detention in political reeducation centers "of all persons deemed dangerous to the state" inflicted hardship and suffering on tens of thousands of people, Communists and non-Communists alike. It did, however, succeed in decimating the Communist party structure in the South. By the summer of 1956, approximately 90 percent of all cells in one province had been smashed; other provinces showed similar results. Many Vietminh cadres surrendered to the government, and some went into hiding. The cadres never forgot the fear and uncertainty that nearly disintegrated the party:

A great many cadres were arrested, and the ones remaining were extremely afraid. Anyone who had been in the resistance was captured on sight. I fled to Saigon. Nobody knew I was a former resistant there. I was trying to get away from my friends.

As this cadre sought refuge in the city, others fled

to former Vietminh strongholds in the remote mountains and jungle areas of the Ca Mau Peninsula and near the Cambodian border. There they banded together and began to reorganize. The cadres always remembered those days of desperation and the lessons it taught them: secrecy and mutual loyalty.

In those days you could say we were 'based' in the mountains, but these were bases for survival. We had no arms at all and barely the means of existence. . . . Control was so close that it was impossible for us cadres to live among the people. But we came down from the hills at night to try to make contacts.

The political struggle for Vietminh cadres was drawing rapidly to a close.

Armed propaganda: a step toward war

October 22, 1957. At 7:25 A.M., as American officers prepared to leave their quarters on the outskirts of Saigon to report for duty, a bomb hidden in a flowerpot outside their building exploded. Two minutes later and a quarter of a mile away, a bomb went off beneath a bus being boarded by American enlisted men. Early that afternoon another blast ripped through the deserted reading room of the United States Information Service library in Saigon. Although eight servicemen were hospitalized—two in critical condition—no one died from the bombings, which the U.S. State Department labeled "part of a Communist plot . . . to embarrass Vietnam's

A revolutionary study group in a South Vietnamese jungle area. Vietminh cadres who stayed behind in the South after the Geneva Agreement met regularly to discuss the revolutionary political theories of Mao and other Communist leaders.

pro-Western president, Ngo Dinh Diem, and to strain relations between his country and the United States."

The bombings were part of a pattern that had begun to emerge months earlier. The Vietminh were back on their feet, this time playing a deadlier game, armed propaganda. There were no longer any illusions about elections, which Diem refused to hold, and the stakes were high: ultimate control of the government of South Vietnam. How did the Vietminh cadres in the South bounce back from what many believed was the brink of extinction? As resilient as it had been against the French, the party managed to turn seeming defeat by imprisonment, reeducation camps, and denunciation into a victory of sorts. It purged itself of "passive, undependable elements," becoming a smaller but more effective and more secret organization. Known party members disappeared to areas where their identities could be hidden. The perhaps 10 or 20 percent of the cadres not exposed or caught by the government practiced the first principle of revolutionary warfare: survival. They formed new cells to rebuild the party structure.

The armed propaganda movement entailed the systematic intimidation and assassination of those in the villages associated with the government. It involved a continuous battle for the allegiance of village peasants between the Vietminh cadres and

Guards arrest a would-be assassin after his attempt to shoot Ngo Dinh Diem at Ban Me Thuot on February 23, 1957.

handfuls of returnees from the North on the one hand and local government officials, militiamen, and the South Vietnamese army on the other. The insurgents correctly identified local government personnel as the weakest link in Diem's chain of command and attacked them with efficiency. Diem himself, by replacing elected village officials with appointed bureaucrats, had made it easier for the Vietminh to inflame peasant resentment against the "outsiders." An authoritative observer stated that "as early as 1957 the cream of village officials had been murdered by the Communists."

The major difference between the Vietminh and the government agents, whether soldiers, Civil Guard, or militia, was that Vietminh cadres went to great lengths to demonstrate the political objectives of their violence to peasants, while the government did not. Although this difference meant nothing to the dead, the living were bound to take notice. A striking example of the cadres' techniques is given in this account of a young peasant villager:

I was not home when my father was killed. I came home at 11:00 P.M.; my father had been killed at about 9:00 P.M.

He was beheaded in front of the house with a sword. The VC [Vietcong] left behind the verdict of the people's court saying that he had perpetrated bloody crimes against the people . . . my first thought was that he was innocent. . . . After the killing the VC often came to my house to educate me. . . . They analyzed my father's crimes. They said my father was a lackey paid by the enemy to harm the people. . . . Thereafter I had no more hatred for the VC because my father was guilty, and had to pay for his crime. I did not believe in his innocence anymore, and I forgot about his death.

Soon afterward, this young man joined the insurgents.

A few bad omens

Saturday, February 23, 1957, was a beautiful sunny day in Ban Me Thuot, and President Diem was savoring every moment of it. His tour of the highlands had been a resounding success. Everywhere he was greeted by cheering crowds, gala receptions, and publicity befitting a leader everyone seemed to admire. Now the president's triumph was approaching. He would address tens of thousands of adoring highlanders in a speech witnessed by the top American brass in South Vietnam. As Diem made his way through the crowds toward the rostrum, attended by a tribal honor guard of mountain warriors armed with spears, a sense of deep pride swelled within him—perhaps he was performing a miracle in South Vietnam after all.

Then, as if out of nowhere, a young man in the crowd raised a weapon and fired at the president. The assassin's submachine gun, leveled at Diem's back, fired rapidly, furiously, spraying bullets all around him. Members of Diem's entourage fell wounded, but somehow the bullets missed the president. When the machine gun jammed, security agents tackled the young man, later described as a Communist, and dragged him away. Diem, seemingly unperturbed, to the wonderment of spectators continued to the rostrum and delivered his speech as if nothing had happened.

Soon other troublesome incidents disturbed Diem's tranquility. Remnants of the Binh Xuyen, now in league with the Vietminh, began marauding along the Saigon River. Within a year there were more brazen attacks. In 1958 a predawn raid of Binh Xuyen bandits supported by Vietminh guerrillas devastated a rubber plantation. For five hours, the raiders sustained a reign of terror, systematically destroying the plantation's power plant, offices, storage buildings, and processing rooms. Their sabotage halted 10 percent of South Vietnam's rubber production and cost the lives of eight South Vietnamese security guards. Similar raids became more frequent toward the end of 1958.

Diem was perplexed. Were not the denunciation campaigns, reeducation camps, and restrictive ordinances working, stamping out the last vestige of Communist activity in the South? Hadn't he convinced the Americans that his "miracle" was real, that his leadership and regime were secure? As before in his career, Diem faced a dilemma. To admit the existence of stepped-up Communist activity would be to acknowledge the failure of his extravagant promises to the people and the Americans. But to ignore the situation could have the most dangerous consequences, giving a freer hand to the Communists and inviting further deterioration of government control in the countryside.

When a Saigon newspaper raised the specter of renewed Communist terrorism, printing an article critical of the government's handling of security problems, Diem made his decision: to cover up the matter. The government shut down the newspaper and fined the editor. The exasperated editor fumed at Diem's "bury your head in the sand" response to what many perceived as a worsening crisis: "I only exercise the right of a free press by warning the authorities, often too much optimistic, against the threat that really exists."

Hanoi: "Let the revolution in the South begin!"

The southern cadres' aggressive tactics also presented party leaders in Hanoi with a dilemma: to urge them on with direction and support or to restrain them, if possible, until North Vietnam was ready to launch the revolution on its own terms. When Hanoi in 1954 had withdrawn most southern fighting forces to the North, the idea was to select the best of them to meet the manpower needs of the regime. In a letter to the regroupees, Ho thanked his southern brothers for their services to the People's Army and to the revitalization of the North:

Since the day you were regrouped here, you have regarded the North as your home . . . and eagerly taken part in the construction of the North. Everyone has endeavored to do his duty.

Ho, however, was confident of victory in the 1956 elections and believed that a military solution to reunification would not be necessary. He stressed to all Vietnamese, especially the southern cadres, that the political struggle for reunification would ultimately be successful:

The regroupment in two regions is a temporary measure: It is a transitional step for the implementation of the armistice and negotiation of peace, and paves the way for national reunification through general election. Regroupment in regions is in no way a partition of our country. . . .

When the political struggle for elections failed, Ho was in a quandary. Southern regroupees in the North were growing restless, and cadres in the South were being steamrollered by Diem's anti-Communist campaign. Le Duan, the party secretary, known to have been in the South in 1956, communicated to Hanoi the plight of the cadres there. According to captured documents, Le Duan expressed his conviction that Diem would eradicate the Communist movement in the South unless Hanoi took action. He felt that Hanoi was "wasting time" in hoping Diem's government would fall and asserted that Diem should be "forcibly overthrown" as soon as possible. Ho and other party leaders, however, chose a different course. Although permitting a trickle of homesick cadres to go south, they continued to play the waiting game.

Even after Moscow's declaration of 1957—which spelled out the "nonpeaceful transition to socialism"

and, Le Duan argued, "created favorable conditions for the revolutionary movement in South Vietnam"— Hanoi hung back. Party leaders still feared conditions in the South were not ripe, that acting too soon might endanger later success. Then in late 1958 Le Duan returned to the South and reported to Hanoi that cadres fighting for their lives there were ready to go ahead with the revolution, with or without the North. This time Hanoi responded positively to Le Duan's assessment of the situation in the South. North Vietnam was finally emerging from the economic doldrums of the mid-1950s, its gross national product (GNP) growing at a healthy rate of 6 percent a year. Foreign aid, Chinese and Russian, was readily available, and foreign trade was up markedly. A "guns and butter" policy was now a viable option.

In May 1959, at the Fifteenth Plenum of the Central Committee of the North Vietnamese Communist party, Hanoi's fateful decision was announced. It called for a "strong North Vietnamese base for helping the South Vietnamese to overthrow Diem and expel the United States." The party's resolution charged the U.S. with being "the main obstacle to the realization of the hopes of the Vietnamese people and an enemy of peace." Southern cadres applauded the resolution, praising it as the turning point in the struggle of all Communists, North and South, to unify the country by force. As for the regroupees, it was time to go home, not to enjoy "peace and unity," but as the vanguard in a bloody war for which few South Vietnamese or Americans were prepared.

Vietminh regroupees from the South meet President Ho Chi Minh in 1957.

A Nation at War

Dusk fell quickly over the quiet crossroads town of Bien Hoa, twenty miles north of Saigon, on July 8, 1959.

For Major Dale Buis of Imperial Beach, California, the steamy humidity of Vietnam was going to take some getting used to. Major Buis had arrived in Bien Hoa only two days before to join the Military Assistance Advisory Group seven-man detachment advising South Vietnam's Seventh Infantry Division. Now, inside a gray stucco sawmill recently converted into an American mess hall, Major Buis showed snapshots of his three young sons to Major Jack Hallet of Baton Rouge, Louisiana, and Captain Howard Boston of Blairsburg, Iowa. Master Sergeant Chester Ovnand finished a letter to his wife in Coppers Cove, Texas, and dropped it in the mess hall mailbox. Two of the Americans drifted off to play tennis. The other six decided to watch a Jeanne Crain movie, *The Tattered Dress*, on a home movie projector.

Absorbed in the first reel of the film, the men didn't hear the six guerrillas who crept out of the darkness alongside the makeshift theater. They didn't hear them ready a French MAT submachine gun in the rear window, push two rifle muzzles through the pantry screens, and take up positions covering the Vietnamese guards at the front of the mess hall. At about 7:00 P.M. the first reel came to an end. Sergeant Ovnand stood up and snapped on the lights.

Instantly high-caliber bullets tore across the mess hall from every direction, killing Ovnand and Buis, and seriously wounding Captain Boston. Major Hallet leaped across Ovnand's body to turn off the lights; otherwise all six Americans might have perished. In the darkness outside, two Vietnamese guards and the mess cook's eight-year-old son, who had been watching the movie through a side window, lay dying.

By the time reinforcements reached the compound fifteen minutes later, the guerrillas had slipped away into the night.

"A nation at war"

Coming as it did during the week of the fifth anniversary of the Diem government, the attack on Bien Hoa was a calculated attempt to embarrass the government and intimidate the Americans. In both respects it was successful. Diem expressed the "profound regret" and "indignation" of the Vietnamese people and staged a protest rally at Bien Hoa where thirty thousand people listened to speakers denounce the "Communist crime" and demand the death penalty for the perpetrators. The guerrillas had already termed July "anti-American month." Now security guards were doubled at the homes and offices of some two thousand American officials and at the MAAG offices in Saigon. American cars were placed under surveillance to prevent the attachment of booby traps, and all packages addressed to Americans were searched. At Bien Hoa the five remaining Americans were on duty the day following the attack. Before they had been unarmed; now each carried a .45 automatic.

For all the publicity it received, however, Bien Hoa was only the most notable of a growing number of in-

cidents during the summer of 1959. Guerrilla units held up a bus, stripped the passengers of their valuables, then demanded "three cheers for Ho Chi Minh." Twenty miles from Saigon, rebels seized a village, then painted propaganda slogans in the streets and on the walls of buildings. During August, a peasant rebellion broke out in Quang Ngai Province in central Vietnam.

In the countryside, assassinations of village officials escalated sharply. From mid-1959 to mid-1960, approximately twenty-five hundred officials were killed, twice the number slain during 1958. American agricultural machinery in villages near the Cambodian border was systematically destroyed. Insurgents conducted vigorous campaigns against schoolteachers, particularly in Long An, Dinh Tuong, and Kien Hoa provinces, kidnapping some, killing a few, and intimidating many. By the end of 1959 thousands of local schools had been forced to close. Terrorism, sabotage, and subversion were no longer sporadic and isolated, but continual, concentrated, and ominous.

More disturbing even than these events, however, was the growing number of armed attacks on villages, highway traffic, and government military outposts. Six former Vietminh bases became the focal points of renewed insurrection. Along the Cambodian border, at the southern tip of the Mekong Delta, and in the forested region north of Saigon, insurgent bands no longer content to pursue political agitation had commenced active rebellion. When guerrillas fell on the government outpost of Trang Sup in Tay Ninh Province, Diem told a French correspondent, "Vietnam is a nation at war."

Some of the insurgent actions during these months represented the continuing resistance of non-Communist groups, including scattered remnants of the Cao Dai and Hoa Hao sects. Unrest also struck the highlands, where government efforts to transplant lowland Vietnamese into paramilitary settlements met increasing montagnard resistance. The energy behind the new insurgency, however, came primarily from Vietminh veterans and from ordinary peasants—beleaguered, disaffected, and increasingly willing to take arms against the Diem regime.

The infiltrators

The insurgent forces, numbering perhaps five thousand by the end of 1959, were in part indigenous and

---

Preceding page. A South Vietnamese Marine patrols the coast in Ben Tre Province looking for junks carrying contraband or soldiers from North Vietnam.

The Infiltrators

The journeys of organized military units from North Vietnam into South Vietnam along the nascent Ho Chi Minh Trail before 1962 have long been secretive and controversial. The infiltrators themselves, however, suffered the same fatigue and fear, hunger and heat that dogged other soldiers in Vietnam. Their scribbled diary entries offer a glimpse into the lives of the dedicated guerrillas.

On July 18, 1961, a sixty-man Vietcong guerrilla unit slipped into South Vietnam's central plateau from Laos. Commanding officer Captain Nguyen Dinh Kieu proclaimed in his dog-eared diary: "From this day on, I am in the Fatherland again." His unit had endured a hard month's hike of over two hundred miles from the North through cold mountainous jungles and soaking monsoon rains, moving each day from one secret camp to the next. Along the way, two of his men had gotten drunk, and Captain Nguyen, worried that deserters or poor discipline would alert South Vietnamese Rangers, had punished them severely. Enemy planes flew overhead constantly once they were inside the South. When some of his men shrank from the sight of bloodshed, Lao Dong party member Nguyen

wrote: "This can be remedied only by intense political activity."

In August, his unit reached its destination, Kon Brai, having suffered only two losses. Nguyen met with district party committee members to map strategy. Soon the squad began to "gather all military power in Safe Base Number 1, then launch[ed] simultaneous attacks all over the mountain area."

Captain Nguyen filled his journal with proverbs echoing those of Chairman Mao and General Giap: "Respect the local population and never touch their property. ... Be extremely friendly with local comrades and very parsimonious with the food supply they give us. ... There will be long marches, no transportation, little food. ... Beware of relations with women. ... Never leave packages of cigarettes at campsites. ... Observe absolute secrecy and discipline. ... Only attack when victory is certain." On September 26, 1961, Captain Nguyen broke that last rule. In a reckless foray against the government-held village of Da Ka Koi, he was killed.

"For two days we have been short of food and had only glutinous rice," Vietcong medical officer Mai Xuan Phong noted in his diary. It was mid-May of 1961, and his unit had just crossed Route 9 west of the DMZ, in Laos. "This portion of our route is really hard," he lamented. "The sun is burning hot. We do not have enough drinking water." Ordered to head further south, Mai reached Darlac Province on August 7 and was attached to a newly formed two-squad unit of mountain tribesmen led by infiltrators from the North. He wrote, "There are no conditions or means for me to operate. There is not sufficient medicine. Life on this base is really difficult." Nevertheless, the unit's "armed propaganda" effort—attacks on land development centers around Ban Me Thuot and mass propaganda—were successful. "We have awakened these people after the dark

years they lived under My-Diem [the American-supported Diem regime]," he wrote. "We seized many documents and much military equipment." On October 3, ARVN forces overran the Vietcong camp and Mai's crude infirmary, capturing a diary but not its author.

Do Luc infiltrated the South in June of 1961. A romantic and lonely man dedicated to the cause, Do Luc had left his girl friend behind in the North. He opened his diary with a message he wished she had sent him: "We are in love and we have talked about that many times. Even though mountains and rivers separate us, I shall wait until the revolution succeeds!"

A native of the highlands, he had joined the Vietminh in March 1954 and went north the following year "a victorious fighter," leaving his family behind. There he became a DRV army regular, working with his comrades to construct factories "under a bright sky and under the superior socialist regime." From December 1960 until May 1961, the veteran Communist guerrilla was in Laos helping the Pathet Lao "annihilate the reactionary clique of Phoumi Nosavan and Boun Oum." And then, Do Luc wrote,

For the third time my life turned to war again. For the liberation of our compatriots in the South, a situation of boiling oil and burning fire is necessary! A situation in which husband is separated from wife, father from son, brother from brother is necessary. I joined the ranks of the liberation army in answer to the call of the front for liberation of the South. Now my life is full of hardship—not enough rice to eat nor salt to give a taste to my tongue, nor enough clothing to keep myself warm. But in my heart I keep loyal to the party and to the people. I am proud and happy.

On September 3, 1961, in a battle near Daktrum, Do Luc was shot and killed.

in part regrouped southern Vietminh infiltrated back into South Vietnam.

When those southerners were regrouped to the North under the Geneva accords of 1954, they entered special North Vietnamese Army regiments that later spearheaded the reinfiltration. Those chosen to return to the South were well prepared. Most had combat experience, and many had learned technical skills in such specialties as communications, demolitions, and medical aid. The regroupees were familiar with the people, culture, and geography of the South and had powerful reasons for wishing to return. They deeply resented what the Diem regime had done to their families and compatriots. Virtually all longed to return home, as the words of two soldiers attest:

I was joyous to learn of my assignment to go south. I was eager to see my home village, to see my family, to get in contact with my wife.

When I received my orders to go south it was the happiest moment of my life, for I would fight, suffer, and win with the people.

At training centers like Xuan Mai near Hanoi, they attended courses lasting from several weeks to several months. Once trained, the regroupees formed into units of from forty to four hundred. A few infiltrated by boat. But most made an arduous one- to two-month trek into South Vietnam, first by truck from North Vietnam into Laos and then by foot along the Ho Chi Minh Trail, a network of relay bases and jungle paths crossing the most inaccessible parts of Laos. By the end of 1959, the southern guerrilla ranks had been bolstered by perhaps a thousand regroupees.

Pacification: the army

How had this relative handful of guerrillas managed to launch and maintain an armed rebellion? They had to their advantage a country ideally suited to guerrilla warfare: impenetrable forests and inaccessible mountains, a vast river delta of endless rice fields crisscrossed by canals and a spider web of footpaths, with safe havens just across the border in the jungles of Laos and Cambodia. They also had in their favor the disorganization and unpopularity of the government. In Diem, they confronted a man of conservative, even reactionary, temper in a social and economic climate demanding radical solutions. Even more valuable, perhaps, was the continued unwillingness of the Diem regime to admit publicly the

full extent of rebellion until insurrection had become civil war.

Nonetheless, South Vietnam was not without the means to defend itself. Ranged against the guerrillas was the military and political establishment of the government of South Vietnam, a nationwide administrative apparatus, a regular army of one hundred and fifty thousand and paramilitary forces totaling an additional ninety thousand men. All this was backed by the military assistance, economic aid, technical cooperation, and political support of the United States.

Nor was Saigon prepared to give in to the rebels. On the contrary, during 1959 and 1960 Diem set in motion a number of pacification measures designed to frustrate the insurgents—military counteroffensives, the resettlement of the civilian population, the establishment of special courts to hunt down Communist agents, and more. That the rebellion continued to grow despite these efforts was not for lack of sufficient resources, but because of peasant hostility, military and administrative incompetence, and a political vision restricted to the single end of keeping the ruling family in power. In fact, much of the government's pacification program proved counterproductive. The resistance increased in proportion to the repression employed by Saigon.

From the beginning of the Diem regime the Army of the Republic of Vietnam (ARVN) had been the government's principal tool for controlling the population. Diem was not prepared to alienate the influential landlord class by carrying out real social reform. Even if he had been willing to take the political risk, he was unlikely to win peasants to his cause by redistributing land they had already received from the Vietminh. As a result, most ARVN operations had less to do with locating the scattered bands of insurgents than with intimidating local villagers into obedience to Saigon.

Trained and equipped by the United States to resist an invasion from North Vietnam, the army was ill equipped to fight a guerrilla war. Many of the regular South Vietnamese divisions occupied static defense positions along the North Vietnamese and Laotian borders. Deployed in part to give validity to southern claims of northern aggressiveness, in part to divert attention from official repression in the coun-

The GVN looked first to the army in its efforts to pacify the countryside and then to a variety of paramilitary groups. This patrol contains both local Civil Guard (in black) and regional Bo An (in khaki) militiamen.

Many villagers felt imprisoned rather than protected in the government's "fortified villages." Here residents of Tam Khanh pose for a village portrait.

tryside, these forces absorbed the bulk of Diem's available military manpower. Those units that did conduct active operations rarely pursued the insurgents into the jungles and paddies. Lacking an adequate intelligence network, traveling in trucks, weapons carriers, and jeeps, the army almost never left the safety of the roads.

The ARVN suffered as well from a divided chain of command. Assessing the risk of weakening the pacification effort as less dangerous than the risk of making a coup easier, Diem refused to delegate military authority to his generals. Instead, he divided it between the generals and the thirty-eight province chiefs, each one directly answerable to him. The same fears led the president to promote officers on the basis of their loyalty to his family rather than their military competence or experience and to rotate senior officers so regularly that no consistent counterinsurgency effort could be mounted.

At U.S. insistence, efforts were made during 1959 to remedy some of these deficiencies. The government began to retrain and reequip the Civil Guard and added ranger units to regular divisions to make the army more operationally flexible. The GVN constructed an enlarged network of bamboo and concrete forts manned by the Civil Guard and the Self-Defense Corps. A Republican Youth Corps was created to help defend hamlets and villages. Simultaneously, American advisers were made available down to regiment and battalion levels.

The army also mounted several major counter-offensives. The most successful was a campaign in the guerrilla-ridden Ca Mau Peninsula carried out by American-trained marines. In two weeks government forces killed three hundred insurgents, captured four hundred, and accepted the surrender of seven hundred more. When the ARVN launched a series of full-scale operations into the Plain of Reeds and eastern Cochin China, however, it met stiff resistance, including resistance from the inhabitants themselves.

Here was the crux of the military's dilemma: the ARVN was a conventional army intent on the conventional objective of defeating the enemy's military forces in the field. At the same time, the army had principal responsibility for maintaining government control over a restive peasant population. When civilians impeded military operations, they were searched, brutalized, their food stolen, their property destroyed, their women assaulted, their lands seized, their families resettled. But the guerrillas were fighting a different war, a political war for political objectives. Their strategy was not to defeat the ARVN in battle, but to gain the support of the civilian population. In turn, the population would become a source of food, clothing, recruits, and operational intelligence. Avoiding confrontations with the numerically superior government troops, using terror selectively, the guerrillas concentrated on destroying the administrative and economic fabric of the Diem regime and on winning over the peasants of the countryside.

Pacification: resettlement

If the army alone could not control the peasants, alternative means had to be found. Another strategy adopted by the government was the resettlement of large numbers of peasant families into fortified villages in the most active insurgent areas.

At the beginning of 1959 the government began to regroup scattered montagnard tribes into defensible communities. This program had the long-run effect of focusing montagnard discontent against the GVN, thus making it easier for the insurgents to subvert the tribes. In an area southwest of Saigon, resettlement was undertaken along political lines. Families with ties to the Vietminh or Vietcong, or suspected of harboring pro-Vietcong sympathies, were grouped into one type of new settlement. Into others the government grouped "loyal" families. Almost immediately peasant opposition developed, and within a few months the action was halted.

In its place emerged the "agroville" program, a concept much hailed in Vietnam and the United States despite its meager success. Borrowed from the British in Malaya, where thousands of ethnic Chinese jungle squatters had been resettled away from guerrilla activity, the agrovilles were to be centers of economic development, political security, and military communication. Each settlement was designed for 400 families (two to three thousand people) with a surrounding cluster of smaller agrovilles of 120 families each. But unlike the British version, each would be built astride a known corridor of Communist infil-

Fortifications in the villages ranged from barbed wire and concrete guard towers to moats bristling with bamboo stakes.

157

tration or in an area of guerrilla concentration. Their construction would be accomplished through the forced labor of peasants, who would then receive a house and a plot of land. The agrovilles were to offer schools, a market center, hospitals, a public garden, electricity, and other amenities of urban life.

Agrovilles were expected to spark the economic development of the rural areas and promote the social revolution of the countryside. Most important, they would "protect" the peasants from the Communists. No longer would the guerrillas "come to the people at night to pester them extorting money and paddy," as one glowing newspaper account read, "and feed them with false propaganda."

To the peasants, who were already angry with the Diem regime because of its land reform policies and

its abolition of village elections, the agrovilles were only another source of discontent. They objected to the forced labor necessary to build them. They objected even more to being uprooted from their ancestral land, from their homes, their tombs, their developed gardens and fields, and sent to strange and often desolate places.

The government master plan called for the completion of eighty agrovilles, sixteen by the end of 1960. By then only eight had been built. Eventually peasant resistance and insurgent attacks led to the abandonment of the program, with only twenty-two completed. After the war it was discovered that the architect of the agroville scheme, Colonel Pham Ngoc Thao, had been a key Communist operative. "His purpose was to antagonize peasants and alienate them from the Diem regime," recalled one of Thao's old comrades, "and it worked."

A South Vietnamese prisoner works in one of Diem's many "reeducation" camps (left). By the late 1950s the camps held an estimated fifty thousand people, most of them anti-Communist opponents of the Diem regime or citizens arrested on "suspicion." Ironically, the poster above this prisoner portrays inmates of a North Vietnamese prison.

Men and women alike were collected for reeducation. Despite the prohibition against mingling of the sexes, children frequently were born and raised in the camps.

Pacification: repression

When Diem was asked about the government's use of force to compel peasants to live in the new settlements, he observed that "coercion has had a vital role in most change." The president rarely displayed any reluctance about using force against the civilian population. Even before the outbreak of active rebellion, Diem had employed the tools of repression to hunt down suspected Communists and anyone else who might challenge his regime. His government sent mobs to wreck the offices of newspapers critical of government policies; established the Can Lao, an elite political police organization; and initiated the Denunciation of Communists Campaign, which sent thousands of Vietnamese to prisons and "reeducation" camps, where torture, blinding, and mutilation were common.

During 1959 the government intensified and expanded the scope of official repression. The denunciation campaign continued apace. In the province of An Xuyen with a population of three hundred thousand, a five-week campaign resulted in the surrender of 8,125 Communist agents and the "denunciation" of 9,806 other agents and 29,978 "sympathizers." The government's semiofficial newspaper, the *Cach Mang Quoc Gia* (National Revolution Daily), outlined a new program, the "radiating" plan, which called for the concentration of military, paramilitary, and police units in a selected number of centers. From these centers government forces would "radiate" out to arrest suspects, using lists compiled during the denunciation campaign, supplemented by names supplied by secret informers in the villages. "Let us mercilessly wipe out the Vietcong," clamored *Cach Mang*, "no longer considering them as human beings."

The heart of the new campaign, however, was the notorious Law 10/59. Under this measure special military courts were established which, upon their own authority, could summon anyone who "commits or *intends to commit* crimes with the aim of sabotage or of infringing upon the security of the State," as well as "whoever belongs to an organization designed to help to prepare or to perpetrate these crimes" (emphasis added). Trial took place within three days of a charge, often within twenty-four hours. The tribunals, accompanied by portable guillotines, rendered one of three decisions: not guilty, life imprisonment, or death. There was no provision for appeal.

American observers often faulted the Diem government for its inefficiency in confronting the insurgents and in promoting social and economic reforms. In so doing, they failed to understand that for Diem the real enemy had never been the sects, the bandits, or the Vietminh. The real enemy had been the people, and particularly the peasants. Against this enemy the government moved with ruthless efficiency. Small wonder then, amid wholesale "denunciations," arbitrary arrests, secret police, drumhead courts, political prisons, forced resettlement, and the depredations of government troops, that terrified peasants would have looked with increasing favor on the only group capable of resisting the Diem regime, the veteran cadres of the Vietminh.

The Caravelle manifesto

The systematic elimination of non-Communist political opposition to the Diem regime left peasants, and other ordinary Vietnamese, with nowhere else to turn. The 1959 elections for the National Assembly are a case in point. In deference to western opinion, the government permitted some independent candidates, like Dr. Pham Quang Dan, the leader of the Free Democratic party, to run for election in Saigon while seeing to it that they could not win. Press censorship kept their names and positions out of the newspapers; the Public Meetings Law prevented them from addressing groups of more than five people; and supporters putting up posters were arrested. Independent candidates were subject to prosecution for any number of fictitious offenses. One candidate was taken to court because a moustache had been drawn on one of her billboard pictures. Another was fined because several of his posters were outlined in red. Other candidacies were invalidated because posters were too big or too small. In all, eight candidates in the Saigon area were disqualified on such grounds.

In the provinces, meanwhile, government officials threatened to arrest would-be candidates and haul them before military courts as Communists unless they withdrew. One National Assembly aspirant recalled:

The 1959 election was very dishonest. Information and Civic Action cadres went around at noon when everyone was home napping and stuffed the ballot boxes. If the results still didn't come out right they were adjusted at district headquarters. . . . The Cong An [special police] beat people and used the "water treatment" [forcing water down a person's throat, or holding his head underwater]. But there was nothing anyone could do. Everyone was too terrified.

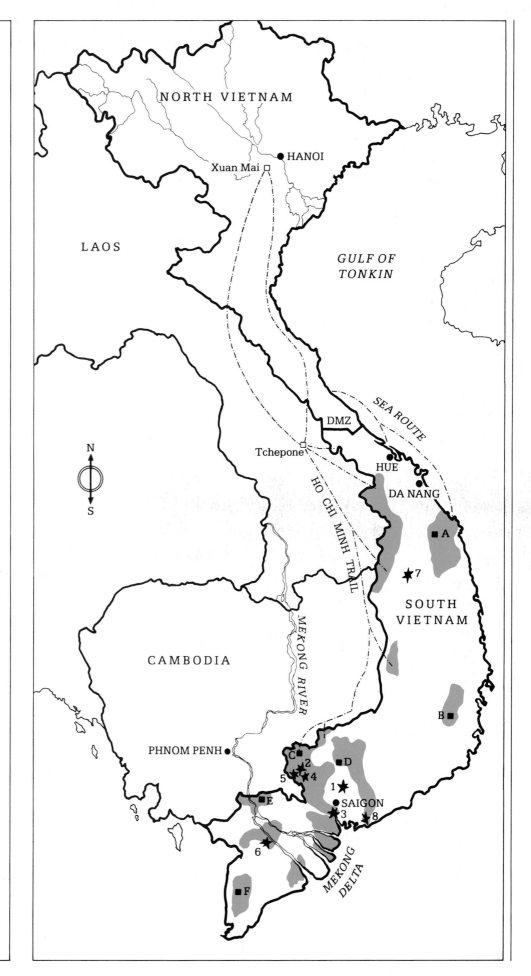

Insurgency in the South

1959–1960

▨	Areas of Insurgent Concentration
✶	Insurgent Attacks (date) (1)
■	Insurgent Bases (A)
□	Infiltration Bases
—·—·—	Infiltration Routes

A	Mang Kim
B	To Hap
C	Duong Minh Chau
D	Phuoc Thanh/Binh Duong
E	Ban O Qua
F	Kien Lam

1	Bien Hoa (7-8-59)
2	Trang Sup (10-59)
3	Can Duoc Dist. (1-60)
4	Tua Hai (2-60)
5	Tay Ninh City (4-60)
6	Can Tho (6-60)
7	Kontum (10-21-60)
8	Long Hai (10-60)

Miles

0   100

A mourner in a Catholic village near Tay Ninh, an area under repeated insurgent attack, burns candles on the coffin of a village guard killed by the guerrillas.

Despite such harassment and intimidation, Dr. Dan won election to the National Assembly, outpolling the government candidate six to one. Diem still had him barred on the trumped-up charge of violating the campaign laws by exceeding his quota of speeches. When Dan entered the assembly and demanded his seat, he was forcibly removed.

By the beginning of 1960, anti-Communist nationalists feared that unless Diem's arbitrary methods were restrained, the Communists would quickly win the sympathy of the people. On April 26 a group of eighteen notables—ten of them former government ministers—assembled at the Caravelle Hotel in Saigon to issue a manifesto warning of the impending catastrophe. Declaring that South Vietnam faced "a situation that is extremely dangerous to the very existence of the nation," the petition charged the government with denying civil liberties, copying "dictatorial Communist methods," conducting one-party rule, and maintaining a corrupt and inefficient bureaucracy. These were, the petitioners admitted, "bitter and harsh truths." But unless the government responded swiftly, the truth would "burst forth in irresistible waves of hatred on the part of a people subjected for a long time to terrible suffering, and a people who shall rise to break the bonds which hold it down."

The Caravelle group announced they would form a national front and attempt to register as a political group. Diem refused to acknowledge their manifesto. Vietnamese newspapers did not report their demands. The petitioners, without a sizable political following of their own and tainted by their earlier association with the French colonial government, got nowhere. It proved to be the last civilian effort to bring the Diem government to heel.

The insurrection: South or North?

A month earlier another manifesto had been hurled at the Diem regime, not by Saigon political figures, but by the insurgents. In a "Declaration of the Veterans of the Resistance," the guerrillas described a reign of terror and declared that Diem had "driven the people of South Vietnam to take up arms in self-defense." Calling for a "democratic government of National Union" to replace "the fascist dictatorship of the Ngo family," the manifesto urged the "full and energetic implementation" of the Geneva accords and the initiation of negotiations with North Vietnam "with a view to the peaceful reunification of the Fatherland." The declaration demanded the elimi-

Village hero: With his handmade machete, Ouk Ton killed six guerrillas attempting to organize his Mekong Delta village.

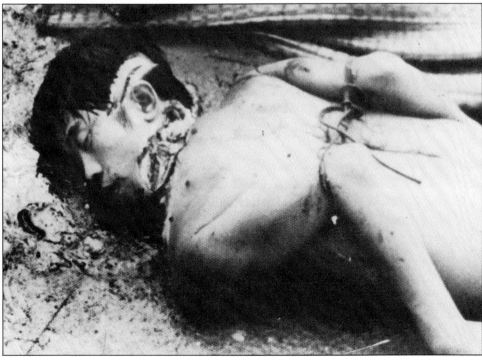

A nearly decapitated victim of the terror campaign waged by Communist insurgents to "punish" those who cooperated with the Diem government. Vietnamese tradition holds that losing one's head condemns the spirit to an eternity of restless wandering.

nation of all United States bases, the expulsion of American military advisers, and an end to American interference in South Vietnam.

Although broadcast over the insurgents' clandestine radio, the Veterans Declaration remained unknown to most Vietnamese. Yet it raises one of the most persistent questions about the origins of the Vietnam War and the assumptions upon which American involvement rested.

The United States government accepted as an absolute political boundary what most Vietnamese, North and South, regarded as nothing more than an artificial and temporary line of demarcation. American officials consistently asserted that the insurrection was conceived and directed by one sovereign nation, North Vietnam, against another, South Vietnam. In testimony before Congress in 1965, Secretary of State Dean Rusk maintained that Hanoi had opted for armed struggle in 1959 because it had given up hope of taking over the rest of Vietnam in any other way and because the South was "far outstripping" the North socially and economically. According to Rusk, Hanoi waited until 1959 to initiate its aggressive program because of continuing domestic difficulties and because the Lao Dong party needed time to organize its forces in the South.

Hanoi, after all, had never regarded the partition of Vietnam as either legitimate or acceptable. By the end of the 1950s the northern regime had sufficiently stabilized its political base to turn its attention once more to reunification. Shortly after Le Duan's trip through the South in late 1958, a South Vietnamese branch of the Vietnamese Communist party was established. And it was soon after the meeting of the Fifteenth Plenum of the Central Committee in Hanoi in May 1959 that the level of fighting in the South increased markedly. It is clear that during the latter part of 1959 Hanoi began to send former Vietminh regroupees and a few northern agents back to the South. By September, Hanoi radio broadcasts termed recent insurgent forays "our attacks" and praised the "skill of our commander and the good will of our soldiers." As for the Declaration of the Veterans of the Resistance, Communist defectors later told an American investigator that the manifesto had been drafted at the direction of the Central Committee of the Lao Dong party and designed with the dual purpose of arousing support in the South for the revolution while obscuring the true leadership of the rebellion.

Others have argued that the insurrection was southern-rooted, a reaction against the repressive measures of the Diem regime; that the North had little choice but to take advantage of a situation of seething discontent. An American anthropologist working in a village in the Mekong Delta reported that by 1958 the area had already experienced the activities of a new political movement called the Mat Tran Dan Toc Giai Phong Mien Nam Viet Nam (National Front for the Liberation of Vietnam). A clandestine radio calling itself the Voice of the South Vietnam Liberation Front began broadcasts in the South in the middle of 1958, calling repeatedly for "struggle against oppression by the dictatorial American Diemists." These broadcasts were denounced by Radio Hanoi as provocations by Saigon and American agents. But they may have been regarded by the northern Communists as a challenge to their established policy which did not call for armed rebellion.

Contrary to official U.S. pronouncements, by 1959 social and economic conditions in South Vietnam were rapidly deteriorating. Diem's failures—not his vaunted miracle—had provided the opportunity for successful insurrection. At the same time, Diem's crude, often brutal pacification efforts were not without result. One veteran Vietminh cadre later recalled the last months of 1959 as "the darkest period for the party in the South, when if you did not have a gun you could not keep your head on your shoulders."

This period was the darkest because of Law 10/59, because of the various political organizations such as the National Revolutionary Movement and the rural youth organizations, and because of the constant military campaigns. There was no place where party members could find rest and security. Almost all were imprisoned and shot.

It was against this background, and the continuing desire for reunification, that the demand for armed resistance grew. The French journalist Jean Lacouture has recorded that an agent from the North attended the meeting of the resistance veterans in March 1960 and reported back that it represented a popular movement that Hanoi would not be able to ignore. Emissaries sent south to test public opinion after the Veterans Declaration were badly received by Vietminh cadres. Lacouture concluded that the leadership in Hanoi did not decide to support armed insurrection "except at the specific demand and under the moral pressure of the militants in the South."

While debate continues over the precise level of Hanoi's involvement in South Vietnam between 1956 and 1960, the totality of the evidence available today suggests that the insurrection was southern-rooted, and that an overwhelming majority of the insurgents was either living in the South at the outbreak of the rebellion or returned to the South from the North where they had been regrouped in 1954. There can be little doubt that the ground was fertile in South Vietnam for armed revolt. It is equally apparent, however, that Hanoi seized on southern discontent at a relatively early date, coordinated overall strategy, provided technical assistance and a modest amount of supplies, and beginning in November 1959, conducted a propaganda offensive that would culminate thirteen months later in the formation of the National Front for the Liberation of South Vietnam.

Direct aggression

In November 1959 orders from the Central Committee in Hanoi reached the district and village level in the South. Armed bands sprang up everywhere and in late January, at the beginning of the celebration of Tet, they attacked. Insurgents raided rubber plantations and government outposts. They broke into a battalion headquarters near the Cambodian border and made off with arms and ammunition. In Long An Province, south of Saigon, a wave of attacks and assassinations turned the holiday period into a week of horror. During the entire previous year, only 3 persons had been assassinated in the province. Now, in the space of a week, 26 people were killed. Many more were slated for execution, but escaped. After a few days of terror a typical police report read: "Five armed men surrounded the home of the hamlet chief, but he had already fled the hamlet several days before." In Long An's Can Duoc District, 90 out of 117 hamlet chiefs resigned, while the rest huddled in market towns near government military outposts. Vietnamese newspapers reported coordinated attacks and individual acts of terrorism all over the delta: 140 army and civilian casualties; 15 kidnapped or missing; 53 Communist deaths; and 323 suspects arrested.

In Kien Hoa Province, Vietminh cadres under the leadership of Madame Nguyen Thi Dinh provoked the first *dong khoi* (concerted uprising) of the insurrection. Insurgent peasant bands isolated government posts, captured government agents, and destroyed the Tan Thoi agroville. Within days the rebellion had spread throughout the province. The insurgents abolished the government village apparatus and redistributed land belonging to "reactionary landlords" to poor peasants. With the weapons they

seized, the peasants established an armed company which, along with scattered guerrilla units from the villages, resisted a large government counterattack.

Government forces suffered their biggest defeat during this Tet offensive at Trang Sup in Tay Ninh Province. The fortress at Trang Sup, a thousand yards long by eight hundred yards wide, surrounded by seven-foot-high earthen ramparts with machine-gun towers at each corner, housed the thirty-second ARVN regiment, numbering two thousand soldiers. On the night of the lunar New Year's eve, bombs planted by guerrilla agents shattered the holiday peace, destroying the radio installations and command post and signaling the guerrilla assault. Two hundred insurgents stormed over the ramparts and made their way to the arms depot as government troops ran screaming from barracks going up in flames. Some surrendered, others rushed outside the fortifications. With the help of porters and some government soldiers who defected to the guerrillas, the insurgents made off with one thousand rifles and automatic weapons. The two battalions sent after the guerrillas pursued them only as far as the nearby jungle. The loss of weapons was serious and embarrassing. The psychological impact of the attack, however, was far more decisive. A few days after the battle one hundred frightened ARVN soldiers deserted the garrison, while local government officials began making judicious contact with the insurgents.

Within weeks the People's Liberation Army of South Vietnam (PLA) announced its formation, and the fighting continued to escalate. In March, insurgents killed or kidnapped an average of 25 local officials each week. In April, the PLA engaged ARVN forces 126 times. Insurgents slipped into the army garrison at Tay Ninh City while most of the regiment was on leave, killed 40 of the 300 men on duty, and took three truckloads of arms and ammunition. At the end of the month, a 100-man guerrilla force infiltrated an ARVN training base, ambushing 250 recruits who were practicing river crossings in rubber rafts. The insurgents killed 50 and captured the rest. They marched their prisoners into the jungle, lectured them on the evils of their government, and sent them home stripped to their shoes.

The guerrilla attacks in the southern provinces had a devastating effect on the government's administrative machinery. Before, government agents could move freely through most of the area while Communist agents operated covertly. Now the situation was reversed. The government apparatus withdrew, tax collections fell off, and with the threat of exposure and capture greatly reduced, peasants began moving into insurgent groups in ever larger numbers.

Between June and October the insurgents strengthened their hold on the Mekong Delta, taking advantage of its ideal guerrilla terrain, exploiting the antagonism of local villagers toward the Catholic refugees from the North who had been resettled there, and cautiously distributing arms to four regiments of Hoa Hao soldiers. Intelligence reports put the guerrilla forces in the delta at between three thousand and five thousand by the middle of 1960. Simultaneously, guerrilla attacks moved closer to the cities. In Can Tho, on the Mekong River, insurgents blew up a large oil storage depot. In July, government forces killed nearly eighty guerrillas in three battles in the Saigon area.

Meanwhile, infiltration from the North continued, with regroupees moving into the central highlands

---

During the aborted 1960 coup against Diem, an insurgent paratroop captain reports the seizure of the presidential guard barracks.

where they joined indigenous guerrilla units and prepared to open a new front in the spreading rebellion. At the end of October, three heavily equipped battalion-strength guerrilla units attacked Kontum, two hundred and fifty miles northwest of Saigon. Hoping to establish a military foothold in the strategic region, or at least erect a protective screen between South Vietnamese garrisons and guerrilla units infiltrating from the North, the insurgent forces overran seven ARVN and Civil Guard posts before being pushed back across the Laotian border by government infantry and paratroop regiments.

On November 8, in the wake of the fierce fighting at Kontum, the Diem government for the first time formally charged North Vietnam with direct aggression, claiming that the enemy had attacked from bases in the North using major units that crossed Laotian territory to reach the battleground. Declaring that the attack "verified" that Laos had become a Communist sanctuary, the government statement warned that "if South Vietnam falls, their victory will be complete in this vital part of the world."

Three days later Diem himself was under attack—not by the guerrillas or the North Vietnamese, but by his own army.

The November coup

In the early morning darkness of November 11, 1960, five crack paratroop battalions, backed by tanks and marines, encircled the presidential palace in central Saigon. There was nothing between them and the overthrow of the Diem regime but a handful of palace guards. Hours later the rebels seized control of the city's radio station and announced that the government had fallen.

The identity of the rebels—part of the Saigon security forces considered most faithful to the president—may have surprised the Saigonese wakened from their sleep by predawn gunfire. But that an attempt should be made to oust Diem came as no shock. For more than a year dissatisfaction with Diem, his government, and his conduct of the war had mounted. The most vocal unhappiness came from the Vietnamese intellectual community, embittered by the president's repressive measures and his refusal to undertake serious administrative reforms. But discontent was most potent within the ranks of the army. American training had made the younger officers, impatient with Diem's absolutism, resentful of presidential favoritism in army promotions, and exasperated with the obstacles Diem placed in their way in the fight against the guerrillas.

Colonel Vuong Van Dong, a leader of the coup, was considered by American military officials to be one of his country's most brilliant young soldiers. But the rebels had blundered badly. Meeting unexpectedly stiff resistance from the Palace Guard, they were content to maintain a cordon around the presidential grounds. Their failure to promptly take over the radio station enabled Diem to prepare a taped appeal to loyal troops which was broadcast at fifteen minute intervals for several hours. Even as thousands of civilians massed before the palace gates carrying banners calling for the ouster of the president and his family, the adroit Diem persuaded the rebels to negotiate their demands. During all-night discussions between the president and Colonel Dong, Diem agreed to dissolve the government, cooperate with the paratroopers' revolutionary council, and join with them in fighting Communist subversives. But by the morning of the twelfth, two infantry divisions loyal to the regime had reached the capital. As they advanced toward the palace grounds, the marines who had fought with the rebels the day before now turned their guns on the insurgents. The paratroopers were driven back to defensive positions around their barracks a half mile away. The rebellion was finished. The coup, in effect, had been talked to death.

On the following morning the *New York Times*, which had frequently complimented Diem on the achievements of his regime, now warned the South Vietnamese president not to ignore the discontent that had provoked the coup attempt. Between insurrection in the countryside and anti-Communist disgust with the authoritarian and reactionary nature of the Diem government, "the president is between two fires, either of which could yet consume him and his regime." Much depended, the newspaper said, on "what reforms he now decides to make to meet such justifiable grievances as may exist among his people."

Diem's concern was less the alleviation of his people's distress, however, than the restoration of his authority. The collapse of the coup was followed by mass arrests of anti-Communists, whether they had

Soldiers loyal to Diem—identified in the confusing battle by red scarves around their necks—relax along a Saigon street after a thirty-hour fight against the insurgent paratroopers.

On December 20, 1960, "somewhere in the South," the National Liberation Front is established. At one of the first meetings, Chairman of the Front Nguyen Huu Tho denounces the U.S.–Diem ("My-Diem") regime.

any connection with the coup or not. Although only one member of the Caravelle group, Tran Van Van, was implicated in the coup, most of the others were immediately rounded up and imprisoned. Dr. Dan, who had thrown in his lot with the conspirators, was arrested, jailed, and tortured.

In the aftermath of the coup, Diem refused to permit any significant troop movements without his personal approval, further crippling the already sagging counterinsurgency efforts. Seeing enemies everywhere, the president withdrew more and more into himself and the narrow circle of his family. Most important of all, with the spectacular failure of the paratroop revolt and the jailing of nationalist opposition leaders, the initiative for change passed wholly to the guerrillas and their Communist allies.

The National Liberation Front

The Communists were ready. The previous twelve months had been a time of escalating armed rebellion. Even more important, it had been a time of intense organizational effort. Down from the North during this period came not only soldiers and supplies but also expertise, experience, and organizational know-how. Beneath the battle that raged throughout the South during the spring and summer of 1960, Communist cadres sounded out potential recruits,

marked likely candidates for leadership roles, held surreptitious meetings, created covert village cells, and made cautious contacts with other disaffected elements. In this effort the Communists worked frequently with non-Communists, muting their ideology in favor of joint hostility to the Diem regime. They drew into their ranks Vietminh veterans, elements of the Cao Dai and Hoa Hao sects, remnants of the Binh Xuyen, university students, farmers from the Mekong Delta, members of the Nationalist party, as well as army deserters, young men fleeing conscription, leaders of splinter political parties, and refugees from the denunciation campaigns. By the end of the year they were prepared to put in place the organization through which the revolution would be carried out.

Meanwhile, North Vietnam had mounted a propaganda campaign that put the blame for the division of Vietnam on the United States. Hanoi denounced American allies in South Vietnam as puppets and lackeys and legitimized northern support for the southern rebellion as a necessary extension of the Vietnamese revolution. In September 1960, the Third Congress of the Lao Dong party publicly committed North Vietnam to the support of the southern insurgency. Delegates to the congress heard Secretary General Le Duan describe the liberation of the South as a "two-stage affair: first, the elimination of the U.S. imperialists and the Ngo Dinh Diem clique, . . . then the establishment of a national democratic coalition government" that would negotiate with the North for reunification. The vehicle for the liberation of the South would be "a united bloc of workers, peasants, and soldiers to bring into being a broad united national front."

On December 20, at a meeting "somewhere in the South" attended by a hundred delegates representing a dozen or more political and religious groups, the National Front for the Liberation of the South—the National Liberation Front (NLF)—was established.

A world away

In Washington, the news made hardly a ripple. The *New York Times* didn't get around to noting the formation of the NLF until the end of March, and then only with a single sentence in the middle of another story. At the beginning of 1961 Americans had other things to occupy their attention: The American-supported regime in Laos was falling apart; mutual hostility had just resulted in the severing of diplomatic relations with Cuba; there was war in Algeria, and crisis in the Belgian Congo. At home the University of Georgia was resisting court orders to desegregate, and the Eisenhower administration had just submitted a record $4 billion welfare appropriation to

Congress. Most diverting of all were the results of the recent national political campaign and the approaching inauguration of the youngest man ever elected to the presidency.

For John Kennedy, too, it was a busy time. There were cabinet selections to be made, a legislative program to begin to pull together, the inaugural address to which he devoted more than a little attention, and endless briefings. President Eisenhower and the young president-elect met twice during the transition. Their last conversation, the day before the inauguration, ranged over a deluge of problems: the balance of payments crisis; the anti-Castro guerrilla forces being trained in Guatemala; and Laos, which Eisenhower described as the key to Southeast Asia. They didn't talk about Saigon or Diem, or the NLF or the Vietcong. And later, when the reins of power had passed into his own hands, Kennedy would recall that final meeting. "You know," he told an aide, with some amazement, "Eisenhower never mentioned it, never uttered the word, Vietnam."

At the Third Congress of the Lao Dong party held in September 1960 in Hanoi, Secretary Le Duan pledged support for the southern insurgency. Liberating the South would be "a two-stage affair: first elimination of the U.S. imperialists and the Ngo Dinh Diem clique ... then the establishment of a national democratic coalition government."

Waging the Cold War

When in the 1950s the American people first focused on the growing conflict in Vietnam, it was through the clouded lens of the Cold War. World War II had left only two nations able to assume global political leadership: the United States and the Soviet Union. Uneasy allies during the war, their basic ideological disagreements fed on the disruptions of the postwar world. Russian domination of Eastern Europe, support for Communist revolutions in Europe and Asia, and successful testing of an atomic bomb provoked fears of Soviet military aggression and world conquest. The United States sought to contain Russian advances by ringing the Soviet sphere with military alliances. With the outbreak of the Korean War in June 1950, this policy was put to a stern test.

Soldiers of Mao Tse-tung's People's Liberation Army, 1951 (left). Although later events would prove otherwise, to most Americans, at the time, Communist China was simply an extension of Soviet military and political power, part of a monolithic world Communist movement controlled from Moscow.

U.S. Marines launch a rocket barrage against Communist positions in Korea. Early victories of United Nations forces (chiefly American and South Korean) were reversed with the Chinese military intervention of November 1950. Although much of the lost ground was made up within six months, warfare continued until an uneasy armistice was signed on July 27, 1953.

Intensification of the Cold War in the early 1950s was accompanied within the United States by a growing fear of Communist "subversion." Between 1947 and 1952, over 6.5 million Americans were checked for security under the Truman loyalty program. Even more ominous were claims made by Wisconsin Senator Joseph McCarthy that hundreds of Communists were at work in the government and armed forces. The denunciation of Alger Hiss, a former State Department official, as a Communist spy and the conviction (and eventual execution) of Ethel and Julius Rosenberg for selling atomic secrets to the Russians, seemed to give credence to McCarthy's charges.

Left. As chairman of a Senate subcommittee, Joseph McCarthy and his demagogic inquiries into alleged Communist penetration of the government bequeathed the epithet "McCarthyism" to the American political vocabulary. The senator's frequently unsubstantiated charges wrecked careers, intimidated officials, and spread an atmosphere of fear and suspicion across the nation before he was finally censured and stilled by his Senate colleagues.

A huge radioactive cloud towers forty thousand feet into the air two minutes after an American hydrogen bomb test in the Pacific in 1951 (above). Russia's acquisition of an atomic bomb in 1949 had ended America's monopoly of nuclear weapons. A new and deadly arms race was underway.

Soviet tanks enter Budapest, November 1956, to crush the Hungarian rebellion. Only months before, Soviet Premier Khrushchev had denounced the "crimes of the Stalin era" in a repudiation of the recent Russian past. But the show of force by Moscow cast doubt on the liberality of Stalin's successors and confirmed American suspicions of Soviet intentions in Europe.

173

U.S. pilot Francis Gary Powers viewing the remains of his U–2 spy plane in a Russian hangar. Powers pleaded guilty to espionage before a high Soviet military tribunal, deepening the chill of the Cold War on the eve of the Kennedy presidency.

A man given to gestures of truculent bravado—he was fond of telling small countries how many bombs it would take to destroy them—Nikita Khrushchev transformed the defensive Cold War waged by Stalin into an aggressive pursuit of Soviet interests around the world.

By mid-decade, America confronted Soviet-style regimes from Berlin to the Pacific. Personifying this Communist colossus in American minds was the new first secretary of the Russian Communist party, Nikita Khrushchev. The son of a Ukrainian miner, Khrushchev rose swiftly through the ranks of the party, gaining effective political control six months after Stalin's death in 1953 and becoming prime minister five years later. Earthy, direct, boastful, and bellicose, Khrushchev alternated between gestures of reconciliation and threats of destruction, calling for "peaceful coexistence" between the Soviet Union and the United States, but warning the western democracies: "We will bury you."

If thoughtful Americans could dismiss Khrushchev's bluster, they could not ignore a series of undeniable Soviet technological achievements: the development of their own hydrogen bomb; the first intercontinental ballistic missile; and Sputnik, the first Earth satellite. Equally striking were Russian political triumphs in Asia, the Middle East, Africa, and Latin America. Meanwhile, the United States was helping to overthrow alleged Communist or pro-Communist governments in Iran (1953) and Guatemala (1954), and helping to install or prop up supposedly prowestern governments in Egypt (1954), Lebanon (1958), and Laos (1959). Six months before the 1960 presidential election, the war of nerves tilted in Russia's direction with the Soviets' announcement that they had shot down an American U-2 spy plane. When President Eisenhower refused to apologize for the incident, Khrushchev made it clear that he would have no serious dealings with Washington until there was a new American president.

An audacious and charismatic figure, Cuba's Fidel Castro marched into Havana in January 1959 pledging a "humanist" revolution that would avoid the errors of both capitalism and communism. But his expropriation of American companies and his growing identification with the Soviet Union angered Washington. Fearing a Russian satellite only ninety miles from American shores, the Eisenhower administration placed an economic embargo on the island nation and began training Cuban exiles for an invasion of their homeland.

Year of Decision

January cold had gripped Washington for a week when the first flakes fell across the capital during the early afternoon of the nineteenth. Within hours icy winds had whipped the heavy snow into drifts, snarling traffic into monumental confusion. Thousands abandoned their cars. Thirty members of the staff found themselves snowbound at the White House, while outside the Kennedy home on N Street, reporters and photographers huddled like patient snowmen, waiting for developments.

But the snow, the wind, even the threat of postponing the next day's events made no visible impression on the young president-elect. From a reception for Eleanor Roosevelt to a concert at Constitution Hall, from an entertainment spectacular at the Armory to a private party at a Washington restaurant, he seemed to defy what nature had hurled across his path. Smiling, laughing, relentless and dominating, unperturbed and indefatigable, he made his way across the city.

An East Berlin soldier breaks for freedom in August 1961, leaping over barbed wire dividing East from West Berlin. The construction of the Berlin Wall in 1961 added to world tension as John Kennedy faced the mounting crisis in Vietnam.

At last toward dawn the snow began to stop. By noon a brilliant sun glittered on the Capitol Plaza. The cold, the snow, the invocation by Boston's Richard Cardinal Cushing, a poem by Vermont's Robert Frost, the rhythmic cadences of the new president as he repeated the oath of office, all echoed a traditional American heritage. "What I want to say," Kennedy had explained to a reporter a week earlier, "is that

Preceding page. Inauguration Day, 1961. "My fellow citizens of the world: Ask not what America will do for you, but what together we can do for the freedom of man."

the spirit of the revolution still is here, still is a part of this country." Now as he addressed the nation, it was to these ideas that he returned.

The torch of leadership had been passed "to a new generation," began the president, "born in this century, tempered by war, disciplined by a hard and bitter peace, proud of our ancient heritage—and unwilling to witness or permit the slow undoing of those human rights to which this nation has always been committed." The world was "very different now" from the world of the first American patriots, but "the same revolutionary beliefs for which our forebears fought are still at issue around the globe."

Let those nations still emerging from centuries of colonialism know our pledge that "one form of colonial control shall not have passed away merely to be replaced by a far more iron tyranny." Let those bil-

At the Vienna Conference of June 1961, JFK meets Soviet Premier Nikita Khrushchev for the first time. The failure of the Vienna meeting to resolve its main issue—the Berlin stalemate—made Kennedy increasingly wary of Soviet expansionism in Asia.

lions struggling daily just to survive know that America is prepared to expend its "best effort" for "whatever period is required."

In all the history of the world, only a few generations had been charged with the responsibility of defending freedom at a moment of genuine peril.

Now the trumpet summons us again—not as a call to arms, though arms we need—not as a call to battle, though embattled we are—but a call to bear the burden of a long twilight struggle. . . .

If the path ahead was long and difficult, if it would demand the utmost of strength and sacrifice, then this was the price the nation would have to pay. "I do not shrink from this responsibility," affirmed the new president, "I welcome it."

The cold war framework

Kennedy's words electrified the throng crowded around the inaugural stand. But amid the cheers and applause, one man sat silently watching. Wrapped in a gray overcoat, his gray hat pulled down over his forehead, Soviet Ambassador Mikhail Menshikov listened impassively, neither frowning nor smiling.

Only two weeks earlier Russian Premier Nikita Khrushchev had thrown down an unmistakable challenge to the new administration. Speaking before the party faithful in Moscow, Khrushchev boasted of com-

179

munism's inevitable triumph and pledged unreserved Soviet support for "wars of national liberation." In Cuba, Algeria, and Vietnam, successful uprisings had already taken place. Soon Asia, Africa, and Latin America would tremble with the shock of revolution. "Communists are revolutionaries," added the premier ominously. "It would be a bad thing if they did not take advantage of new opportunities." As surely as he had inherited the Oval Office and the Lincoln bed, John Kennedy had inherited the Cold War.

Kennedy came into office at a time when the issue of Communist aggression preoccupied American political debate. Global crises, reported *Newsweek* magazine the week of the inauguration, are "stacked up for Mr. Kennedy." Pointing to Europe and the deteriorating situation in Berlin, to Latin America where Castroism was spreading through much of the troubled region, to Africa where Russia was moving "into what once was a Western preserve," the magazine declared that the Communists had "broken through" most of the barriers built by the West to contain them. "The greatest single problem that faces John Kennedy," concluded the report, "and the key to most of his other problems, is how to meet the aggressive power of the Communist bloc."

Kennedy would soon be put to the test. Throughout 1961 the Cold War generated crisis after crisis: the aborted invasion by Cuban refugees at the Bay of Pigs in April; the search for a cease-fire in Laos in May; the truculent summit meeting between Kennedy and Khrushchev in June; the shock of the Berlin Wall in August; and the resumption of Russian atmospheric nuclear testing in September. In these same months Kennedy would be making major adjustments in the defense budget, calling up one hundred and fifty thousand reservists, initiating a national program of fallout shelters for protection against nuclear attack, and orchestrating a new arms build-up to close the so-called "missile gap."

It was in this superheated atmosphere that the first major reappraisal of the American commitment to Vietnam was undertaken. During the course of that year-long review, Kennedy came under intense pressure—from his own advisers, from the Vietnamese, and most of all from the Pentagon—to take decisive military steps to retrieve the situation. For them Vietnam became, more than anything else, a test of will, a line drawn in the sand. Kennedy was himself a cold warrior. Unlike John Foster Dulles, however, he saw that confrontation not as a religious crusade, but

as an ideological contest of power. Wary of casual military involvement, skeptical of the capacity of the United States to police the world, his would be a voice of restraint in the evolution of American policy on Vietnam. But he could never wholly escape the imperatives of the Cold War, never wholly escape his own brave promise to "pay any price, bear any burden, meet any hardship, support any friend, oppose any foe, to assure the survival and the success of liberty."

Situation Vietnam

In the canals of the Mekong Delta and the crowded streets of Saigon, the new president's rhetoric confronted a rapidly deteriorating reality. The National Liberation Front's campaign of terror and propaganda continued unabated. Coordinated military attacks increased as the guerrillas tried to force government troops to withdraw from the villages into the larger towns.

In Washington, the new president had scarcely learned his way around the west wing of the White House, when Vietnam came forcibly to his attention: first in the form of a Counter-Insurgency Plan (CIP) worked up during the last months of the Eisenhower administration; and then in a memorandum on the Vietnam situation from the ubiquitous Colonel, now General Edward Lansdale.

The Counter-Insurgency Plan appeared on Kennedy's desk during his first week in office. It called for additional U.S. aid to support a twenty-thousand-man increase in the ARVN (up to one hundred and seventy thousand men) and to train, equip, and supply a thirty-two-thousand-man addition to the Civil Guard (up to sixty-eight thousand). In exchange, Diem would be asked to consolidate the army chain of command, broaden his government to include opposition leaders in the cabinet, give the National Assembly real power, curb corruption, and launch "civic action" in the countryside to win the loyalty of the peasants. The plan concluded confidently that, if these measures were properly implemented, they would "turn the tide" in the battle against the insurgents.

It was a modest proposal to help the South Vietnamese help themselves, and Kennedy approved the CIP on January 28, virtually without discussion. So it must have been with some impatience that he greeted Walt Rostow four days later, when his adviser brought him the Lansdale memo. His schedule

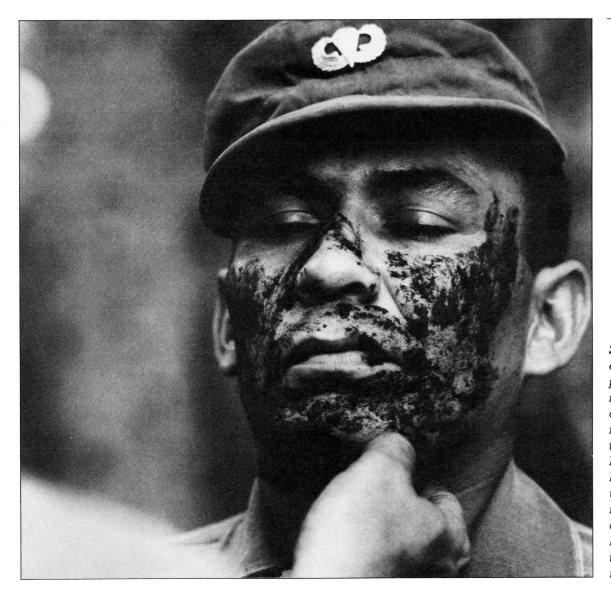

Seven-year army veteran Ace Richardson prepares for night maneuvers in the swamps of North Carolina. During weeks of rugged training, Special Forces volunteers learned how to blow up bridges, parachute into jungle terrain, fire a montagnard crossbow, and choke a sentry to death without making a sound.

was very tight, the president told Rostow. Did he need to read it all? Fifteen minutes later Kennedy looked up. "This is the worst one we've got, isn't it?"

Returning to Washington after several weeks in Vietnam, Lansdale offered a far graver assessment of the situation than had the CIP. South Vietnam was in precarious shape. During the past twelve months the insurgents had swelled in numbers, both through infiltration from the North and through rapid mobilization in the South. They had extended their control over ever-larger sections of the countryside and were now perilously close to a takeover. The South Vietnamese military command was in disarray; the administrative bureaucracy was a shambles. In short, the Diem government was totally unprepared to combat the mounting level of insurrection it now confronted.

Worst of all, in Lansdale's judgment, few in Saigon—Americans or Vietnamese—recognized that South Vietnam faced not merely rebellion, or even

armed aggression directed by Hanoi, but revolutionary war conducted along the lines laid down by Mao and Giap. If South Vietnam was to survive, it would have to radically revise its military thinking. If it was to prevail, it would have to confront the enemy with the tactics and strategy of unconventional warfare.

Kennedy immediately instructed Rostow to find out what the army was doing about counterinsurgency training. He soon learned to his dismay that the Special Forces at Fort Bragg consisted of fewer than a thousand men using outdated training manuals and unsophisticated equipment. Kennedy was determined to do better. At the president's direction the Special Warfare Center began preparing soldiers to challenge guerrillas in the jungles and mountains of the Third World. Training centers in Panama, Okinawa, and West Germany were expanded. The State Department initiated courses in counterinsurgency for Foreign Service officers. The president read works by Mao and the Argentinian guerrilla theorist

Che Guevara, and then pointedly recommended them to all concerned. By the end of the year a Special Group (Counterinsurgency) had been established to coordinate the nation's capacity to wage unconventional warfare.

A confusion of purpose

Meanwhile the administration had to deal with a stubborn ally no less intractable in his way than the shadowy NLF guerrilla. As negotiations over the CIP began in Saigon in mid-February, Washington was determined to gain a commitment from Diem on necessary reforms.

The State Department assumed that essential agreement on the CIP could be reached in two weeks. In fact negotiations lasted nearly three months. Six weeks went by before unanimity had been reached on even the general outlines of the plan. As first MAAG in Saigon and then the Joint Chiefs grew impatient, Washington began to hedge. Since success could not be achieved without the willing cooperation of the Vietnamese, the embassy was instructed not to push Diem too hard. When the long-awaited decrees finally appeared in early May, they were little more than meaningless pieces of paper. Six months later the very same reforms remained high on the administration's agenda. Meanwhile the United States went ahead with the aid package, and Diem got his troops.

Not for the last time did the opportunity to be firm with Diem elude the Kennedy administration. This was due in part to a confusion of purpose within Washington. On the one hand, the State Department believed that only substantial reforms would make it possible for the South Vietnamese to successfully resist Communist insurrection. On the other hand, there was constant pressure from the military, and others, to get on with the war.

For his part, Diem remained an ardent Vietnamese nationalist, suspicious of foreign interference and irritated by the assumption that if only the Vietnamese would listen to American advice their country might amount to something. Increasingly, he avoided having to listen to such suggestions by the simple expedient of doing all the talking himself. Diem's monologues were already legendary, but during 1961 they passed all bounds, frequently lasting six, seven, even twelve hours. Whether this was a tactic or a disease, it made "negotiations" an interminable

process. Perhaps most important, Diem knew he was in the driver's seat. Without a ready alternative—and Diem had seen to it that there was none—Washington either had to live with him or risk "losing" South Vietnam altogether, a politically unacceptable prospect for a Democratic president whose party had paid dearly for "losing" China to communism only a decade earlier.

In any case, the South Vietnamese president had more immediate concerns in the spring of 1961 than the CIP. Presidential elections planned for early April gave him an opportunity to impress Washington with his popular support, but they also offered the insurgents a tantalizing opportunity to embarrass his regime. Diem had nothing to fear from his two obscure opponents—a rubber planter and a doctor of Oriental medicine—but government troops could not prevent the guerrillas from threatening village notables, forc-

ing peasants to tear up voting and identity cards in hopes of minimizing the turnout, and warning of a major offensive on the day of the election. In Saigon, grenades took two lives and wounded more than twenty people, two of them Americans, in the last days before the balloting.

The threatened attack, however, never materialized. Washington issued an election eve statement of support, and Diem was reelected to another six-year term, capturing nearly 80 percent of the vote. But beneath the official reports and the heavy voter turnout lay disturbing signs. Many voters apparently went to the polls to have their registration cards clipped, fearing that the lack of this badge of citizenship might lead to future difficulties with the authorities. Even so, nearly 25 percent of Saigon's seven hundred thousand voters stayed away from the polls. Of those who did vote, fewer than half cast their ballot for Diem.

A new direction

Just before the election the *Times of Vietnam* reported that Washington "has now fully examined" the situation and "decided that the wisest course is to continue to extend its support to the present Vietnam Government." In fact, up to this point the Kennedy administration had simply followed policy lines established during the Eisenhower years. It was only in late April that the new administration began to establish its own policy on Vietnam.

Diem emerged the overwhelming victor in the controlled elections of 1961, thanks in part to these students parading in his behalf. The president faced no serious opposition, and many Saigon intellectual and professional figures refused to vote.

The job of conducting this review was turned over to an interagency task force headed by Deputy Secretary of Defense Roswell Gilpatric. But before Kennedy came to any decision, the State Department and the Joint Chiefs of Staff would have their say, and above the policy battle loomed the imposing figure of General Douglas E. MacArthur.

The task force was established on April 20, the day after the Cuban invasion force had surrendered at the Bay of Pigs, and delivered its report on the twenty-seventh, as the cease-fire in Laos threatened to unravel. From this time on, until Kennedy made his first major decision on Vietnam two weeks later, the Vietnam problem was debated in an atmosphere dominated by events in Laos and by the reverberations of the Cuban disaster.

Kennedy received the task force report on a day of prolonged meetings on the Laos crisis and was little comforted by its conclusion that the security situation in neighboring South Vietnam had become critical. To meet the emergency, the task force recommended U.S. support for a two-division increase in the South Vietnamese army, and, in an unprecedented proposal, recommended breaking through the Geneva-imposed ceiling on American military forces in Vietnam by deploying thirty-six hundred U.S. soldiers to train the new ARVN divisions. In a covering memorandum to the president, Gilpatric added his personal suggestion that General Lansdale proceed to Vietnam as operations officer of the task force to make further suggestions for direct American action.

The recommendations for American troop deployment were a direct response to the Laos situation. The crux of this first effort by the new administration to define a direction of its own in Vietnam, however, was the proposed Lansdale mission. When he set the task force in motion, Kennedy wasn't looking for a new program, but a new man, steeped in the wiles of counterinsurgency, to take command of the old program. Lansdale, the thinly disguised hero of the 1958 bestseller *The Ugly American* (and the villain of Graham Greene's 1955 novel *The Quiet American*), seemed the perfect choice.

But under the impact of Laos, the focus of review shifted from the Pentagon to the State Department, and there the task force report fell into the hands of George Ball.

Presidential program for Vietnam

As deputy undersecretary of state for economic af-

fairs, Ball had spent the first months of the new administration almost wholly on European matters. But he had long been dubious about American involvement in Indochina, let alone any steps that might drag the United States into another land war on the Asian continent. Nor did the undersecretary have any great confidence in Lansdale, a man "whose time had passed," whose solutions were more appropriate to the far less complex Philippine context of the early fifties than to the Vietnam of 1961. During the first week of May, Ball made a series of revisions to the task force report that drastically reshaped the proposed dimensions of American involvement in South Vietnam.

The State Department version of the task force report took a large step backward from the level of commitment proposed by the Pentagon. Lansdale's role was eliminated, the task force itself to be replaced by a new group under State's direction. The Defense recommendation that the U.S. declare its intention to intervene unilaterally if necessary to save South Vietnam from communism was replaced by a proposal to explore a new bilateral treaty. The military actions recommended by Defense were incorporated unchanged, but they were placed in an annex to the State report and labeled a matter for "further study." Deployment of U.S. troops in particular was made less definite: State called it something that "might result" from further discussions with the Vietnamese. And where the Gilpatric draft had avoided any suggestion of demanding reforms from the Diem government in exchange for U.S. aid, State called for a "major alteration in the present government structure of South Vietnam," suggesting that a combination of inducements and pressure might still bring Diem around.

The Pentagon didn't give up without a fight. After receiving the Ball revisions, Gilpatric asked the Joint Chiefs for their views on the commitment of U.S. troops to Vietnam. They replied with an emphatic recommendation for the deployment of sufficient American forces to provide a visible deterrent to further aggression by North Vietnam or China.

Against the clamor for strong American action from the Defense Department and the Joint Chiefs, Kennedy had in State a staunch ally. Now he found another—and a most unexpected one at that—General Douglas MacArthur. At a meeting at the White House on April 28, MacArthur told the president it would be a "mistake" to fight in Southeast Asia. "He thinks our line should be Japan, Formosa, and the

Philippines," the president noted in a private memorandum. Encouraged by the general's advice, Kennedy brought him back to Washington to meet with a group of congressional leaders. MacArthur told the legislators that the United States would be foolish to fight on the Asia continent. The future of Southeast Asia should be determined through negotiation. Maxwell Taylor, Kennedy's senior military adviser, thought that MacArthur's advice had "made a hell of an impression on the president. ... Whenever he'd get this military advice from the Joint Chiefs or from me or anyone else, he'd say, 'Well, now, gentlemen, you go back and convince General MacArthur, then I'll be convinced.' None of us," Taylor added, "undertook the task."

The Presidential Program for Vietnam, as it became known, was embodied in a National Security Action Memorandum dated May 11, 1961, and followed closely State's recommendations. The president directed the Defense Department to undertake a "full examination" of the size and composition of forces that would be necessary should the United States decide to commit troops to Vietnam. The ambassador in Saigon was empowered to open negotiations on a bilateral treaty with Saigon but was explicitly advised to make no commitments without review by the president. To help the South Vietnamese cope with the mounting insurrection, the United States agreed to provide equipment, cooperate on health, welfare, and public work projects, and deploy a four hundred–man Special Forces group to Nha Trang to accelerate ARVN training.

The May decisions

What can we make of these May decisions? Kennedy had inherited a substantial, if not very specific commitment to South Vietnam. For fifteen years the containment of communism had been the keystone of

World War II hero and master strategist General Douglas MacArthur (center) watches what many have called his most brilliant stroke: The September 1950 landing at Inchon Beach, Korea, which crushed the North Korean army's attempted takeover of South Korea. MacArthur later warned President Kennedy against involving the U.S. in another Asian land war, this one in Vietnam.

The Laos Crisis

On the final day of his presidency, Dwight D. Eisenhower led John F. Kennedy into a cabinet room filled with advisers for a last transition meeting in which Ike bequeathed the nation's problems to his successor. The talk—of anti-Castro Cuban exiles training in Guatemala, of the balance of payments crisis—was somber. But the most immediately dangerous "mess" he was passing on, said Eisenhower, existed in Laos. A Communist takeover there would put "unbelievable pressure" on Thailand, Cambodia, and South Vietnam. SEATO nations France and Britain hesitated to act. If no other nation would help, then the United States should be willing to intervene alone. "You might have to go in there and fight it out," Eisenhower suggested.

Kennedy was furious. Eisenhower, the soldier-statesman so proud that no war had started during his eight years in office, was handing a prospective war over to his successor. In the first two months of his presidency, Kennedy devoted more time and task force studies to Laos than to any other problem.

A landlocked country of just over 2 million people, Laos resembles Italy without the heel and toe. Two-thirds of the country is forested, and more than half the population lives in the South, subsisting as farmers along the Mekong River and its tributaries. Little touched by modern civilization, Laos has no railroads; its roads

and trails are limited. The ambition of the apolitical, predominantly Buddhist people, until recent years has been to be left alone. Politics was the preserve of a small elite (many of them related), which had begun a movement for independence from France after World War II.

That movement succeeded in 1954 when Laos gained independence as part of the Geneva Agreement, which also prohibited foreign military aid and bases but permitted exceptions for defense installations. With the French withdrawal (a military training mission remained, however), America moved to turn the country into a "bulwark against communism." By 1960 the United States had pumped nearly $300 million—$150 per

President Kennedy demonstrates the progress of Communist insurgency in Laos during a press conference on March 23, 1961. That day he called the Communist threat to Laos "difficult and potentially dangerous." The crisis in Laos dragged on into 1962.

capita—into this primitive land, 85 percent of which paid for the build-up of the Royal Laotian Army. Under an operation called White Star, the Special Forces trained Meo and other mountainous tribesmen as counterinsurgent guerrillas.

American aid also financed a tide of corruption, bribery, and waste. Imported automobiles crowded the dusty streets of Vientiane, the administrative capital, and army officers lived off American patronage. The widening gap between the affluent capital and the poor countryside allowed the Pathet Lao—a Communist insurrectionist group founded in 1950 by Prince Souphanouvong, under the tutelage of Ho Chi Minh—to gather support in the villages and consolidate control of the two provinces it occupied with the help of the Vietminh.

In 1957 neutralist Prince Souvanna Phouma, leader of the royal forces, negotiated with the Pathet Lao of Prince Souphanouvong (who happened to be his half brother). They signed the Vientiane Agreements, establishing a neutral Laos under coalition government. Displeased with finding Communists in power, the Eisenhower administration, under CIA aegis, set up the Committee for the Defense of the National Interests (CDNI), installing right-wing General Phoumi Nosavan as chief and scuttling the neutralist coalition. Prince Souvanna was ousted and his counterpart, Prince Souphanouvong, was jailed. He soon escaped and led the Pathet Lao back to the mountains. The civil war resumed.

It caused few casualties, however. General Phoumi's handsomely paid army was useless in battle. "Your chief of staff couldn't lead a platoon around the corner to buy a newspaper," the American ambassador once told him. Another diplomat repeated a briefing from an American military adviser who reported great improvements in the Laotian army: "Only a few months ago, the Laotians used to retreat without their weapons; now they take their weapons with them when they run away."

In August 1960, paratroop Captain Kong Le seized Vientiane on a day when Phoumi was out of town. He invited Prince Souvanna to reestablish a neutralist government. Phoumi then proclaimed his own government and marched on the capital in December 1960. Souvanna fled to Cambodia, and Kong Le and his troops joined up with the Pathet Lao.

Having rejected the neutral alternative, the Eisenhower administration drove the neutralist forces into a reluctant alliance with the Communists. In response the Soviet Union was soon airlifting forty-five tons of arms and munitions daily from Hanoi.

In February 1961, a few weeks after Kennedy's inauguration, General Phoumi embarked on a campaign to recover the strategic Plain of Jars in Pathet Lao–controlled north central Laos. Though superior in numbers, the American-trained, American-equipped soldiers broke and ran on hearing that the North Vietnamese were fighting on the other side. Eisenhower's strategy, inherited by Kennedy, was in a shambles and the country lay open.

The Joint Chiefs of Staff warned Kennedy that sending American troops could provoke a Communist escalation in the twin forms of Vietminh pouring across the border and the ultimate possibility of war with China. Either go in full-scale, they said, with sixty thousand soldiers and air cover (and prepare to use nuclear weapons should the Chinese intervene), or back off. Kennedy was reluctant to send in troops. Although he did not think Laos "worthy of engaging the attention of great powers," he recognized that American prestige now was involved. "We cannot and will not accept any visible humiliation over Laos," he said.

On March 23, he held a televised press conference against the backdrop of three maps showing the gains of Communists supported by the Soviet Union. "The security of Southeast Asia will be endangered if Laos loses its neutral independence," he said gravely. "Its own safety runs with the safety of us all." Kennedy alerted combat troops in Okinawa, sent five hundred marines to rest at anchor off Bangkok, Thailand, and moved the Seventh Fleet into the South China Sea.

On April 1, Soviet Premier Nikita Khrushchev expressed his willingness in principle to consider a cease-fire. "Why take risks over Laos?" he said to Ambassador Llewellyn Thompson. "It will fall into our laps like a ripe apple." But Khrushchev delayed, in part to explain his policy to the Pathet Lao and Chinese, in part to allow the Pathet Lao time to capture more territory.

While the diplomats maneuvered, Kennedy faced a crisis—the Bay of Pigs—in which he vetoed any military force. Lest the Soviets misinterpret that restraint, he maintained his aggressive posture in Laos, where fighting continued, by placing ten thousand marines in Okinawa on alert once again. (The Joint Chiefs had increased their troop estimate to one hundred and forty thousand.)

On April 24, the Soviets agreed to a cease-fire which took effect May 1. In the opinion of adviser Arthur Schlesinger, Kennedy, prepared to undertake a limited intervention, had been chastened by the Bay of Pigs. "If it hadn't been for Cuba, we might be about to intervene in Laos," Kennedy had told him.

An international conference attended by fourteen nations convened in Geneva on May 16, 1961. Represented by the skillful diplomat Averell Harriman, the United States pressed for a coalition government. Harriman, who favored Prince Souvanna Phouma as head of state, had managed to persuade the United States that Souvanna, in spite of having accepted aid from the Soviets, was not a Communist. After fourteen grinding months, the Laos accords, signed in late July 1962, established a "government of national union" under Prince Souvanna. Though the neutralist government was given a short life expectancy, the United States had decided that Laos was too fragile a place from which to oppose Communist expansion in Southeast Asia. If the line was to be held, the place to hold it was in nationalist Vietnam.

American foreign policy. On it depended, or so many American officials believed, the continued economic and political preeminence of the United States and its allies. More narrowly, the United States, which had used its considerable influence to neutralize internal opposition to the Diem regime, bore the chief responsibility for the South Vietnamese government. Now the mounting insurrection, Diem's pleas for additional military aid, and the collapse of the American position in Laos created tremendous pressure on the new administration to "do something."

By all accounts, the military situation, though serious, was retrievable. To have simply given up on Vietnam without making any effort to determine whether the situation could be saved at a reasonable cost seemed out of the question to Washington. To have opened negotiations with the Communists with an eye toward establishing a coalition government, as in Laos, appeared similarly impossible. Diem had effectively silenced South Vietnam's sizable neutralist faction. To find a more effective partner than Diem with whom to work meant taking unknown risks. Moreover, in the wake of the American pullback from Laos, it would hardly be reassuring to other Asian anti-Communist leaders to dispense with one of the most heralded among them.

In fact, these initial Kennedy decisions didn't commit the United States significantly further than had the Eisenhower administration. On the question of military assistance in particular, Kennedy had not gone beyond the program in Laos—advisers, material, and some covert combat assistance. Indeed, what marks the May decisions more sharply than anything else is their general tone of almost unqualified American support for Vietnam, hedged in on all substantive issues—the precise nature of American commitment to South Vietnam, U.S. support of the Diem regime, the dispatch of American military forces—by qualifications that left the president a great deal of freedom to maneuver. From the administration's point of view, it was a minimal response. Kennedy was determined to go forward, but slowly. He would see what the South Vietnamese would do for themselves.

The Johnson mission

The man Kennedy dispatched during the second week of May to carry the administration's program to Saigon was Vice President Lyndon Johnson. After talks at the presidential palace, Johnson left Vietnam in an expansive mood. "I have never attended a conference of any kind in thirty years that was more productive or more cordial," he told reporters. "President Diem is the Churchill of the decade. . . . He will fight communism in the streets and alleys, and when his hands are torn he will fight it with his feet."

Back in Washington, Johnson reported to the president that his mission had "arrested the decline of confidence" in U.S. intentions but had not restored the confidence already lost. He had found Diem a man of "admirable qualities . . . surrounded by persons less admirable than he," remote from his people, yet indispensable to American interests. The United States "must decide whether to support Diem," said Johnson flatly, "or let Vietnam fall." The South Vietnamese president had shown no interest in a bilateral treaty. American troops were neither required nor desired. But the U.S. must be prepared to extend increased amounts of military and economic assistance. The fundamental decision, the vice president believed, was "whether to meet the challenge of Communist expansion now in Southeast Asia or throw in the towel in the area and pull back our defenses to San Francisco and a 'Fortress America' concept."

The Johnson trip, a public relations triumph on both sides of the Pacific, confirmed the administration's initial decision to cast its lot with Diem. Despite Diem's reluctance to accept them, it also prompted renewed calls from U.S. military officials for the introduction of American soldiers. The vice president had scarcely left Tan Son Nhut Airport when Lansdale sent a memorandum to Gilpatric pointing out that while Diem had rejected American combat troops, he seemed more willing to accept American soldiers for training purposes. General Lyman L. Lemnitzer, chairman of the Joint Chiefs of Staff, had already let it be known during a trip of his own to Asia that he supported the use of U.S. soldiers against Communist guerrilla activity in Vietnam. Now MAAG Chief General Lionel McGarr weighed in with a request for sixteen thousand American troops whose nominal mission would be to establish ARVN training centers, but who would also be capable of undertaking combat assignments.

This kind of military involvement remained alien to the White House, where the outlines of a new but much less extensive commitment were beginning to take shape. In a note to Secretary of Defense Robert McNamara written during the first week of June, Walt Rostow proposed the force levels needed to support a counterguerrilla war in Vietnam. Rostow cited aircraft, helicopters, communications men, special forces, and militia teachers but did not mention combat units. Not only was the Rostow note a precise description of the kind of military assistance that Kennedy would ultimately dispatch to Vietnam (combat support and advisers, but no independent combat units); it also suggests the growing distance between the Pentagon's wish to go in with as much as possible and the president's desire to defer any steps likely to lead to confrontation on the ground between American soldiers and Vietnamese guerrillas.

But in Saigon, McGarr continued to urge on Diem the necessity of an enlarged U.S. military contingent. During their talks in May, Johnson had requested that South Vietnam outline its military needs. Now, Diem made his wishes known. He told Kennedy that the insurrection in his country "has risen to the scale of a bloody, Communist-inspired civil war." Indicating that he had sought McGarr's advice in drafting the proposals, Diem requested American support for an ARVN force of two hundred and seventy thousand (an increase of one hundred thousand over the CIP proposal only finally agreed upon a month earlier) and a "considerable expansion" of American military personnel to staff training centers for combat leaders and technical specialists.

The Diem request sharpened administration concern over the continuing problem of how Vietnam was to finance its own war effort. But by now the issue of force levels had come to dominate discussion on Vietnam. The Staley mission, a team of economists led by Eugene Staley of Stanford University, went to Vietnam in mid-June to explore how Saigon might take on a greater share of the war's financial burden. They returned with a number of rather vague economic proposals and two specific recommendations on the size of the South Vietnamese army: two hundred thousand men if the insurgency remained at present levels; two hundred and seventy thousand if the level of insurrection increased, or if the Communists gained control of Laos. Meanwhile, on the ground in South Vietnam, the "bloody civil war" continued without rest.

The summer offensive

The Johnson and Staley missions had at least had a bracing effect in Saigon. Through the summer months GVN officials issued daily reports of military success against the guerrillas. In the middle of July, government units took on a five hundred-man NLF force in the marshes of Kien Tuong Province, eighty miles west of Saigon, in the biggest battle since the rebellion began in earnest two years earlier. The large insurgent contingent, armed with mortars, machine guns, rifles, and grenades, blundered into a government ambush where it was pinned down by heavy gunfire and cut to pieces. In the fierce fighting nearly two hundred guerrillas were killed and many more wounded. After the day-long battle, the bodies of the dead lay strewn across two miles of marshland, the flags of the NLF still fluttering in the humid air.

Part of the credit for the government victories could be traced to the stepped-up training being conducted by American advisers. With the help of the additional Special Forces soldiers authorized by President Kennedy in May, four separate commando training centers were put into operation. When they first arrived at the centers, many of the Vietnamese recruits could not read a map or a compass and talked so loudly on patrol that, according to one American instructor, "The dogs in every village were barking for miles around." By the end of the summer some seventy commando companies—nearly seven thousand soldiers—had learned how to scale cliffs, operate cable pulleys, walk noiselessly in the jungle, and kill swiftly. The best units had even launched clandestine operations into North Vietnam.

But for all the new equipment, the Special Forces advisers, and the growing number of South Vietnamese offensives, NLF military units continued to push forward. By midsummer "hard-core" guerrilla forces had grown to over twelve thousand, almost double the number at the beginning of the year. The return of regroupees from the North accounted for some of the additional insurgents. But most were recruited in the villages of the South. From bases north and west of Kontum, NLF units harassed the highlands as far south as Ban Me Thuot, where a guerrilla band ambushed and killed two members of the National Assembly. Just north of Saigon, the front's operations reached from the mountains on the Cambodian border almost down to the sea. The front controlled at least a quarter of the villages in the Mekong Delta and had won nocturnal control of perhaps 70 percent of the countryside. Repeated raids near Saigon had reduced the area of reasonable security to the city's border.

It was from Saigon in late August that the White House received a most discouraging report from the American journalist Theodore White:

The situation gets worse almost week by week. ... The guerrillas now control almost all the southern delta—so much so that I could find no American who would drive me outside Saigon in his car even by day without a military convoy. ...

White reported a "political breakdown of formidable proportions: ... What perplexes the hell out of me is that the Commies, on their side, seem to be able to find people willing to die for their cause. ... I find it discouraging to spend a night in a Saigon nightclub full of young fellows of twenty and twenty-five dancing and jitterbugging, while twenty miles away their Communist contemporaries are terrorizing the countryside." Alluding to the American experience in China, White spelled out the dilemma facing the Kennedy administration. "If a defeat in South Vietnam is to be considered our defeat, if we are responsible for holding that area, then we must have authority to act. And that means intervention in Vietnamese politics." But if we do intervene, he asked pointedly, "have we the proper personnel, the proper instruments, the proper clarity of objectives to intervene successfully?"

"A real war"

Within a few weeks after Kennedy received White's letter, NLF regular forces launched a major offensive in central Vietnam. Units numbering as many as one thousand men attacked government outposts, villages, even provincial towns. Attacks more than tripled, from one hundred and fifty a month to over four hundred and fifty in September. Most spectacular of all was the seizure of Phuoc Vinh, the capital of Phuoc Long Province, on September 18.

Captured guerrillas await interrogation beside the bodies of their dead comrades. Although the action whose results are pictured here took place in 1962, it was similar to numerous earlier South Vietnamese counteroffensives.

Vietnamese soldiers complained of "dancing with death" while their more fortunate peers were "dancing with girls" in Saigon. Eventually a morality law decreed that a prostitute caught three times with different men was subject to arrest.

The insurgents captured the town early in the morning, held it most of the day, publicly beheaded Diem's province chief before a huge crowd, and then departed before government troops could arrive. Phuoc Vinh shattered morale in Saigon, only sixty miles south. Government officials feared that the NLF intended to create a "liberated area" in which it would install a shadow government. When the rebels launched a second heavy attack in Darlac Province on September 22, taking hostage an American aid expert, an atmosphere of crisis took hold in South Vietnam. "It's no longer a guerrilla war," Diem told the National Assembly, "but a real war."

At this point Diem began to change his mind about the nature and amount of American support he required. On October 1 he reversed position and requested a bilateral treaty with the United States. Two weeks later, he asked for an additional fighter-bomber squadron, civilian pilots for helicopters and C-47 transport aircraft, and U.S. combat units for a "combat-training" mission near the demilitarized zone. Diem also broached with Ambassador Frederick Nolting the possibility of stationing American troops in a number of provincial capitals in the highlands as a "symbolic" gesture of support and to free ARVN forces for counterguerrilla operations.

Under Diem's prodding, the question of dispatching U.S. troops reached center stage in Washington. Walt Rostow suggested a 25,000-man SEATO force to guard the Vietnam-Laos border. The Joint Chiefs rejected the proposal, arguing that the troops would be poorly located to halt a potential invasion and stretched too thin to stop infiltration. They favored instead a "concentrated effort" in Laos, but if that were politically unacceptable, the deployment of 20,000 soldiers to the central highlands near Pleiku. The 20,000-man figure, however, was only a stopgap. The Chiefs estimated that 40,000 U.S. soldiers would be required to "clean up the Vietcong threat," and another 128,000 in the event of active North Vietnamese or Chinese Communist intervention. Even the

State Department got into the act. Alexis Johnson, deputy undersecretary for political affairs, "guessed" that three divisions of 13,750 men each would be the ultimate force required to defeat the insurgents.

All of these proposals were considered at a National Security Council meeting on October 11. That afternoon Kennedy announced that his military adviser, General Maxwell Taylor, would go to South Vietnam to make a personal assessment of the situation there.

The Taylor mission

Taylor left Washington for Saigon on October 18, bringing along Walt Rostow as his deputy and a plane full of military experts, State Department observers, and civilian technicians. The fact that the mission was commanded by a general, with a White House aide as deputy, but no figure of comparable rank from the State Department, suggested the extent to which Secretary of State Dean Rusk had left the problem to Kennedy and Defense. If Kennedy acquiesced because of his personal confidence in Taylor, it was a decision that would color the recommendations he received and perpetuate the assumption that Vietnam was primarily a military, rather than a political problem.

Their plane touched down in a Saigon reeling from military and economic blows. Continuing the shift of their activities from the delta to an area north of Saigon, NLF cadres were regrouping into battalions capable of taking on ARVN bases formerly considered secure. Meanwhile floods along the Mekong River had created a twenty-five-hundred-square-mile inland sea, destroying the rice surplus for the next year, killing thousands of livestock, and ruining farm machinery. The devastation left two hundred thousand homes underwater and 1.5 million people with little or nothing to eat. With the floods and the war, rice stocks in Saigon fell to an all-time low, and prices skyrocketed. On the day the Taylor group arrived, Diem went before the National Assembly to proclaim a state of emergency.

What Taylor discovered in Vietnam, he told the president on his return to Washington a week later, was a pervasive crisis of confidence: doubt that America was determined to save Southeast Asia from communism; doubt that Diem's methods could defeat the NLF. Bad tactics and bad administrative procedures had permitted insurgent gains, invited a political crisis, and led to a serious loss of Vietnamese

After an all-night patrol, Master Sergeant Antonio Duarte eats with his Vietnamese army trainees. By mid-1961 several hundred Americans like Duarte were involved in the conflict.

morale. But Taylor found Diem, "with all his weaknesses," a man of "extraordinary ability, stubbornness, and guts" and rejected any suggestion that he be replaced.

Taylor's recommendations rested on two primary assumptions: first, the necessity of a strong, unequivocal military commitment to South Vietnam; and second, the belief that the weaknesses of Diem's regime could be overcome if enough Americans—civilian and military alike—took an active role in showing the Vietnamese how to win the war. By improving its intelligence of NLF activities, by loosening administrative impediments to more effective military action, and by getting the ARVN to take the offensive, South Vietnam could go a long way toward defending itself.

But not, thought Taylor, far enough. There was an American role to play beyond military aid and technical assistance. The United States should "offer" the

South Vietnamese an American military task force of between six thousand and ten thousand men. Introduced for flood control operations in the delta, the task force would be a symbol of American resolve. It would constitute a military reserve on which the ARVN might draw and act as an advance group for whatever additional American forces might later be required. Meanwhile, the task force would "conduct such combat operations as are necessary for self-defense and for the security of the area in which [it] is stationed."

"No limit to our commitment"

Taylor was well aware of the implications of taking such a decisive step. Although American prestige was currently engaged in South Vietnam, it would only become more so by sending troops. Any introduction of U.S. forces would heighten tensions in the region and risk escalation into a major war. But worst of all, the introduction of American forces was a beginning without an end. "If the first contingent is not enough to accomplish the necessary results it will

General Maxwell D. Taylor meets with South Vietnamese Major General Duong Van "Big" Minh in October 1961. A large man with a gap-toothed grin, Minh was critical of Diem's handling of the war. The Taylor mission reported to Kennedy that Diem's methods could not defeat the NLF.

be difficult to resist the pressure to reinforce. If the ultimate result sought is the closing of the frontiers and the cleanup of the insurgents within South Vietnam, there is no limit to our possible commitment."

These disadvantages, however, were outweighed in Taylor's mind by other factors. There could be "no action so convincing of U.S. seriousness of purpose, and hence so reassuring" to our friends and allies in Southeast Asia, as the introduction of U.S. forces into the area. Moreover, Taylor considered South Vietnam "not an excessively difficult or unpleasant place to operate." The risks of backing into a major Asian war were "present but ... not impressive." North Vietnam was "extremely vulnerable to conventional bombing," a weakness that could be diplomatically exploited.

Both North Vietnam and China, argued Taylor, would confront "severe logistical difficulties in trying to maintain strong forces in the field." Finally, there was "no case for fearing a mass onslaught of Communist manpower into South Vietnam and its neighboring states," particularly if our air power was allowed a "free hand" against logistical targets. Taylor concluded that the introduction of a U.S. military task force without delay offered far more advantages than difficulties, far more opportunities than risks. "In fact," he concluded, "I do not believe that our program to save South Vietnam will succeed without it."

But what made Vietnam so important to the United States? To George Ball and a few others at the State Department, what the United States faced in Vietnam was not Soviet aggression but Tonkinese imperialism. The rebellion, as far as Ball was concerned, was a "tribal" war in which the United States took part only at its peril. But to Taylor, as to most of Kennedy's advisers, South Vietnam was falling victim to "a clear and systematic" Communist strategy to extend its power and influence wherever possible, by whatever means necessary. The only thing that could halt this onrushing catastrophe was "a hard U.S. commitment to the ground in Vietnam," and soon.

The Vietnam program: first phase

Reflecting later on the reception of his report, Taylor couldn't recall "anyone who was strongly against, except one man and that was the president. The president just didn't want to be convinced that this was the right thing to do." All year long Kennedy had been under pressure—on Cuba, on Laos, on Berlin, and now on Vietnam—to confront with forceful action

what was perceived as Communist aggression. But for all his own cold war rhetoric, Kennedy saw America's role in somewhat different terms. In a speech delivered during Taylor's absence in Vietnam, Kennedy had asked Americans to "face the fact that the United States is neither omnipotent nor omniscient," that there "cannot be an American solution to every world problem." Pointing out that Americans comprised only 6 percent of the earth's people, he reminded his countrymen that they had neither the right nor the capacity to impose their will on the rest of the world. After he received Taylor's report, he told a presidential adviser: "They want a force of American troops. They say it's necessary in order to restore confidence and maintain morale. But it will be just like Berlin. The troops will march in; the bands will play; the crowds will cheer; and in four days everyone will have forgotten. Then we will be told we have to send in more troops."

Others shared the president's misgivings, especially at the State Department. Averell Harriman, Kennedy's choice to head the U.S. delegation at the Laos peace conference, disputed the Taylor conclusion that the crisis of confidence was military in origin, arguing instead that the gravity of the situation in Vietnam was the result of a political failure: Diem's unwillingness or incapacity to serve the needs of the villages, and his repressive response to a peasant-based insurrection.

Perhaps most far-seeing of all was Sterling Cottrell, chairman of the Vietnam Task Force, who had also traveled to Saigon with the Taylor group. Cottrell pointed out that the war going on in Vietnam was waged in the villages. The battle must be joined and could only be won at that level. But foreign soldiers could not themselves win the battle at the village level. He concluded it would be a fundamental mistake for the United States to commit itself irrevocably to the defeat of communism in South Vietnam.

But Defense had one last round to fire. In a memorandum to the president on November 8, McNamara recommended that "we do commit the U.S. to the clear objective of preventing the fall of South Vietnam to communism, and that we support this commitment by the necessary military actions." The secretary of defense asserted that the fall of Vietnam would have "extremely serious" strategic implications worldwide and that the chances were probably "sharply against" preventing that fall without the introduction of U.S. troops. But success could not be guaranteed; and McNamara was at pains to spell out the "ulti-

195

mate possible extent" of American military commitment: six divisions and support units, or about two hundred and five thousand men.

This was not what the president wanted to hear, nor was it altogether satisfactory to Secretary of State Rusk. Almost certainly with the blessing, if not at the direction of the president, Rusk persuaded McNamara to reconsider his position. The memorandum they jointly produced on November 11 retained the commitment of the United States to prevent the fall of South Vietnam to communism and included contingency planning for military action against "the source of aggression in North Vietnam." But any decision to commit combat ground forces to South Vietnam was deferred. Instead, the military courses of action were divided into two phases. Under Phase A, the United States would immediately dispatch support troops and equipment, including helicopters, transport aircraft, air reconnaissance equipment, small craft, and intelligence equipment, along with the uniformed and civilian advisers necessary for training and operations. Phase A also called for administrators and advisers to assume positions in the governmental machinery of South Vietnam. Phase B projected the further study and possible deployment of major ground forces at a later date. In return, Diem would be expected to carry out military, political, economic, and social reforms much like those requested in May, and, in addition, join in a "limited partnership" with American military and embassy officials in the conduct of the war.

Kennedy now had a joint recommendation from his secretaries of defense and state telling him almost exactly what he wanted to hear. With one crucial deletion—their recommendation that the United States formally commit itself to saving South Vietnam—the Rusk–McNamara memo became on November 15 the First Phase of Vietnam Program, the guiding recommendations for the next two years and more of American involvement in South Vietnam.

The November decisions

When Taylor returned to Washington in early November, three questions remained to be answered. What level of formal commitment would the United States give to South Vietnam? What conditions, if any, would be attached to new American aid? Would the combat task force recommended by Taylor be deployed?

Intelligence estimates that North Vietnam would respond to increased American support for the Diem regime with increased support for the insurgents, plus his experience with Diem over the past year, dissuaded the president from any open-ended commitment to the defense of the South. Nor was Kennedy inclined to increase substantially American aid to the Saigon regime without putting pressure on Diem to move forward on social and economic reforms.

As vital as these questions were, the central issue had become the question of troops. There were a number of possible reasons for Kennedy's negative decision: his concern that the introduction of combat units would upset the negotiations over Laos; his lack of confidence in the advice of his military advisers— even his hand-picked military advisers—after Cuba and Laos; his conviction that, in the end, fighting the insurgents was primarily a South Vietnamese job; and his fear that, once the first soldiers were on the ground and taking casualties, the pressure to send more troops would be intense.

"Within five years we could have three hundred thousand men in the paddies and jungles and never find them again," George Ball had warned the president in early November. At the time, Kennedy had replied with some asperity: "George, you're just crazier than hell. That just isn't going to happen." But he too had his doubts about introducing troops. "It's like taking a drink," he remarked. "The effect wears off and you have to take another."

John Kennedy began his administration with a call for international firmness and domestic sacrifice. Eager to recapture an image of decisiveness in the wake of the Bay of Pigs fiasco, the Vienna summit, and the Laos crisis, yet doubtful about the prospects for long-term success, he adopted the strategy of doing what was minimally necessary to forestall a Communist takeover of South Vietnam. Like George Ball he regarded Vietnam as a quagmire, but unlike Ball he was confident that he could maintain control over events.

The November decisions were designed to keep the U.S. commitment within bounds and Kennedy's options open. He did not tie military assistance

The Departments of State and Defense disagreed over the level of U.S. commitment to South Vietnam in the first months of the Kennedy administration. But Secretary of State Dean Rusk (left) and Secretary of Defense Robert McNamara temporarily ended the debate with their joint memorandum of November 11. It called for U.S. commitment to South Vietnam but not for the dispatch of American troops.

directly to political reforms but rejected a larger U.S. military presence because of the absence of such reforms. He deferred the introduction of combat units but did not rule them out as a future alternative. He escalated his rhetoric about the importance of Vietnam but carefully avoided any formal, open-ended commitment.

Presidents could not talk about Vietnam being vital to American interests, however, without making its defense an article of American faith. Nor could they encourage planning within the government for greatly increased levels of military and political involvement and assume that such planning would not take on a life of its own. Throughout 1961 the president contended with what Leslie Gelb, the editor of the *Pentagon Papers*, has called a "preconceived consensus to go on." By November the issue had boiled down to a simple equation: the costs of pulling out—in American prestige abroad, in political consequences at home—seemed much greater to Kennedy than the costs of going forward. He had inherited what he took to be a political and national responsibility. If all it required was a few thousand advisers and a bit more military aid to meet that responsibility, it seemed a small step to take. It was a step, however, that maintained the momentum of American involvement, a momentum which would prove exceedingly difficult to arrest.

Washington and Saigon

Whatever the reasoning behind Kennedy's decision, it was taken by press and public alike as a decision to defer a decision. The general outlines of the package of American assistance that would be dispatched to South Vietnam had been the subject of public discussion for so long that it stirred little concern and even less interest. A number of other crises—at the UN, in the Congo, on nuclear testing, and in Berlin where a symbolic confrontation between Soviet and American tanks had just taken place—preoccupied public attention. Sending equipment and advisers to South Vietnam, even in much greater numbers, seemed by comparison small potatoes.

In Saigon the mood was considerably less sanguine. Kennedy had ended up offering Diem less than he was expecting, and at a steeper price than he was prepared to pay. Diem was especially disappointed that the Taylor task force was scrapped, wondering aloud if the U.S. was getting ready to back out of Vietnam, as it had already done in Laos. An anti-American campaign broke out in the gov-ernment-controlled Vietnamese press. One Saigon newspaper published an eight-column headline reading: "Republic of Vietnam Is Not a Guinea Pig for Capitalist Imperialism." Diem's brother Nhu objected bitterly that American insistence on social, economic, and political reforms was interference in Vietnamese internal affairs and irrelevant to the main task of defeating the insurgents.

In the end, Washington backed down. Diem's unhappiness at the new American demands for reform had already provoked an awkward public squabble and might lead to renewed pressure on the president to send the combat task force after all. So instead of a "limited partnership," Washington now asked only that "in operations directly related to the security situation, one party will not take decisions or actions affecting the other without full and frank prior consultations." Once the U.S. backed away, Diem proved amenable to a statement of agreed principles

Destination: Vietnam. The arrival of these thirty-three American helicopters in Saigon in December 1961 raised the level of U.S. participation in the civil war raging across the Vietnamese countryside.

and measures. Whether this would result in anything more substantial than similar statements in the past remained to be seen. Meanwhile, the promised additional military support had already begun to arrive.

A beginning without an end

On December 11, the aircraft ferry Core reached Saigon carrying thirty-three (C) H–21C twin-rotor helicopters, their pilots and ground crews. The aircraft were to be assigned to support South Vietnamese units but would remain under U.S. Army control and operation. The four hundred men in the two helicopter companies raised the total number of United States military personnel in Vietnam to fifteen hundred. "Many more," the New York Times reported, "are expected."

By November 1963, there would be more than 16,000 American soldiers in South Vietnam. Between 1961 and 1963, American forces would participate in hundreds of armed confrontations, chalk up some seven thousand air sorties, lose twenty-three aircraft, and suffer the deaths of 108 men. Americans at home would learn of "strategic hamlets" and "open zones." They would read reports of a new exodus of refugees. And they would watch with confusion as Buddhist bonzes set themselves afire and military conspirators, with American approval, overthrew the Diem regime in a bloody coup. Most of all, they would be bewildered by the tenacity of the elusive, pajama-clad figures the soldiers called "Victor Charlie."

Already by the time the first American contingent reached South Vietnam, regular NLF forces numbering fifteen thousand were organized into at least twenty-seven main force battalions operating from well concealed fortified bases and war zones scattered throughout the South. They had extended their influence in varying degrees to about 80 percent of the countryside. Attacking now in battalion, as well as company and platoon strength, the insurgents destroyed charcoal kilns and disrupted convoys creating an acute fuel shortage in Saigon, hacked to pieces the north-south railroad leading from the capital to the northern frontier, ambushed and killed forty Civil Guards in Phu Yen Province, and derailed a train from Saigon to Nha Trang. Every government soldier on the train vanished. At year's end, the war was consuming a thousand lives a week.

Whatever the fate of the new advisers would be, their presence in Vietnam, in numbers greatly in ex-

Following page. Sergeant William Bowen, one of the first of the new American advisers, conducts an operational training mission with Vietnamese volunteers. The Kennedy administration hoped that advisers like Bowen would make deeper U.S. military involvement unnecessary.

cess of what the Geneva accords permitted, was something of a diplomatic embarrassment. In December the State Department released a white paper entitled A Threat to the Peace, ostensibly documenting massive violations of the Geneva accords by North Vietnam. According to the white paper, which had been in preparation for several months, the NLF was simply a creature of the northern Communists, Hanoi was supporting the southern insurgency with arms and men, and infiltration of military and espionage units had assumed "ominous proportions." In fact, the report grossly exaggerated the amount and significance of outside support for the insurgency, contradicting not only CIA estimates but even internal memoranda of the State Department itself. Nonetheless, a case had been made, and the deployment of equipment and advisers went forward.

As the State Department white paper was being released in Washington, another kind of drama was taking place thousands of miles away in the southern highlands of South Vietnam. The tribesmen of the village of Buon Enao had assembled to affirm their allegiance to the South Vietnamese government. Armed with crossbows and spears, they publicly pledged that no Vietcong would enter their village or receive assistance of any kind. A few days later a seven-man detachment of the U.S. First Special Forces Group arrived to train the people of Buon Enao and to establish a strike force made up of tribesmen from the surrounding villages.

So began America's longest war. Like the Chinese and the French before them, the Americans had come to fight in Vietnam.

Special to the New York Times

WASHINGTON, Dec. 19—United States military men in South Vietnam were understood today to be operating in battle areas with South Vietnamese forces that are fighting Communist guerrillas.

Bibliography

I. Books and Articles

Abbas, Ferhat. *Guerre et Revolution: La Nuit Coloniale.* Julliard, 1962.

Adair, Gilbert. *Vietnam On Film.* Proteus Books, 1981.

Alsop, Joseph. "A Reporter at Large." *The New Yorker,* (1955), p. 48.

American University. *Case Studies in Insurgency and Revolutionary Warfare: Vietnam 1941:1954.* Special Operations Research Office, 1964.

Andrews, William R. *The Village War. Vietnamese Communist Revolutionary Activities in Dinh Tuong Province, 1960-1964.* University of Missouri Press, 1973.

Archer, Jules. *Ho Chi Minh: Legend of Hanoi.* Crowell-Collier Press, 1971.

Asprey, Robert Brown. "Guerrilla Warfare." *Encyclopaedia Brittannica Macropaedia,* 1974.

"Atlantic Report." *Atlantic Monthly,* October 1961.

Bain, Chester. *Vietnam: The Roots of Conflict.* Prentice-Hall, 1967.

Berrigan, D. "I Saw the French Losing Indo-China." *The Saturday Evening Post,* March 18, 1950.

Bodard, Lucien. *The Quicksand War: Prelude to Vietnam.* Trans. Patrick O'Brian. Atlantic-Little Brown, 1967.

Bouscaren, A. T. "France and Graham Greene v. America and Diem." *Catholic World,* 181(1955).

Brown, Malcolm W. *The New Face of War.* Bobbs-Merrill Co., 1965.

Burchett, Wilfred G. *Vietnam: Inside Story of the Guerrilla War.* International Publishers, 1965.

Buttinger, Joseph. *Vietnam: A Dragon Embattled.* Vols. 1,2. Praeger, 1967.

Carver, George A., Jr. "The Faceless Viet Cong." *Foreign Affairs,* April 1966, pp. 347-72.

Chen, King C. *Vietnam and China, 1938-1954.* Princeton University Press, 1969.

Cherne, Leo. "Deepening Red Shadow Over Vietnam." *The New York Times Magazine,* April 9, 1961.

Child, F. C. "Vietnam: The Eleventh Hour." *The New Republic,* December 4, 1961.

Cole, Allen, ed. *Conflict in Indochina and its International Repercussions.* Cornell University Press, 1956.

Conley, Michael Charles. *The Communist Insurgent Infrastructure in South Vietnam: A Study of Organization and Strategy.* Center for Research in Social Systems, American University, 1968.

"Conversation with General Giap On the Battle of Dienbienphu." *Vietnamese Studies,* 3(1965), pp. 8-21.

Cooper, Chester. *The Lost Crusade: America in Vietnam.* Fawcett, 1972.

Corley, Francis. "Vietnam Since Geneva." *Fordham University Quarterly,* 33(1958-59).

Crozier, Brian. "Diem Regime in Southern Vietnam." *Far Eastern Survey,* 24(1955).

Davidson, W. P., and Zasloff, J. J. *A Profile of Viet Cong Cadres.* Rand Corporation RM-4983-1, 1966.

"Defense of Vietnam." *Commonweal,* October 20, 1961.

Denton, F. *Volunteers for the Viet Cong.* Rand Corporation RM-5647, 1968.

Devillers, Philippe. "The Struggle for the Unification of Vietnam." *The China Quarterly,* 9(1962), pp. 2-23.

Devillers, Philippe, and Lacouture, Jean. *End of a War: Indochina, 1954.* Trans. Alexander Lieven and Adam Roberts. Praeger, 1969.

Dooley, Tom. *Deliver Us From Evil.* Farrar, Strauss, and Cudahy, 1956.

Dorsey, John T. "South Vietnam in Perspective." *Far Eastern Survey,* 27(1958).

Doyon, Jacques. *Les Soldats Blancs de Hô Chi-Minh.* Fayard, 1973.

Draper, Theodore. *Abuse of Power.* Viking Press, 1967.

Du Berrier, Hilaire.
 Background to Betrayal. Western Islands, 1965.
 "Report from Saigon." *American Mercury,* 87(1958).

Du Chatelle, Maj. R. Ronssin. "The War in Indochina." *Military Review,* February 1966.

Duncanson, Dennis J. *Government and Revolution in Vietnam.* Oxford University Press, 1968.

Eden, Anthony. *Full Circle: The Memoirs of Anthony Eden.* Houghton Mifflin, Co., 1960.

Encyclopedia Americana, s.v. "Foreign Legion."

Encyclopaedia Brittanica, s.v. "French Foreign Legion."

Fall, Bernard B.
 Dien Bien Phu: Un Coin D'Enfer. Trans. Michel Carrière. Robert Laffout, 1968.
 Hell in a Very Small Place: The Siege of Dien Bien Phu. Pall Mall Press, 1967.
 "Indochina, The Last Year of the War: Communist Organization and Tactics." *Military Review,* October 1956.
 "Indochina, the Last Year of the War: The Navarre Plan." *Military Review,* December 1956.
 "Indochina: The Seven-Year Dilemma." *Military Review,* October 1953.
 Political Development of Viet-Nam: VJ Day to the Geneva Cease-Fire. 3 Vols. Ann Arbor, Mich.: University Microfilms, 1955.
 "South Viet-Nam's Internal Problems." *Pacific Affairs,* 31(1958), pp. 241-60.
 Street Without Joy. The Stackpole Co., 1964.
 "The Political Religious Sects of Viet-Nam." *Pacific Affairs,* 28(1955), pp. 235-53.
 The Two Viet-Nams: A Political and Military Analysis. Praeger, 1963.
 The Viet Minh Regime: Government and Administration in the DRVN. Institute of Pacific Relations, 1956.
 Viet-Nam Witness: 1953-1966. Praeger, 1966.
 "Viet-Nam's Chinese Problem." *Far Eastern Survey,* 27(1958), pp. 65-72.
 "Will South Viet-Nam Be Next?" *Nation,* May 31, 1958.

Fauvet, Jacques. *La Quatrième République.* Fayard, 1959.

Fishel, Wesley R.
 "Free Vietnam Since Geneva." *Yale Review,* 49(1959), pp. 68-79.
 "Vietnam's War of Attrition." *New Leader,* December 7, 1959.

Fishel, Wesley R., ed. *Vietnam: Anatomy of a Conflict.* F. E. Peacock Publishers, Inc., 1968.

FitzGerald, Frances. *Fire in the Lake: The Vietnamese and the Americans in Vietnam.* Atlantic-Little Brown, 1972.

Gettleman, Marvin E., ed. *Vietnam.* Fawcett, 1965.

Gheddo, Pierro. *The Cross and the Bo-Tree: Catholics and Buddhists in Vietnam.* Trans. Charles Underhill Quinn. Sheed & Ward, 1970.

Giap, Vo Nguyen.
 Dien Bien Phu. Foreign Languages Publishing House, 1962.
 People's War, People's Army: The Viet Công Insurrection Manual for Under-developed Countries. Praeger, 1962.

Gittinger, J. "Rent Reductions and Tenure Security in Free Vietnam." *Journal of Farm Economics,* 39 (1957).

Goodman, G.J.W. "Unconventional Warriors." *Esquire,* November 1961.

Graebner, Norman A. *Nationalism and Communism in Asia: The American Response.* D.C. Heath, Co., 1977.

Grant, J.A.C. "The Vietnam Constitution of 1956." *American Political Science Review,* 56(1958), pp. 437-63.

Grauwin, Paul. *Doctor at Dienbienphu.* J. Day Co., 1955.

Greene, Graham.
 "Indo-China." *The New Republic,* April 5, 1954.
 The Quiet American. Penguin Books, 1955.
 "To Hope Till Hope Creates." *The New Republic,* April 12, 1954.
 Ways of Escape. Simon & Schuster, 1980.

Greenhouse, Lee. *Hollywood's Wartime Depiction of Vietnam.* Harvard College Honors Thesis, 1978.

Gurtov, Melvin. *The First Vietnam Crisis: Chinese Communist Strategy and United States Involvement, 1953-54.* Columbia University Press, 1967.

Halberstam, David. *The Best and the Brightest.* Random House, 1972.

Hammer, Ellen J.
 "Parties and Politics in Vietnam." *Foreign Affairs Reports,* 2(1954), pp. 145-58.
 "Progress Report on South Vietnam." *Pacific Affairs,* 30(1957), pp. 221-35.
 The Struggle for Indochina. Stanford University Press, 1954.
 "Vietnam, 1956." *Journal of International Affairs,* 10(1956), pp. 28-48.

Henderson, William. "South Vietnam Finds Itself." *Foreign Affairs,* 35(1957), pp. 283-94.

Hickey, Gerald C. *Village in Vietnam.* Yale University Press, 1964.

Ho Chi Minh. *Selected Works.* Vols. 1-4. Foreign Languages Publishing House, 1960.

Hoang Van Chi. *From Colonialism to Communism—A Case History of North Vietnam.* Praeger, 1964.

Hoang Van Thai, Lt. Gen. *Some Aspects of Guerrilla Warfare in Vietnam.* Foreign Languages Publishing House, 1965.

Honey, P. J., ed. *North Vietnam Today.* Praeger, 1962.

Hoopes, Townsend. *The Devil and John Foster Dulles.* Little, Brown & Co., 1973.

Hotham, David.
 "South Vietnam—Shaky Bastion." *The New Republic,* 1957.
 "U.S. Aid to Vietnam—A Balance Sheet." *The Reporter,* (1957), pp. 30-3.

Isaacs, Harold. "Peace Comes to Saigon." *Harpers,* March 1946.

Jumper, Roy.
 "Mandarin Bureaucracy and Politics in Southern Vietnam." *Pacific Affairs,* 30(1957), pp. 47-58.
 "Sects and Communism in South Vietnam." *Orbis,* 3(1959), pp. 85-96.
 "The Communist Challenge to South Vietnam." *Far Eastern Survey,* 25(1956), pp. 161-8.

Kahin, George McTurnan, and Lewis, John W. *The U.S. In Vietnam: An Analysis in Depth of the History of American Involvement in Vietnam.* Dell, 1967.

Karnow, Stanley. "Communists Infiltrated Old Viet Regime." *The Boston Globe,* March 26, 1981.

Kelly, Colonel Francis J. *U.S. Army Special Forces, 1961-1971*. Department of the Army, 1973.
Knoebl, Kuno. *Victor Charlie: The Face of War in Viet-Nam*. Trans. Abe Farbstein. Praeger, 1967.

Lacouture, Jean.
　Ho Chi Minh: A Political Biography. Trans. Peter Wiles. Random House, 1968.
　Vietnam: Between Two Truces. Random House, 1966.
Lancaster, Donald. *The Emancipation of French Indo China*. Oxford University Press, 1961.
Langlais, Pierre. *Dien Bien Phu*. Editions France-Empire, 1963.
Lartéguy, Jean. *The Centurions*. E. P. Dutton & Co., 1962.
Lederer, William J., and Burdick, Eugene. *The Ugly American*. W.W. Norton & Co., 1958.
Le Duan. *The Vietnamese Revolution*. International Publishers, 1971.
"Le Duan." *Who's Who in the Socialist Countries: A Biographical Encyclopedia of 10,000 Leading Personalities in 16 Leading Communist Countries*. Borys Lewytzkyi and Juliusz Straynowski, eds. K. G. Saur Publishing Inc., 1978, p. 347.
Leites, Nathan. *The Viet Cong Style of Politics*. Rand Corporation RM-5487, 1969.
Lewy, Guenter. *America in Vietnam*. Oxford University Press, 1978.
Lindsay, F. A. "Unconventional Warfare." *Foreign Affairs*, January 1962.

Maneli, Mieczyslaw. *War of the Vanquished*. Harper & Row, 1971.
Masse, B. L. "Revolt in Vietnam." *America*, December 26, 1960.
McAlister, John T., Jr.
　"Mountain Minorities and the Viet Minh: A Key to the Indochina War." *Southeast Asian Tribes, Minorities and Nations*. Edited by Peter Kunstadter, Princeton University Press, 1967.
　Vietnam: The Origins of Revolution. Alfred A. Knopf, 1969.
McAlister, John T., Jr., and Mus, Paul. *The Vietnamese and their Revolution*. Harper & Row, 1970.
Murphy, Marvin. "Overcoming Resistance to Major Change: Vietnamese Budget Reform." *Public Administration Review*, 20(1960), pp. 148-51.
Murti, B.S.N. *Vietnam Divided*. Asia Publishing House, 1964.

Nguyen Khac Huyen. *Vision Accomplished? The Enigma of Ho Chi Minh*. Collier Books, 1971.
Nguyen Tuyet Mai. "Electioneering—Vietnamese Style." *Asian Survey*, 2(1962), pp. 11-8.
Nguyên Van Thong, et al. *Return to Dien Bien Phu and Other Stories*. Foreign Languages Publishing House, 1961.

O'Ballance, Edgar.
　The Indo-China War 1945-1954: A Study in Guerrilla Warfare. Faber & Faber, 1964.
　The Wars in Vietnam. 1954-1973. Hippocrene Books, Inc., 1975.

Pettit, Clyde E., ed. *The Experts*. Lyle Stuart, Inc., 1975.
Pike, Douglas. *Viet Cong: The Organization and Techniques of the National Liberation Front of South Vietnam*. MIT Press, 1966.
Porter, Gareth. *Vietnam: The Definitive Documentation of Human Decisions*. Vols. 1,2. Earl M. Coleman Enterprises, 1979.

Race, Jeffrey. *War Comes to Long An*. University of California Press, 1972.
Raskin, Marcus G., and Fall, Bernard B., eds. *The Viet-Nam Reader*. Random House, 1965.
Rocolle, Pierre. *Pourquoi Dien Bien Phu*. Flammarion, 1968.
Rose, Lisle Abbott. *Roads of Tragedy: The United States and the Struggle for Asia, 1945-1953*. Greenwood Press, 1976.
Rosie, George. *The British in Vietnam: How the Twenty-five Years War Began*. Panther, 1970.
Rostow, W. W.
　"Guerrilla Warfare in Underdeveloped Areas." *Marine Corps Gazette*, January 1962.
　The Diffusion of Power, 1957-1972. Macmillan, 1972.
Roy, Jules. *La Bataille de Dien Bien Phu*. René Julliard, 1963.
　The Battle of Dien Bien Phu. Trans. Robert Baldick. Harper & Row, 1965.

Sainteny, Jean.
　Histoire d'une Paix Manquée. Fayard, 1953.
　Ho Chi Minh and his followers: A Personal Memoir. Trans. Herman Briffault. Cowley Book Co., 1968.
Samuels, Gertrude. "Passage to Freedom in Vietnam." *National Geographic*, June 1955.
Scheer, Robert. "The Genesis of U.S. Support to Ngo Dinh Diem." In *Vietnam*, edited by Marvin Gettlemann, Fawcett, 1965.
Schlesinger, Arthur M.
　A Thousand Days: John F. Kennedy in the White House. Houghton Mifflin Co., 1965.
　Robert Kennedy and His Times. Houghton Mifflin Co., 1978.
Schoenbrun, David. *As France Goes*. Gollancz, 1957.
Scigliano, Robert.
　South Viet-Nam: Nation Under Stress. Houghton Mifflin Co., 1963.
　South Viet-Nam Since Independence. Michigan State University Press, 1963.
Shabad, Theodore. "Economic Development in North Vietnam." *Pacific Affairs*, 31(1958), pp. 36-53.

Shaplen, Robert.
　"Enigma of Ho Chi Minh." *The Reporter*, 12(1955), pp. 11-9.
　The Lost Revolution: The U.S. in Vietnam, 1946-1966. Rev. ed. Harper & Row, 1966.
Simpson, H. R. "Slow Boat to Freedom." *Commonweal*, 61(1955), pp. 426-8.
Sinclair, Andrew Annandale. "Guevara, 'Che.'" *Encyclopaedia Brittanica Macropaedia*, 1974.
Sorenson, Theodore C. *Kennedy*. Harper & Row, 1965.

Tanham, George Kilpatrick. *Communist Revolutionary Warfare: From the Vietminh to the Viet Cong*. Rev. ed. Praeger, 1967.
"The Dien Bien Phu Campaign." *Vietnam*, 2(1964), pp. 9-11.
Truong Chinh. *Primer for Revolt: The Communist Takeover in Vietnam*. Praeger, 1963.
Turnbull, Lt. Col. P.E.X., M.C. "Dien Bien Phu and Sergeant Kubiak." *The Army Quarterly and Defense Journal*, 90(1965), pp. 97-103.
Turner, Robert F. *Vietnamese Communism: Its Origins and Development*. Hoover Institute Press, 1975.

Vietnam: A Reporter's War. The Australian Broadcasting Commission, 1975.

Warner, Denis. *The Last Confucian*. Macmillan, 1963.
Werth, Alexander. *France 1940-1955*. Beacon Press, 1956.
White, P. T. "South Vietnam Fights the Red Tide." *National Geographic*, October 1961.
White, Theodore H.
　"Indochina—The Long Trail of Errors." *The Reporter*, June 22, 1954.
　The Making of the President 1960. Pocket Books, 1961.
Woodruff, Lloyd W. *Study of a Vietnamese Rural Community*. 2 vols. Michigan State University Press, 1960.
Wurfel, David. "Agrarian Reform in the Republic of Vietnam." *Far Eastern Survey*, 26(1957), pp. 81-92.

Yacano, Xavier. *Les Etapes De La Décolonisation*. Presses Universitaires de France, 1971.

Zasloff, Joseph J.
　"Origins of the Insurgency in South Vietnam, 1954-1960: The Role of the Southern Vietminh Cadres." Rand Corporation RM-5163/2-ISA/ARPA, 1968.
　"Political Motivation of the Viet Cong and the Vietminh Regroupees." Rand Corporation RM-4703/2 ISA/ARPA, 1968.
　"The Role of the Sanctuary in Insurgency: Communist China's Support to the Viet Minh 1946-1954." Rand Corporation RM-4618-PR, 1967.

II. Government Publications
Department of Defense. *United States-Vietnam Relations, 1945-1967*. U.S. Government Printing Office, 1971.
Futrell, Robert F. *The United States Air Force in Southeast Asia. The Advisory Years to 1965*. U.S. Government Printing Office, 1981.
Government of South Vietnam. *Victory of Rung Sat*. 1955.
Nalty, Bernard C. *Air Power and the Fight for Khe Sanh*. Office of Air Force History, USAF, 1973.
Shore, Captain Moyers S., II, USMC. *The Battle for Khe Sanh*. History and Museums Divisions, Headquarters, U.S. Marine Corps, 1977.
U.S. Congress: Senate Committee on Foreign Relations. *Report on Indochina*. U.S. Government Printing Office, 1954.
U.S. Congress: Senate Committee on Foreign Relations. *U.S. in Vietnam—1944-47*. Staff Study No. 2, U.S. Government Printing Office, 1972.
U.S. Department of State. "A Threat to the Peace: North Viet-Nam's Effort to Conquer South Viet-Nam." Far Eastern Series 110, Pts. 1 and 2, Bureau of Public Affairs, 1961.

III. Newspapers and periodicals
The authors consulted the following newspapers and periodicals:
Business Week, 1954-1961.
LIFE Magazine, 1945-1961.
New Republic, 1955-1961.
Newsweek Magazine, 1945-1962.
The *New York Times*, 1945-1961, 1981.
Time Magazine, 1945-1962.
The *Times of Vietnam*, 1956-1961.
U.S. News and World Report, 1948-1962.

IV. Archival Sources
John Foster Dulles Papers. Sealey G. Mudd Library Princeton University, Princeton, N.J.
Dwight David Eisenhower Library, Copies of John Foster Dulles Files, Gettysburg, PA.

V. Interviews
George W. Ball, former undersecretary of state, on April 15, 1981.

Photography Credits

Cover Photos:
Top right, Ernst Haas–Magnum; bottom right, Larry Burrows, LIFE Magazine © 1963, Time Inc.; left bottom, Howard Sochurek; top left, UPI.

Asia in Revolt
p. 6, top, Johnny Florea–LIFE Magazine, © 1946, Time Inc.; bottom, Wide World. p. 7, Johnny Florea–LIFE Magazine, © 1946, Time Inc. p. 8, top, Wide World; bottom, Keystone. p. 9, Wide World. p. 10, left, H. Cartier-Bresson–Magnum; right, Wide World. p. 11, Tallandier.

Chapter I
p. 13, Tallandier. p. 14, Imperial War Museum. p. 15, Keystone. p. 16, Tallandier. p. 17, Keystone. p. 18, Photographique Bibliothèque Nationale Paris. p. 19, Ngo Vinh Long Collection. p. 21, Keystone. pp. 23, 26, Ngo Vinh Long Collection.

Images of War
pp. 28–30, Howard Sochurek. p. 31, Robert Capa–Magnum.

Chapter II
p. 33, Indochine Sud-Est Asiatique. p. 35, National Archives. p. 36, Keystone. p. 37, Ernst Haas–Magnum. p. 39, Photo Almasy. p. 40, René Dazy. p. 41, Agence France-Presse. p. 42, U.S. Air Force. p. 43, Agence France-Presse. p. 44, E.C.P. Armées–France. p. 45, Eastfoto. p. 47, Courtesy of The Library of Congress. p. 49, Keystone.

The Legion Was Their Country
p. 52, Paris Match. p. 53, Howard Sochurek–LIFE Magazine, © 1951, Time Inc. p. 54, top, Howard Sochurek–LIFE Magazine, © 1951, Time Inc.; bottom, Photo Almasy. p. 55, Robert Capa–Magnum.

Chapter III
p. 57, Agence France-Presse. p. 59, Roger Viollet. p. 61, Daniel Camus–Paris Match. p. 63, Ngo Vinh Long Collection. p. 64, Daniel Camus Collection–Paris Match. pp. 65–6, Jean Rondy. p. 67, François Sully–Black Star. pp. 68–71, Jean Rondy. p. 72, French Information Service. p. 73, Jean Rondy. p. 78, E.C.P. Armées–France. p. 79, Jean Rondy. p. 80, Wide World. p. 81, top, Agence France-Presse; bottom, Daniel Camus Collection–Paris Match. p. 83, Wide World.

Chapter IV
p. 87, Howard Sochurek–LIFE Magazine, © 1954, Time Inc. p. 89, Liberation News Service. p. 91, Howard Sochurek–LIFE Magazine, © 1954, Time Inc. p. 92, Agence France-Presse. p. 95, U.S. Air Force. p. 96, Howard Sochurek–LIFE Magazine, © 1954, Time Inc. p. 97, top left, Tallandier; top right, François Sully–Black Star; bottom, Keystone. p. 99, Agence France-Presse.

Chapter V
p. 101, Marc Riboud Collection. p. 103, Keystone. pp. 105–6, Eastfoto. pp. 107–9, Ngo Vinh Long Collection. p. 111, Eastfoto. p. 112, Ngo Vinh Long Collection. p. 113, Arts and Music Publishing House, Hanoi. p. 115, Black Star. pp. 116–9, The Museum of Modern Art–Film Stills Archive.

Chapter VI
p. 121, Howard Sochurek–LIFE Magazine, © 1955, Time Inc. p. 123, Keystone. pp. 124–5, Howard Sochurek–LIFE Magazine, © 1955, Time Inc. p. 127, UPI. p. 129, François Sully–Black Star. p. 130, Howard Sochurek–LIFE Magazine, © 1955, Time Inc.

Chapter VII
p. 135, Paris Match. p. 137, François Sully–Black Star. p. 139, Tallandier. pp. 140–1, UPI. p. 143, E.C.P. Armées–France. p. 144, Tallandier. p. 146, Eastfoto. p. 147, Black Star. p. 149, Ngo Vinh Long Collection.

Chapter VIII
p. 151, Nicholas Tikhomiroff–Magnum. p. 155, Nicholas Tikhomiroff–Magnum. p. 156, François Sully–Black Star. p. 157, U.S. Army. pp. 158–59, Black Star. p. 162, Nicholas Tikhomiroff–Magnum. p. 163, top, Wide World; bottom, UPI. p. 166, François Sully–Black Star. p. 167, Black Star. p. 168, Nihon Denpa News, Ltd. p. 169, Ngo Vinh Long Collection.

The Cold War
p. 170, Wide World. p. 171, UPI. p. 172, Eve Arnold–Magnum. p. 173, top, Wide World; bottom, Keystone. p. 174, top, Sovfoto; bottom, UPI. p. 175, UPI.

Chapter IX
p. 177, UPI. p. 178, Wide World. p. 179, Cornell Capa–Magnum. p. 181, Burt Glinn–Magnum. p. 183, Nicholas Tikhomiroff–Magnum. p. 187, U.S. Army. p. 188, Wide World. p. 191, François Sully–Black Star. p. 192, Robert Ellison–Black Star. p. 193, John Dominis–LIFE Magazine, © 1961, Time Inc. p. 194, François Sully–Black Star. p. 197, John F. Kennedy Library. p. 199, Howard Sochurek–LIFE Magazine, © 1962, Time Inc. p. 200, Wide World.

Map Credits

p. 46—Map by Diane McCaffery. From The Quicksand War: Prelude to Vietnam by Lucien Bodard, translated and abridged by Patrick O'Brian, © 1967 by Little, Brown and Co., Inc. Reproduced by permission of Little, Brown and Co. in association with the Atlantic Monthly Press.
p. 48—Map by Diane McCaffery. From an article by Bernard Fall entitled, "Indochina: The Seven-Year Dilemma," appearing in the October 1953 issue of Military Review. Reproduced by permission from Military Review.
p. 74—Map by Mary Reilly. Source: Dien Bien Phu, Third Edition, by Vo Nguyen Giap. Foreign Languages Publishing House, 1964.
p. 75, top—Map by Mary Reilly. From a map by Daniel Camus appearing in La Bataille de Dien Bien Phu by Jules Roy, © 1963 by René Julliard. Reproduced by permission.
p. 75, bottom—Map by Mary Reilly. Composite map from pp. 166, 212, 254, 380 in Hell in a Very Small Place: The Siege of Dien Bien Phu, by Bernard B. Fall (J.B. Lippincott Company), Copyright © 1966 by Bernard B. Fall. Reprinted by permission of Harper & Row, Publishers, Inc.
p. 76, top left—Map by Mary Reilly. From Pourquoi Dien Bien Phu? by Pierre Rocolle, © 1968 by Edition Flammarion. Reproduced by permission.
p. 76, top right—Map by Mary Reilly. From Pourquoi Dien Bien Phu? by Pierre Rocolle, © 1968 by Edition Flammarion. Reproduced by permission.
p. 76, bottom—Map by Mary Reilly. Source: Map by John Carnes.
p. 76, bottom (inset)—Map by Mary Reilly. From Pourquoi Dien Bien Phu? by Pierre Rocolle, © 1968 by Edition Flammarion. Reproduced by permission.
p. 80—Map by Diane McCaffery. From The Two Vietnams: A Political and Military Analysis, second revised edition, by Bernard Fall. Copyright © 1963, 1964, 1967 by Frederick A. Praeger, Inc. Reprinted by permission of Holt, Rinehart and Winston, CBS College Publishing.
p. 94—Map by Diane McCaffery. © 1954 by The New York Times Company. Reprinted by permission.
p. 122—Map by Diane McCaffery. From an article by Bernard Fall entitled, "The Political Religious Sects of Vietnam," appearing in Pacific Affairs 28 (1955). Reproduced by permission.
p. 126—Map by Diane McCaffery. © 1955 by The New York Times Company. Reprinted by permission.
p. 161—Map by Diane McCaffery.

Acknowledgments

Boston Publishing Company wishes to acknowledge the kind assistance of the following people: Catherine Antoine, Paris; Nancy Bressler, Curator, Sealey G. Mudd Manuscript Library, Princeton University; Charles W. Dunn, Professor and Chairman, Department of Celtic Languages and Literature, Harvard University; Nathaniel Gray and Robert Lyons, Lumière, Florence, Mass.; Howard Sochurek, New York; David Stern, Able Art, Boston, Mass.; and Frantz Braamcamp, Phillippe Majescas, Gilbert Pepin-Malherbe, and other members of the Association des Combattants de l'Union Française—the French Indochina veterans organization—who wish to remain anonymous.

Index

Names, Acronyms, Terms

Annam—central section of Vietnam; French protectorate from 1893 to 1954.

ARVN—Army of the Republic of Vietnam. The army of South Vietnam.

Binh Xuyen—bandit army that at one time controlled half of Saigon. Led by Bay Vien (Le Van Vien).

Cao Dai—religious sect formed in 1925 by a group of civil servants in Cochin China. A spirit revealed itself to them as the "Cao Dai," or supreme god of the universe.

CIA—Central Intelligence Agency. It replaced in 1947 the OSS, the World War II U.S. intelligence agency.

CIP—Counter-Insurgency Plan. 1961 plan calling for additional U.S. aid to support a 20,000 man increase in the ARVN and to train, equip, and supply a 32,000-man addition to South Vietnam's Civil Guard.

Cochin China—southern section of Vietnam; French colony from 1863 to 1954.

Cold War—description of struggle between Western powers and Communist bloc from the end of World War II until the early 1960s.

collectivization—grouping together of laborers and poor farmers to cultivate state-owned land.

Dien Bien Phu—site of French defeat in 1954 signaling the end of their power in Vietnam. Located west of Hanoi on Laotian border.

DMZ—demilitarized zone. Established according to the Geneva accords of 1954, provisionally dividing North Vietnam from South Vietnam along the seventeenth parallel.

DRV—Democratic Republic of Vietnam. The government of Ho Chi Minh, established on September 2, 1945. Provisionally confined to North Vietnam by the Geneva accords of 1954.

French Expeditionary Corps—colonial army of France. Made up chiefly of soldiers from French colonies and commanded by an all-volunteer force from France. The use of conscripts in Indochina had been banned by the French parliament.

GCO—general counteroffensive. The third stage of Mao's outline for military victory. After being on the defensive and demoralizing the enemy, a revolutionary army uses the third stage—the GCO—consisting of a frontal attack on the enemy troops.

GVN—government of South Vietnam. Also referred to as the Republic of Vietnam. Provisionally established by the Geneva accords in 1954.

hedgehogs—isolated outposts in which the French high command concentrated troops.

Hoa Hao—religious sect headed by Huynh Phu So, who began preaching in 1939 toward a reformed Buddhism involving internal faith rather than outward ritual.

ICC—International Control Commission. Mandated by Geneva accords of 1954 to supervise implementation of the agreement. Consisted of representatives of Poland, India, and Canada.

Lao Dong party—Vietnam Worker's party (Communist party). Founded by Ho Chi Minh in May 1951. Absorbed the Vietminh and was the ruling party of the DRV.

MAAG—Military Assistance Advisory Group. U.S. military advisory program to South Vietnam beginning in 1955.

montagnards—the mountain tribes of Vietnam, wooed by both the North and the South because of their knowledge of the rugged highland terrain.

MSU Advisory Group—Michigan State University team led by Dr. Wesley Fishel that in 1955 attempted to reorganize Diem's administration, police, and Civil Guard.

Muong soldiers—hill tribesmen used by the French in their counterattack against the Vietminh.

napalm—incendiary used in Vietnam by French and Americans both as defoliant and antipersonnel weapon. Shot from a flame thrower or dropped from aircraft, the substance adheres while it burns.

National Revolutionary Movement—Diem's following, dominated by his brothers Nhu and Can.

NLF—National Liberation Front, officially the National Front for the Liberation of the South.

Formed on December 20, 1960, it aimed to overthrow South Vietnam's government and reunite the North and the South. The NLF included Communists and non-Communists.

NSC—National Security Council. Responsible for developing defense strategies for the U.S. Situated in the White House, it exerts general direction over the CIA.

Operation Lea—unsuccessful French attempt to end the Vietminh rebellion in fall 1947 and capture Ho Chi Minh.

Operation Vulture—operation conceived but never mounted by American and French military in Vietnam in 1954 to relieve the siege at Dien Bien Phu. It called for American bombers to raid the perimeter of the valley cutting Vietminh communications and artillery installations.

OSS—Office of Strategic Services. Created in 1942 under the U.S. Joint Chiefs of Staff to obtain information about enemy military operations. Disbanded in 1945, many of its functions were absorbed by the CIA.

Pentagon Papers—a once-secret internal Defense Department study of U.S.-Vietnam relations from 1945 to 1967. Made available to the *New York Times* in 1971 by Daniel Ellsberg and later released by the Pentagon.

PLA—People's Liberation Army of South Vietnam, the army of the NLF.

psywar—psychological warfare.

psyops—psychological warfare operations.

RC 4—Route Coloniale 4. French road near Chinese border connecting hedgehogs in northeast Vietnam. Scene of heavy fighting and major French defeat in 1950.

seventeenth parallel—temporary division line between North and South Vietnam established by the Geneva accords of 1954 pending unification election scheduled for July 1956. Elections were never held and division remained until 1975.

Tonkin—northern section of Vietnam; French protectorate from 1883 to 1954.

USAID—United States Agency for International Development.

Vietcong—derogatory contraction of Vietnam Cong San (Vietnamese Communist). In use since 1956.

Vietminh—coalition founded by Ho Chi Minh in May 1941 and ruled the DRV. Absorbed by the Lao Dong party in 1951.

Vietnamization—term given to President Nixon's phased withdrawal of U.S. troops and transfer of their responsibilities to South Vietnamese.

VPA—Vietnam People's Army. North Vietnam's army, led by Vo Nguyen Giap.